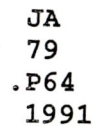

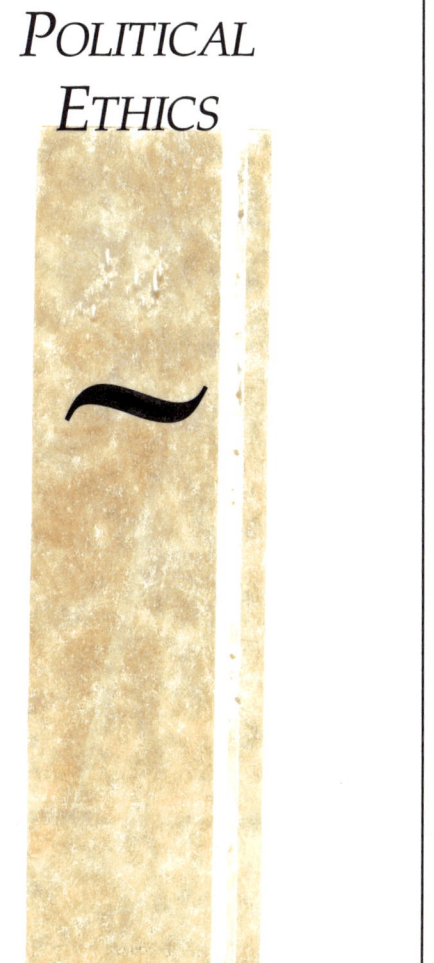

POLITICAL ETHICS

*This is Volume 12 in a series of studies
commissioned as part of the research program
of the Royal Commission on Electoral Reform
and Party Financing*

POLITICAL ETHICS
A CANADIAN PERSPECTIVE

Janet Hiebert
Editor

Volume 12 of the Research Studies

ROYAL COMMISSION ON ELECTORAL REFORM
AND PARTY FINANCING
AND CANADA COMMUNICATION GROUP –
PUBLISHING, SUPPLY AND SERVICES CANADA

DUNDURN PRESS
TORONTO AND OXFORD

© Minister of Supply and Services Canada, 1991
Printed and bound in Canada
ISBN 1-55002-108-7
ISSN 1188-2743
Catalogue No. Z1-1989/2-41-12E

Published by Dundurn Press Limited in cooperation with the Royal Commission on Electoral Reform and Party Financing and Canada Communication Group – Publishing, Supply and Services Canada.

All rights reserved. No part of this publication may be reproduced, stored in a retrieval system, or transmitted in any form or by any means, electronic, mechanical, photocopying, recording, or otherwise (except brief passages for purposes of review) without the prior written permission of the Minister of Supply and Services.

#004074627

Canadian Cataloguing in Publication Data

Main entry under title:
Political ethics

(Research studies ; 12)
Issued also in French under title: L'éthique et la politique au Canada.
ISBN 1-55002-108-7

1. Political ethics – Canada. I. Hiebert, Janet, 1960– . II. Canada. Royal Commission on Electoral Reform and Party Financing. III. Series: Research studies (Canada. Royal Commission on Electoral Reform and Party Financing) ; 12.

BJ55.P64 1991   172'.0971   C91-090524-X

Dundurn Press Limited
2181 Queen Street East
Suite 301
Toronto, Canada
M4E 1E5

Dundurn Distribution
73 Lime Walk
Headington
Oxford, England
OX3 7AD

Contents

Foreword	ix
Introduction	xi
Preface	xvii

1. Ethical Issues in the Debate on Reform of the *Canada Elections Act*: An Ethicological Analysis — 3
　Pierre Fortin

Reasons for Reform	5
Ethical Issues Raised by Perceptions of Democracy in Canada	14
The Right to Vote	19
Representation	24
Selection of Candidates	28
Political Parties and their Financing	34
Interest Groups	39
Regulating Election Expenditures	43
The Voters List	45
Role of the Media in the Electoral Process	50
Opinion Polls During an Election Period	55
The Election Campaign and the Conduct of the Vote	57
Poll Closing Times and the Disclosure of Election Results	61
Conclusion	62
Appendix	66
References	72

2. Public Sector Ethics — 73
　Vincent Lemieux

A Concept of Public Sector Ethics	73
Public Sector and Private Sector Ethics	77
Patronage, Corruption and Conflict of Interest	78
Participants' Perceptions	82
The Practical Implications of Public Sector Ethics	91
Recommendations	97
References	98

3. ALLEGATIONS OF UNDUE INFLUENCE IN CANADIAN POLITICS — 101
IAN GREENE

Methodology — 101
The Meaning of Undue Influence — 103
Perceptions of Undue Influence — 107
Recommendations and Conclusion — 122
Appendices — 127
Notes — 161
References — 164

4. NEGATIVE POLITICAL ADVERTISING: AN ANALYSIS OF RESEARCH FINDINGS IN LIGHT OF CANADIAN PRACTICE — 165
WALTER I. ROMANOW, WALTER C. SODERLUND, RICHARD G. PRICE

Definitions — 167
Historical Experience — 169
Canadian Practice — 179
Views on Regulatory Options — 184
Conclusion — 187
Notes — 188
Interviews — 189
References — 190

5. CITIZENSHIP AND EQUITY: VARIATIONS ACROSS TIME AND IN SPACE — 195
JANE JENSON

Definitions of Citizenship: Some Fundamental Tensions — 197
The Power of Discourse: Disputing Citizenship — 202
Citizenship and Equity in Canadian Politics — 205
Place-Sensitive Citizenship: Equity for "Island Communities" — 206
Nationwide Citizenship: Equity for Individuals — 211
A Fragmented Citizenship: Categorial Equity — 218
Notes — 222
References — 225

6. FAIRNESS, EQUITY AND RIGHTS — 229
KATHY L. BROCK

Key Points of Contact — 230
A New Canadian Consciousness — 234

Contents

The Conflict between Rights and Fairness	242
Conclusion	253
Notes	255
Bibliography	257

7. A CODE OF ETHICS FOR POLITICAL PARTIES — 265
JANET HIEBERT

Codes of Ethics	267
Corporate Use of Codes	268
Benefits of Articulating the Values of a Party	270
Considerations when Developing a Code	273
Addressing the Political Context in which Parties Operate	275
Conclusion	277
Appendix	278
Acknowledgements	278
Bibliography	278

FIGURES

1. ETHICAL ISSUES IN THE DEBATE ON REFORM OF THE *CANADA ELECTIONS ACT*: AN ETHICOLOGICAL ANALYSIS

1.1	Principal ethical issue: how can we encourage more equitable participation in the electoral process by all citizens?	65

3. ALLEGATIONS OF UNDUE INFLUENCE IN CANADIAN POLITICS

3.K1	Allegations of undue influence by year	161

TABLES

3. ALLEGATIONS OF UNDUE INFLUENCE IN CANADIAN POLITICS

3.K1	All allegations of undue influence, 1979–90	158
3.K2	All allegations of undue influence, 1979–90, by level of government	159

FOREWORD

~

THE ROYAL COMMISSION on Electoral Reform and Party Financing was established in November 1989. Our mandate was to inquire into and report on the appropriate principles and process that should govern the election of members of the House of Commons and the financing of political parties and candidates' campaigns. To conduct such a comprehensive examination of Canada's electoral system, we held extensive public consultations and developed a research program designed to ensure that our recommendations would be guided by an independent foundation of empirical inquiry and analysis.

The Commission's in-depth review of the electoral system was the first of its kind in Canada's history of electoral democracy. It was dictated largely by the major constitutional, social and technological changes of the past several decades, which have transformed Canadian society, and their concomitant influence on Canadians' expectations of the political process itself. In particular, the adoption in 1982 of the *Canadian Charter of Rights and Freedoms* has heightened Canadians' awareness of their democratic and political rights and of the way they are served by the electoral system.

The importance of electoral reform cannot be overemphasized. As the Commission's work proceeded, Canadians became increasingly preoccupied with constitutional issues that have the potential to change the nature of Confederation. No matter what their beliefs or political allegiances in this continuing debate, Canadians agree that constitutional change must be achieved in the context of fair and democratic processes. We cannot complacently assume that our current electoral process will always meet this standard or that it leaves no room for improvement. Parliament and the national government must be seen as legitimate; electoral reform can both enhance the stature of national political institutions and reinforce their ability to define the future of our country in ways that command Canadians' respect and confidence and promote the national interest.

In carrying out our mandate, we remained mindful of the importance of protecting our democratic heritage, while at the same time balancing it against the emerging values that are injecting a new dynamic into the electoral system. If our system is to reflect the realities of Canadian political life, then reform requires more than mere tinkering with electoral laws and practices.

Our broad mandate challenged us to explore a full range of options. We commissioned more than 100 research studies, to be published in a 23-volume collection. In the belief that our electoral laws must measure up to the very best contemporary practice, we examined election-related laws and processes in all of our provinces and territories and studied comparable legislation and processes in established democracies around the world. This unprecedented array of empirical study and expert opinion made a vital contribution to our deliberations. We made every effort to ensure that the research was both intellectually rigorous and of practical value. All studies were subjected to peer review, and many of the authors discussed their preliminary findings with members of the political and academic communities at national symposiums on major aspects of the electoral system.

The Commission placed the research program under the able and inspired direction of Dr. Peter Aucoin, Professor of Political Science and Public Administration at Dalhousie University. We are confident that the efforts of Dr. Aucoin, together with those of the research coordinators and scholars whose work appears in this and other volumes, will continue to be of value to historians, political scientists, parliamentarians and policy makers, as well as to thoughtful Canadians and the international community.

Along with the other Commissioners, I extend my sincere gratitude to the entire Commission staff for their dedication and commitment. I also wish to thank the many people who participated in our symposiums for their valuable contributions, as well as the members of the research and practitioners' advisory groups whose counsel significantly aided our undertaking.

Pierre Lortie
Chairman

INTRODUCTION

THE ROYAL COMMISSION'S research program constituted a comprehensive and detailed examination of the Canadian electoral process. The scope of the research, undertaken to assist Commissioners in their deliberations, was dictated by the broad mandate given to the Commission.

The objective of the research program was to provide Commissioners with a full account of the factors that have shaped our electoral democracy. This dictated, first and foremost, a focus on federal electoral law, but our inquiries also extended to the Canadian constitution, including the institutions of parliamentary government, the practices of political parties, the mass media and nonpartisan political organizations, as well as the decision-making role of the courts with respect to the constitutional rights of citizens. Throughout, our research sought to introduce a historical perspective in order to place the contemporary experience within the Canadian political tradition.

We recognized that neither our consideration of the factors shaping Canadian electoral democracy nor our assessment of reform proposals would be as complete as necessary if we failed to examine the experiences of Canadian provinces and territories and of other democracies. Our research program thus emphasized comparative dimensions in relation to the major subjects of inquiry.

Our research program involved, in addition to the work of the Commission's research coordinators, analysts and support staff, over 200 specialists from 28 universities in Canada, from the private sector and, in a number of cases, from abroad. Specialists in political science constituted the majority of our researchers, but specialists in law, economics, management, computer sciences, ethics, sociology and communications, among other disciplines, were also involved.

In addition to the preparation of research studies for the Commission, our research program included a series of research seminars, symposiums and workshops. These meetings brought together the Commissioners, researchers, representatives from the political parties, media personnel and others with practical experience in political parties, electoral politics and public affairs. These meetings provided not only a forum for discussion of the various subjects of the Commission's mandate, but also an opportunity for our research to be assessed by those with an intimate knowledge of the world of political practice.

These public reviews of our research were complemented by internal and external assessments of each research report by persons qualified in the area; such assessments were completed prior to our decision to publish any study in the series of research volumes.

The Research Branch of the Commission was divided into several areas, with the individual research projects in each area assigned to the research coordinators as follows:

F. Leslie Seidle	Political Party and Election Finance
Herman Bakvis	Political Parties
Kathy Megyery	Women, Ethno-Cultural Groups and Youth
David Small	Redistribution; Electoral Boundaries; Voter Registration
Janet Hiebert	Party Ethics
Michael Cassidy	Democratic Rights; Election Administration
Robert A. Milen	Aboriginal Electoral Participation and Representation
Frederick J. Fletcher	Mass Media and Broadcasting in Elections
David Mac Donald (Assistant Research Coordinator)	Direct Democracy

These coordinators identified appropriate specialists to undertake research, managed the projects and prepared them for publication. They also organized the seminars, symposiums and workshops in their research areas and were responsible for preparing presentations and briefings to help the Commission in its deliberations and decision making. Finally, they participated in drafting the Final Report of the Commission.

INTRODUCTION

On behalf of the Commission, I welcome the opportunity to thank the following for their generous assistance in producing these research studies – a project that required the talents of many individuals.

In performing their duties, the research coordinators made a notable contribution to the work of the Commission. Despite the pressures of tight deadlines, they worked with unfailing good humour and the utmost congeniality. I thank all of them for their consistent support and cooperation.

In particular, I wish to express my gratitude to Leslie Seidle, senior research coordinator, who supervised our research analysts and support staff in Ottawa. His diligence, commitment and professionalism not only set high standards, but also proved contagious. I am grateful to Kathy Megyery, who performed a similar function in Montreal with equal aplomb and skill. Her enthusiasm and dedication inspired us all.

On behalf of the research coordinators and myself, I wish to thank our research analysts: Daniel Arsenault, Eric Bertram, Cécile Boucher, Peter Constantinou, Yves Denoncourt, David Docherty, Luc Dumont, Jane Dunlop, Scott Evans, Véronique Garneau, Keith Heintzman, Paul Holmes, Hugh Mellon, Cheryl D. Mitchell, Donald Padget, Alain Pelletier, Dominique Tremblay and Lisa Young. The Research Branch was strengthened by their ability to carry out research in a wide variety of areas, their intellectual curiosity and their team spirit.

The work of the research coordinators and analysts was greatly facilitated by the professional skills and invaluable cooperation of Research Branch staff members: Paulette LeBlanc, who, as administrative assistant, managed the flow of research projects; Hélène Leroux, secretary to the research coordinators, who produced briefing material for the Commissioners and who, with Lori Nazar, assumed responsibility for monitoring the progress of research projects in the latter stages of our work; Kathleen McBride and her assistant Natalie Brose, who created and maintained the database of briefs and hearings transcripts; and Richard Herold and his assistant Susan Dancause, who were responsible for our research library. Jacinthe Séguin and Cathy Tucker also deserve thanks – in addition to their duties as receptionists, they assisted in a variety of ways to help us meet deadlines.

We were extremely fortunate to obtain the research services of first-class specialists from the academic and private sectors. Their contributions are found in this and the other 22 published research volumes. We thank them for the quality of their work and for their willingness to contribute and to meet our tight deadlines.

Our research program also benefited from the counsel of Jean-Marc Hamel, Special Adviser to the Chairman of the Commission and former

Chief Electoral Officer of Canada, whose knowledge and experience proved invaluable.

In addition, numerous specialists assessed our research studies. Their assessments not only improved the quality of our published studies, but also provided us with much-needed advice on many issues. In particular, we wish to single out professors Donald Blake, Janine Brodie, Alan Cairns, Kenneth Carty, John Courtney, Peter Desbarats, Jane Jenson, Richard Johnston, Vincent Lemieux, Terry Morley and Joseph Wearing, as well as Ms. Beth Symes.

Producing such a large number of studies in less than a year requires a mastery of the skills and logistics of publishing. We were fortunate to be able to count on the Commission's Director of Communications, Richard Rochefort, and Assistant Director, Hélène Papineau. They were ably supported by the Communications staff: Patricia Burden, Louise Dagenais, Caroline Field, Claudine Labelle, France Langlois, Lorraine Maheux, Ruth McVeigh, Chantal Morissette, Sylvie Patry, Jacques Poitras and Claudette Rouleau-O'Toole.

To bring the project to fruition, the Commission also called on specialized contractors. We are deeply grateful for the services of Ann McCoomb (references and fact checking); Marthe Lemery, Pierre Chagnon and the staff of Communications Com'ça (French quality control); Norman Bloom, Pamela Riseborough and associates of B&B Editorial Consulting (English adaptation and quality control); and Mado Reid (French production). Al Albania and his staff at Acart Graphics designed the studies and produced some 2 400 tables and figures.

The Commission's research reports constitute Canada's largest publishing project of 1991. Successful completion of the project required close cooperation between the public and private sectors. In the public sector, we especially acknowledge the excellent service of the Privy Council unit of the Translation Bureau, Department of the Secretary of State of Canada, under the direction of Michel Parent, and our contacts Ruth Steele and Terry Denovan of the Canada Communication Group, Department of Supply and Services.

The Commission's co-publisher for the research studies was Dundurn Press of Toronto, whose exceptional service is gratefully acknowledged. Wilson & Lafleur of Montreal, working with the Centre de Documentation Juridique du Québec, did equally admirable work in preparing the French version of the studies.

Teams of editors, copy editors and proofreaders worked diligently under stringent deadlines with the Commission and the publishers to prepare some 20 000 pages of manuscript for design, typesetting and printing. The work of these individuals, whose names are listed elsewhere in this volume, was greatly appreciated.

Our acknowledgements extend to the contributions of the Commission's Executive Director, Guy Goulard, and the administration and executive support teams: Maurice Lacasse, Denis Lafrance and Steve Tremblay (finance); Thérèse Lacasse and Mary Guy-Shea (personnel); Cécile Desforges (assistant to the Executive Director); Marie Dionne (administration); Anna Bevilacqua (records); and support staff members Michelle Bélanger, Roch Langlois, Michel Lauzon, Jean Mathieu, David McKay and Pierrette McMurtie, as well as Denise Miquelon and Christiane Séguin of the Montreal office.

A special debt of gratitude is owed to Marlène Girard, assistant to the Chairman. Her ability to supervise the logistics of the Commission's work amid the tight schedules of the Chairman and Commissioners contributed greatly to the completion of our task.

I also wish to express my deep gratitude to my own secretary, Liette Simard. Her superb administrative skills and great patience brought much-appreciated order to my penchant for the chaotic workstyle of academe. She also assumed responsibility for the administrative coordination of revisions to the final drafts of volumes 1 and 2 of the Commission's Final Report. I owe much to her efforts and assistance.

Finally, on behalf of the research coordinators and myself, I wish to thank the Chairman, Pierre Lortie, the members of the Commission, Pierre Fortier, Robert Gabor, William Knight and Lucie Pépin, and former members Elwood Cowley and Senator Donald Oliver. We are honoured to have worked with such an eminent and thoughtful group of Canadians, and we have benefited immensely from their knowledge and experience. In particular, we wish to acknowledge the creativity, intellectual rigour and energy our Chairman brought to our task. His unparalleled capacity to challenge, to bring out the best in us, was indeed inspiring.

Peter Aucoin
Director of Research

PREFACE

THE ROYAL COMMISSION'S research on political ethics was designed to assess standards of political behaviour in regard to electoral democracy and to point to those values and principles that are recognized as characterizing the highest standards of ethical conduct. The performance of our institutions and elected representatives is judged by the ethical standards held by the public. If our political institutions and processes for selecting representative government are to retain legitimacy, it is essential that political practices conform to evolving ethical norms.

Public confidence requires that basic election rules be clearly articulated in a fair and transparent regulatory framework. Fulfilling normative expectations, however, may not be satisfied exclusively by complying with laws. This is because laws represent the minimum standards that must be adhered to without penalty. Consequently, demands to regulate a greater range of political activities may arise if the actions of political parties depart significantly from public expectations of appropriate conduct or if parties are perceived as being incapable of or unwilling to regulate their own activities.

The objective in this volume is to develop an understanding of the ethical concerns associated with political practices and to suggest ways candidates and parties can respond to these more demanding ethical expectations.

Pierre Fortin describes the ethical component of the submissions to the Commission. This study draws attention to the values and principles underlying public concerns and discusses why certain political practices are perceived to be contrary to public ethical expectations.

In the second study, Vincent Lemieux evaluates ethical concerns associated with patronage, corruption and conflict of interest. The study argues that the foundation for ethical reform lies in the ethical norms of the private sector, which foster competition and responsibility.

Ian Greene analyses the concept of undue influence in the electoral process by reviewing newspaper stories related to incidents or allegations. The study reveals that one of the incidents most likely to generate publicity involves the public's perception that political donations are exchanged for favours.

In the fourth study, Walter Romanow, Walter Soderlund and Richard Price examine negative political advertising. Based on interviews with Canadian political strategists, advisers and pollsters, the authors find that not only is negative advertising considered effective but that party activists anticipate greater reliance on this advertising method in future campaigns.

Jane Jenson analyses the linkage in Canada between equity and citizenship. Jenson argues that while earlier political understanding emphasized the equitable treatment of regions, contemporary views call for a renegotiation of citizenship to be more representative of new social groups.

The sixth study, by Kathy Brock, examines how a new rights discourse, encouraged by the *Canadian Charter of Rights and Freedoms*, is influencing how Canadians view the electoral system. The Charter has introduced a tension between rights and perceptions of fairness and equity that must be resolved, the author argues, if the legitimacy of the electoral process and system of political representation are to be maintained.

The final study in the volume, by Janet Hiebert, proposes codes of ethics for political parties as instruments for self-reform. The study argues that a code of ethics would give a party's leadership the tools for enforcement and members a clearer sense of their obligations to the fundamental principles of the party.

What emerges from these studies is the view that Canadian political candidates and parties have a significant impact on how Canadians assess and respond to the political process. The insights provided by the seven studies in this volume make a valuable contribution to the process of evaluating the ethical performance of political participants.

I am grateful to the contributors to this volume, who responded admirably to the requests that they examine the various ethical dimensions of Canadian politics. In addition to those who wrote studies in the volume, I would like to acknowledge the insights and suggestions of Peter Aucoin, Director of Research of the Royal Commission on Electoral Reform and Party Financing.

Janet Hiebert
Research Coordinator

POLITICAL
ETHICS

~

1

ETHICAL ISSUES IN THE DEBATE ON REFORM OF THE CANADA ELECTIONS ACT
An Ethicological Analysis

Pierre Fortin

THE ROYAL COMMISSION on Electoral Reform and Party Financing (RCERPF) provided us with the briefs it received so we could make an ethicological analysis of them, clearly identifying the main ethical issues in the debate on the topics in its mandate.

Of the 801 briefs received by the Commission, 52 percent were submitted by individuals, 26 percent by various associations and groups with no political affiliations and 22 percent by political personalities and groups. These briefs came from across Canada: 38 percent from Ontario, 17 percent from British Columbia and the Yukon, 11 percent from Manitoba and Saskatchewan, 11 percent from the Atlantic provinces, 11 percent from Quebec, 10 percent from Alberta and the Northwest Territories. Finally, 2 percent of the briefs were written by Canadian citizens living abroad.

Ethicology is a method of reading that sets out the moral or ethical dynamics of a text and identifies the issues it contains. What do we mean by an ethical issue? Ethical issues are involved where the following factors come into play:

- the application of laws, standards or rules to specific practices – in this case, regulation of the electoral process and party financing;
- the articulation of certain values that are conveyed in these laws, standards or rules and that inspire such regulation;

- the referral of these values to the concepts of democracy and citizens' rights and freedoms that justify such regulation.

Thus, the reform proposals contained in the submissions to the Commission are not neutral: they are inspired by specific values that they promote in any suggestion dealing with regulation of the electoral process or party financing.

In our study, we examined the briefs from four perspectives that enabled us to define the ethical issues contained in the briefs' suggestions, proposals and recommendations:

- First, from the practical perspective, we examined the actual reform proposal or correction involving a particular aspect of the present *Canada Elections Act* or of party financing.
- Next, we worked from the perspective of the standard or rule that was rejected or proposed as a means of regulating the electoral process or party financing.
- Then, from the axiological perspective, we examined the values that inspired a person or group of people to make their proposals.
- Finally, from the perspective of justification, of legitimizing the proposed reforms, we sought the democratic model that inspired them.

The ethicological analysis of the briefs presented to the Commission made it possible to identify the principal values promoted through the diverse proposals made to the Commission, and to draw attention to both the content of these same values and the justification for them. In so doing, we were able to draw out the concepts of democracy that were advocated or rejected in the briefs, and the dynamic of the opposing values involved in various aspects of regulation relating to electoral reform and party financing.

Our analysis also enabled us to identify several major ethical issues. Each is inherent in various problems identified by individuals, groups or associations who expressed their views on reforming the *Canada Elections Act* and on party financing. Our study in no way claims to outline what all Canadians think of the current state of democracy in our country, nor does it claim to express all the suggestions made to the Commission in their most minute detail. It was designed not in the theoretical framework of quantitative studies but from a qualitative perspective. By defining the ethical issues in the debate on reforming the *Canada Elections Act*, we wished to draw attention to the main elements of the debate as expressed in the 801 submissions to the Commission so as to bring out the ethical dynamics.

The following pages set out a summary-synthesis of each of the 13 sections of our research report:

1. Reasons for reform;
2. Perceptions of democracy in Canada and the ethical issues they raise;
3. The right to vote;
4. Representation;
5. The selection of candidates;
6. Political parties and their financing;
7. Interest groups;
8. Regulating election spending;
9. The voters list;
10. The role of the media in the electoral process;
11. Opinion polls during an election period;
12. The election campaign and the conduct of the vote;
13. Poll closing times and the disclosure of election results.

The quotations in this synthesis illustrate views widely shared by those who made presentations to the Commission. However, they do not convey the full richness of the debate.

REASONS FOR REFORM

The first questions that concerned us from the perspective of ethicology were the following: What motivated people to come before the Commission to call for reform of a given aspect of the *Canada Elections Act*? On what basis do they call for this reform? What values are invoked in their arguments? What is the justification for the desired reform?

In a very large number of the briefs presented to the Commission (see the list in the Appendix), we found a severe diagnosis of the state of health of the Canadian political system. For example, one reads:

> We have improved our processes over the last century. And we did start with one of, if not the, finest democratic structures in the world: the British parliamentary system combined with universal suffrage. However, our society has evolved in close step with the American society and in increasing estrangement from our British origins. We have been shaped by our regionalism, as well, which makes us different from our centralist cousins, but which has led to a deterioration of the quality of both government and democratic representation. Many of our basic practices and conventions have become inadequate to ensure the kind of quality democratic representation an advanced

country like ours deserves. This has increased the opportunity for distortions and abuses of our democratic process, by self-interested individuals and groups. Some are of goodwill, but too many are without conscience or any vision, or respect for democracy. (B-239-P)*

Democracy, it is sometimes felt, no longer works: "Canadians are beginning to say that the democratic system is no longer working" (B-371-P). Abuse, distortions, lies and corruption have led to a loss of confidence in political personalities by the public, which in the end causes a decline in citizen participation. Three submissions, among others, passionately decried the loss of confidence in politicians, which is felt by a majority of the population: "I have lost hope in our politics and politicians. Our politic is all lies and our politicians are a bunch of crooks ... people ... have no trust in politicians" (B-437-I). "There is a need to return to democracy and do away with the aristocratic system that has become entrenched in Ottawa. The Canadian public no longer trust their representatives who have taken on an air of arrogance and are often embroiled in suspicious if not corrupt activities" (B-113-I). "There is a decreasing value attached to the election process. The man on the street says about politicians 'They're all the same, in it for themselves, can't be trusted'" (B-666-A).

Some claimed that the current electoral process is faulty and that it undermines the quality of democratic life. The weaknesses of the electoral system discourage citizen participation and fair representation of the population:

> The first-past-the-post system of voting is archaic, unfair, undemocratic, and unrepresentative. As an electoral system, its three chief failings are that it lacks:
>
> - accountability both to the elector and to other opinions within the political spectrum;
> - legitimate representation both in broad terms of proportionality and to the constituent elector, but also in terms of issue and regional conflict; and
> - an ability to provide for real consensus ...
>
> Our current system of single member constituencies elected by plurality is inflexible, unstable and unrepresentative. It throws into question the legitimacy of our democratic institutions, which in turn

---

* These numbers refer to the list of briefs appended to this study.

seriously inhibits their ability to govern. It provides no basis for consensus and has traditionally provided little opportunity for public input into decision making. (B-520-I)

In addition to participation and fair representation, the Commission was asked to draw inspiration from the values of fairness, equality and effectiveness. In the name of these values, there were frequent calls for electoral reform to counter cynicism about the government:

> The survival of a healthy democratic system is everyone's concern, and this commission on electoral reform must ensure the survival of a healthy and fair democratic process in our nation. There is often a feeling of cynicism and lethargy exhibited by citizens towards government, and in the process of electing governments. (B-574-P)

According to several briefs, minorities and regions are not really part of the process. It is thus necessary to encourage more active participation by ordinary citizens in the electoral process by giving them all the means needed to participate fully:

> For some elections, the field of candidates, though seemingly wide, has been limited to the three principal political parties. This situation can be explained by the fact that not all the registered political parties are able to make their options known. The high costs of election campaigns and the financial risks for individuals who run for office reduce individual participation in the debates of our society, and permit only the richest political parties to take important initiatives. We must provide the means, as a democratic society, for all duly registered political parties and their representatives to get themselves heard by the public. Canadians' democratic choices must not be limited to the established political parties. The need is growing urgent, because during the last two elections we witnessed the Americanization of our campaign styles, which had the result of limiting our democratic and political choices: after all, only the leaders are visible in this type of campaign ... To prevent a deepening apathy of the public toward the electoral process, we must give it the tools needed to facilitate active participation in every riding, at the grassroots of our political system. To enable ordinary citizens to react and to act. (B-741-P)

Principal Threats to Canadian Democracy

From the briefs to the Commission, we have isolated seven principal factors that are alleged to threaten Canadian democracy or, more specifically, the democratic ideal to which Canadians aspire. These factors are:

1. the negative feelings shown by the population toward the electoral process;
2. the lack of response by the current electoral system to changes occurring in Canadian society;
3. the marginalization of large sectors of the population in the democratic process;
4. the lack of sensitivity to the needs and aspirations of Canadians on the part of political parties;
5. difficulties arising from the increasingly pluralistic nature of Canadian society;
6. problems arising from the lack of attention paid to certain regions of the country or to their population; and
7. an interpretation on the part of election officers that runs counter to the letter and the spirit of the *Canada Elections Act*.

To illustrate each of these factors, here are some reflections drawn from briefs presented to the Commission.

Negative Feelings Toward the Electoral Process
One citizen argued before the members of the Commission: "After the last three elections – federal, provincial and municipal – that I had been involved in as a voter it is easy to come to the conclusion that each of these elections had been 'bought' by business interests" (B-229-I). One organization more or less shared this assessment:

> As you are well aware, there is a popular perception that business and government generally participate in a "you scratch my back, I scratch yours" arrangement. While some may argue that this perception is a misconception advanced by partisan interests and general cynicism, we regretfully cannot accept that. We believe that the astute political observer will agree that the arrangements with government and business ... [are] not as open and above board as they should be. Not only is this an ethical problem, but it also results in popular cynicism and a general mistrust for the entire public process. (B-622-A)

Lack of Response by the Current Electoral System to Societal Change
Some contributors felt that recent social changes have transformed political institutions and forms of participation in the electoral process, as well as political attitudes and behaviour:

> The Canadian political culture has changed dramatically in the course of the last two decades. Technological, demographic and lifestyle changes are transforming the way Canadians view their political

institutions and how they participate in the political process. We are a less deferential, less ideological, and increasingly pragmatic people and our decisions today are more likely to be driven by information than by instinct or by loyalty to a product or a political party.

Institutions, governments, private corporations, and individuals face intense daily scrutiny, rising expectations, and seemingly contradictory signals from the public. We have become a more critical and sceptical people and the media – particularly television – have made Canadians one of the most aware and best informed societies in history.

At the same time, there are those who say that the Canadian electoral process is under duress and that it is time we stop and take stock of what is happening. (B-619-A)

Marginalization in the Democratic Process

There is also worry that domination of political life by a select minority leads to social and economic inequities, as well as contributing to the marginalization of large sectors of the Canadian population:

> The perception that "it won't make any difference," and that "politics is a rich man's game" (read: white, middle class, able-bodied, heterosexual, male), is widely held. This "perception" is solidly grounded in a political tradition which has perpetuated social and economic inequities and marginalized whole segments of Canadian society. Equality for women and other disadvantaged groups is not a top priority for the present federal government ... Lack of access to relevant information is another obstacle which both entrenches voter indifference and impedes the exercise of the right to vote ... Lack of means to educate voters is not the problem; it is the political will to provide funding to ensure it happens that is missing. Given sufficient financial support, community-based groups would serve as excellent information conduits to their constituent members. (B-423-A)

Political Insensitivity to Canadian Needs and Aspirations

Several briefs insisted that political parties need to be reminded forcefully of interests of the population that they do not seem to share. According to a member of Parliament: "The perception left with voters is that the political parties are essentially led by interests rather than [by] the ordinary citizen, for whom government should work" (B-267-P).

Pluralism and Problems in Canadian Society

That various ethnic groups play only a minor role in politics is an important concern:

- Minority groups are far from being politically integrated in Canada.
- Their relative exclusion from the Canadian political system threatens their social, cultural and economic integration.
- The political marginalization of minority groups runs counter to the principle of multiculturalism enshrined in the *Canadian Charter of Rights and Freedoms*.
- Unquestionably, what constitutes "political" representation for minority groups involves notions and categories that are foreign to the majority of Canadians.
- When observing the political reality of minority groups, one may well perceive a very different and disturbing political world.
- Any reform of electoral mechanisms cannot ignore these factors. (B-496-I)

Lack of Attention to Certain Regions and Peoples

Canada is a complex country, and this has an impact on our practice of democracy. According to some submissions, we must begin to take account of regional representation, a notion that our present political system lacks:

> Although rule by the majority is the first principle of democracy, Canada is not a homogeneous country. The views of a majority of citizens often differ by area. The governing system must be seen as fair by most citizens. Even the citizens of central Canada can see that a system which they dominate, irrespective of the views of the other regions, is not fair. Therefore Canada needs regional representation when laws are made. (B-203-I)

The loss of confidence in the democratic process is also felt by native peoples. They too experience a deep sense of alienation and rejection by other Canadians. On this subject, the Assembly of First Nations wrote:

> Our faith in Canada is weakening. We have, as individuals and collectively as a people, a deep sense of alienation and rejection. There is a growing opinion among our leaders that we are wasting our energy and resources trying to find acceptance and friendship in a home that does not want Indians. (B-572-A)

The president of the Native Council of Nova Scotia raised the difficulty of speaking of a truly democratic Canada as she cast a critical eye over the Canadian political system:

I know that none of us in this room can in all honesty say that our political process of representative government under either the current electoral representative model – [or] a party financing system [with] southern geographic constituency boundaries stretching northerly into areas where other peoples may be a majority – can justify the international norm for calling Canada a democracy. A democracy meaning by the people for the people – especially when everyone here knows that the present system excludes representation for so many other distinct peoples in the House of Commons. (B-769-A)

Violations of the Canada Elections Act *by Election Officers*
A member of Parliament from the West believes that "nothing is more important to a democratic society than the structure of its electoral system" (B-516-P). Basing their arguments on the same principle, others proposed a profound re-examination of the entire electoral system, particularly of the power of bureaucrats who violate the spirit and the letter of the *Canada Elections Act*. Some citizens stressed that "powerful and 'all knowing' bureaucrats interpret and abuse their role in administering the ... [law] according to both the spirit and the letter" (B-018-I). "We believe that it should be the mandate of Elections Canada to maximize voter participation in our elections. Wherever possible bureaucratic obstacles to participation should be dismantled" (B-607-A).

Principal Criteria Guiding *Canada Elections Act* Reform
Having brought out the principal factors that those who appeared before the Commission see as threatening democracy in Canada, we will now identify the criteria that must be given priority in any reform of the *Canada Elections Act* to ensure a better quality of democratic life for Canadians. These can be classified into three categories:

1. criteria concerning the aims of the electoral process;
2. criteria to encourage more voter participation; and
3. criteria that deal with the basic formulation of the *Canada Elections Act* to make it more acceptable.

We will now consider how these criteria are formulated in suggestions proposed to the Commission.

Aims of the Electoral Process
In his brief, one citizen insisted on the importance of drawing inspiration from the *Canadian Charter of Rights and Freedoms* in electoral reform and the regulation of party financing to promote four fundamental

freedoms: freedom of conscience and religion; freedom of thought, belief, opinion and expression, including freedom of the press and other communication media; freedom of peaceful assembly; and freedom of association (B-422-I). Referring to these fundamental freedoms, the writer of a brief from Calgary observed that:

> The new constitutional law of elections is comprised of both freedoms and rights. In particular:
>
> (1) the freedom of expression;
> (2) the freedom of association;
> (3) the right to vote in an election of members of the House of Commons and a legislative assembly; and
> (4) the right to qualify for membership in the House of Commons and a legislative assembly.
>
> These four constitutional rights and freedoms may be limited by the state only in response to a pressing and substantial concern. The limitation on the right or freedom must be proportional to the societal interest that is invoked to justify any limitation. Proportionality means that the limitation on the right or freedom is rationally connected to the objective and that it is carefully tailored to achieve the objective without otherwise infringing on the constitutional values of a free and democratic society. (B-676-I)

The author of another brief believes that the "pursuit of a process of opening up a democracy of quality in Canada" should follow the "principles of accessibility, openness, effectiveness, and respect for the individual" (B-488-P). He justifies each of these values in the following manner:

> Physical accessibility is imperative today and will be even more imperative tomorrow with the aging of our population. We must find other ways to enable those who worked throughout their lives to build the Canada of today to show their electoral preference for one political grouping or another.
> Openness is more important than ever in a world where political credibility, at one time so strong, has become so fragile: our democracy will always need committed citizens to insure its durability.
> Effectiveness is an unyielding condition of the technological world in which we already live, and will be more so tomorrow.
> Finally, respect for the individual is, of course, the great contem-

porary victory of humanism: it has managed to enshrine respect for individual differences in our institutions and to raise it to the ranks of the important values of our time. (ibid.)

A returning officer stated that "the Canadian electoral system is based on the confidence and impartiality that the electorate and political parties display." As is the case "in matters of fairness," "the electoral system must not only be fair and neutral, it must also have the appearance of fairness and neutrality" (B-241-I).

Citizen Participation

In determining reforms of the *Canada Elections Act* to be submitted to the government, the Commission has been advised to set three objectives based on the values of participation, responsibility, equality and fairness:

1. To encourage and facilitate the fullest possible participation by Canadians in all aspects of the democratic process.
2. To encourage Canadians to take greater responsibility for participating in the democratic process.
3. To ensure equality and fairness in the conduct of election campaigns without imposing an unreasonable regulatory or administrative burden upon volunteer campaign workers. (B-331-P)

A citizen from Calgary requested that, while reforming the electoral process, the Commission tackle the delicate question of equity:

The present electoral system presents most voters with a hopeless perception of a money-power election process. This causes many to stay away from the polls because persons of wealth with business connections dominate the process to a large extent. To reform the system, money needs to be removed from the process so that all candidates have equal access to voters on the basis of platforms and ideas rather than advertising and poster power. (B-062-I)

Making Electoral Law More Accessible

Those submitting briefs frequently lamented excessive control of the electoral process: "In my view, elections – like so many other aspects of Canadian life – are overregulated; in fact, there are nine different Acts that contain provisions relevant to the electoral system, and it is a too cumbersome and expensive process." Hence the request to simplify the electoral system: "There must be a way of simplifying it. It should be your goal to try and make the system simpler and less expensive to run" (B-074-I).

Several briefs asked that future versions of the *Canada Elections Act* be written in simple, accessible language, and be made easier to understand and more workable. Here are two reflections on the subject:

> It is fundamental that the language in which this act is expressed is both unambiguous and simple. The excision of ambiguity will probably never be achieved totally but it is a worthy goal. The matter of using simpler and more readily-understandable language cannot be over-emphasized. It is critical, for example, that the "average" candidate or citizen be able to read and understand the act. I'm sure that the daunting language forms used in the act are a deterrent to its broader understanding. (B-672-P)

> The right to vote, and the smoothness with which an electoral system functions, are very important to the democratic system. It also reflects on the image of the profession of politics itself. Wherever there is criticism of the operations of an electoral system, or the conditions of officials and candidates operating within that system – there will be negative repercussions. Therefore, all rules and regulations must be practical and workable. Onerous technical details should be eliminated in order to reduce the paper burden and frustration. (B-366-P)

The criteria most often cited in reform proposals for the *Canada Elections Act* referred to promotion of the *Canadian Charter of Rights and Freedoms*; it was even said that the future of democracy in Canada depends on furthering the Charter. There were calls for greater access to the electoral process for minority groups as well as a strong desire that the electoral system be less regulated and that the *Canada Elections Act* be simplified.

The principal ethical issue at stake in the debate on reforming the *Canada Elections Act* – one that appears central to our analysis – can be expressed in the form of a question: How can we encourage more equitable participation by all citizens in the entire electoral process?

ETHICAL ISSUES RAISED BY PERCEPTIONS OF DEMOCRACY IN CANADA

The debate on the democratic ideal that ought to inspire, support and justify the desired reforms of the *Canada Elections Act* has highlighted five principal perceptions of democracy:

1. Democracy is an ideal to be promoted.
2. Democracy is ensured by its electoral system.

3. Democracy requires that referendums and plebiscites be held.
4. Democracy is a matter of education.
5. Certain groups of citizens do not see themselves in this democratic ideal.

The reflections that follow illustrate each of these points.

Democracy: An Ideal to Be Promoted

Our democratic system is often seen as resting on two convictions, trust and faith in this system: "Without trust and faith in the system of democracy there can be no democracy." This trust and this faith also imply the responsibility of every individual to search for the common good: "We have democracy only in so far as we trust each other to act responsibly for the common good" (B-569-I). According to one brief, we thus unite the three fundamental principles on which democracy is based: "I believe democracy is based on three fundamental principles: the laws represent the views of the majority of citizens; each citizen's view is of equal weight; the means to influence the views of other citizens is equally available to each citizen" (B-203-I).

But the democratic ideal is not the same for everyone, as demonstrated by three different positions in the debate. According to the Reform Party of Canada, this is how the democratic ideal should be formulated:

> We believe that public policy in democratic societies should reflect the will of the majority of the citizens as determined by free and fair elections, referendums and the decisions of legally constituted and representative Parliaments and Assemblies elected by the people. We believe in the common sense of the common people, their right to choose their own leaders and to govern themselves through truly representative and responsive institutions and their right to directly initiate legislation for which substantial public support is demonstrated. We believe in accountability of elected representatives to the people who elect them and that the duty of elected members to their constituents should supersede their obligations to their political parties. Finally, we affirm our commitment to the rule of the law and to the concept that governments and law-makers are not above the law. (B-660-P)

Another brief described the democratic ideal in the following way:

> A truly democratic society must be founded on fundamental principles that promote fairness, participation and empower members of society:

- Promotion of local democracy
- Responsive and accountable institutions
- Promotion of freedom and the exercise of basic democratic rights
- A fair voting system
- Guaranteed voice for minority and critical opinions, both in Parliament and in the media
- Use of referendums and plebiscites to strengthen direct democracy
- Party financing system that prevents well-financed interest groups from influencing elections, the Government or any Member of Parliament. (B-774-P)

The Green Party of Canada bases its concept of the democratic ideal on ecological principles:

> The Green vision includes a responsibility to create both a healthy environment and a healthy society, both of which are fundamentally interrelated. The following is the party's Basis of Unity as well as the party's values. These values should be reflected in all Green policies and activities.
> 1. Non-violence and Military Disarmament ...
> 2. Ecologically Sustainable Economy ...
> 3. Preservation and Restoration of Ecosystem Diversity ...
> 4. Eco-feminism ...
> 5. Cultural and Multi-racial Diversity ...
> 6. Consensual Decision-making Process ...
> 7. De-Centralized Decision Making ...
> 8. Holistic Community through Personal and Global Responsibility. (B-419-P)

Ensuring Democracy through the Electoral System

According to the chief electoral officer of Quebec, democracy "rests on the free vote of electors" (B-624-I). This view was echoed in another brief: "Free elections are the foundation of democracy, and yes, they must be honestly and properly run to ensure that this foundation remains sound and enduring" (B-544-I). According to most contributors, participation and freedom of speech are two fundamental values that the electoral system must promote. It is also considered essential to safeguard "the fundamental recognition of the principle of equality among participants in the political process" (B-751-A).

The Need for Referendums and Plebiscites

Referendums and plebiscites must be held because politicians and bureaucrats have assumed too much power over the people (B-552-I).

Three particularly representative briefs conveyed this view well:

> The citizens of Canada have a right to be consulted individually on matters of such critical concern to them and the future of their country ... Voters who believe that their opinions are heeded and realize that they can effect change will be more willing to participate in the electoral process. Apathy and active distrust of politicians will decline as individuals are personally involved in deciding their own futures. (B-124-P)

> A referendum of the people that is held on important questions, as is held in Italy frequently for instance, is never practised in our country. This is wrong, the people should have more access to actively participating on important issues. I am also of the opinion that any one decision that would cost more than two million dollars should be ok'd first by the people in each riding. Too much waste of taxpayers' money is perpetrated by each government. (B-095-P)

> One of the most attractive aspects of the system of citizen-initiated referendums is the process itself. The very process of gathering hundreds of thousands of names on a petition to put an initiative on the ballot and the subsequent campaign on the issue itself further the political education of the voting public in a major way. (B-547-A)

These positions were criticized, however, because a referendum can paralyze the democratic life of a country (B-579-I).

Role of Education in Maintaining Democracy

The democratic ideal cannot thrive without an educational plan to inspire new generations and give them some understanding. "There should be no greater endeavor than to increase the public's knowledge of the importance of exercising their right to vote on election day. Students are an intricate part of the system, and if we begin with the youth, the cycle of apathy may not continue" (B-653-A). Several briefs stressed the importance of the initiation of high school students into the rules of democracy. It was also suggested that greater emphasis be placed on the education of all citizens in the democratic process, and that new Canadians be well informed about the Canadian electoral process.

Groups Excluded from the Democratic Ideal

Most of the briefs presented by Aboriginal people stated emphatically that they do not see themselves in the democratic ideal held by whites in this country, and moreover, that this ideal undermines their dignity and violates their rights:

> I won't dwell on the historical litany and current revelations of my people's preclusion from your Canada [of] our family. I am sure you have read, heard, seen, felt, and know: that we were not invited to help you build on our lands the federation to be known as Canada. That we would come to learn that you would not uphold and honour your Crown's pledges to us in treaty and proclamations. That your democracy for Canada, even with another family of a different speaking people, the French, did not trust itself to one vote for one man, and built in a majority rule by the English – you still can't remedy that and would rather self-destruct than accommodate. I am sure you have already heard that you feel my people to be less than your four-year-old child, and that you have had to consolidate into one Act, the *Indian Act*, all your charity for us. That even after you allowed my people to vote for your party, your candidates, you did not change your north-south geographically favoured electoral boundaries to accommodate our northern Aboriginal majority to elect Aboriginal candidates of Aboriginal parties or to make other affiliations to your Parliament. That you still believe that your majority, which is now a minority in Canada, should still rule this federation by spending millions of dollars to elect your favoured candidate and party. You still believe that since your system never allowed us meaningful representation as a minority that the majority rules, and that we have fair and responsible government in a democracy called Canada.
>
> I am sure that you have heard by some that Canadians don't want to see a real federation to be known as Canada, that is, a true democracy, where all migrating families to this land, and the original inhabitants, the Aboriginal peoples, can all prosper, flourish, share, and live in harmony, because to do so would allow all these "foreigners and Indians" to take away our jobs and resources and leave us with nothing. For those Canadians will you let this Indian have some air, or will I take too much too? (B-769-A)

The Commission's attention was drawn frequently to the importance of ensuring better representation of women, visible minorities and new Canadians:

> There are those who argue that the Parliament of Canada is not reflective of Canadian reality. In some ways, they are correct. Until such time as the parliamentarians who serve in the House of Commons

and Senate of Canada include more women, more Canadians of colour, more native Canadians, in fact, represent the true mosaic that is Canada, we cannot pride ourselves on having a truly representative Parliament ... The challenge then is to make Parliament more representative of the Canadian reality. (B-784-P)

The analysis of perceptions of democracy has enabled us to identify a twofold question present in the debate on the democratic ideal: How do we realize, in law and in practice, the stated ideal? Even more important, how can we implement it so that the whole Canadian population sees itself as participating in this ideal? This twofold question has led us to identify two major ethical issues. To encourage the most equitable participation possible in the electoral process, how do we articulate the different moral values of freedom, fairness and respect for differences? What legislation will respond to the imperatives of these moral values in a socially constructive way to ensure the integrity of the Canadian democratic system?

THE RIGHT TO VOTE

Once certain major principles and the values in the debate on the democratic ideal are brought out, it is necessary to tackle the problems of the right to vote. Who can vote? Who can actively participate in the electoral process? How is it that some people are excluded? Why are they refused this right? Should they be given the vote? Under what conditions? These are the main questions that we have come away with.

The right to vote, and the substance and goals of the right to vote, preoccupied almost everyone who submitted briefs to the Commission. First, we considered the perception of the right to vote that emerged from each of the briefs, focusing on the values advanced to justify this right. Next, we examined the right to vote of inmates, people with mental and physical disabilities, the sick, the illiterate and the homeless, as well as citizens occupying particular positions or living under special conditions. The presentation of the debate over the right to vote concludes with an overview of a number of suggestions concerning the voting age. Let us look briefly at each of these points.

All briefs presented to the Commission stated that the right to vote is a fundamental right recognized by all of Canadian society and sanctioned by major legal documents. The right to vote is frequently considered to be something sacred. Questions were raised, however, about the true significance of this right and its impact on the Canadian population, principally with respect to groups of people in special situations or belonging to minorities. As well, there were concerns about the application of this right. Most of the briefs stressed that the sacrosanct principle of the right to vote is often violated in Canadian society. This statement expresses a widely held position and effectively summarizes several presentations on the subject: "In Canada, we are led to believe that *every Canadian citizen* over the age of eighteen has the right to vote. On paper, this is true; our *Charter of Rights and Freedoms* stipulates that all Canadians are guaranteed this right. However, in practice, this is far from true" (B-267-P).

For some people, three other rights are linked to the right to vote: the right to stand for election, the right to a secret ballot and the right of access to all necessary information so that the voters' decisions will be as enlightened as possible. It should not be forgotten that responsibility is linked to the exercise of these rights.

Some contributors did not accept that the right to vote is universal; hence the following debate that developed around certain values and their impact on the entire electoral process.

Inmates and the Right to Vote

The author of one brief effectively summarized the debate on this question: "One of the most controversial areas in election law concerns the right of prisoners to vote. While some people argue that a person who commits a crime has forfeited his rights as a citizen and must temporarily be denied this privilege, others argue that voting is a right and that sending a person to prison is enough punishment since that person's rights to freedom of movement and assembly, etc. ... have been cut off. Although the *Charter of Rights and Freedoms* provides every Canadian citizen the right to vote, the *Canada Elections Act* does not" (B-742-P).

In fact, some people would refuse inmates the right to vote. The principal arguments can be outlined as follows:

1. People who are incarcerated have forfeited their right to vote because they have not respected the objectives of society and its laws. In breaking these laws, they have broken the social contract. It is, therefore, fair to punish them in this way.
2. They have lost the privilege of voting because of their crimes.
3. They have not contributed anything of significance to society, so why accord them such a right?

In contrast, there are those who feel that, in a democratic system, such a fundamental right cannot be taken away from an inmate. The following five arguments support this position:

1. The right to vote is a fundamental right that imprisonment cannot take away.
2. Preventing an inmate from voting contravenes the *Canadian Charter of Rights and Freedoms.*
3. Denying inmates the right to vote punishes them twice.
4. Depriving inmates of the right to vote runs counter to Canada's correctional philosophy, which emphasizes rehabilitation.
5. Depriving inmates of their right to vote prevents them from fulfilling their civic duties.

Some briefs distinguished between inmates who should maintain the right to vote and those who should forfeit it. Some were prepared to give the vote to inmates of provincial prisons, but not to inmates of federal institutions. Moreover, some held that, instead of placing all inmates on an equal footing, account must be taken of inmates' particular situations, to avoid depriving them of this fundamental right too easily.

In acknowledging inmates' right to vote, the contributors made reference not only to the *Canadian Charter of Rights and Freedoms* and to the *Universal Declaration of Human Rights* but also to the very principle of a democratic Canada (B-224-A; B-423-A; B-535-A), all while asserting that the right to vote is a duty incumbent on all citizens (B-498-A).

People with Mental Disabilities and the Right to Vote

Several interveners raised the question of whether people with mental disabilities should have the right to vote. We will first outline the arguments advanced by those who wish to deny people with mental disabilities the right to vote. We will then present some of the common positions, in order to draw attention to arguments in favour of the right to vote for such people.

Some briefs claimed that these people should not vote. What prompted this position? The briefs claimed that people with mental disabilities are not competent to correctly exercise their right to vote: "Seriously mentally deranged people should also not be allowed to vote – people must be competent, responsible and know what they are doing" (B-342-I; see also B-567-P).

Moreover, they claimed that people with profound mental distress are easily manipulated by their families or by those who are responsible for their care: "Giving them the vote would make about as much sense as giving it to three-year-olds" (B-493-I). A court finding of mental incapacity is sufficient to take away the right to vote.

Even contributors who would not go so far as to call for giving the vote to all people with mental disabilities worried about their vulnerability to discrimination: "A uniform definition is required on how to determine voting competence by the mentally handicapped. We found substantial differences within our group as to how this was measured" (B-497-I). There were some attempts to propose criteria for avoiding discrimination against those capable of voting.

According to others who came before the Commission, people with mental disabilities must be allowed to integrate themselves as much as possible into the community. The right to participate in the democratic process is an important part of their social integration. The main arguments for their participation were inspired by the values of dignity, freedom and autonomy of the individual, open-mindedness toward people with disabilities, respect for life, and the full and complete integration of such people into society: "The social integration and development of the social role of persons living with an intellectual deficiency constitutes a true social project: Canadian citizens must be provided with the means to actualize their rights without discrimination or privilege" (B-513-A).

People with Physical Disabilities and the Right to Vote

The briefs also suggested facilitating the exercise of the right to vote by people with physical disabilities in the interest of dignity and the autonomy of the individual, solidarity, equity and participation by all in democratic life. "In concrete terms, it is up to society to foster the autonomy of persons in difficulty, within their own immediate setting, to improve, through human solidarity, their physical and social environment" (B-475-A). It is thus important to ensure that these people can participate actively in the democratic life of the country.

People Who Are Ill and the Right to Vote

Although there is no question of denying the right to vote to the sick because of the state of their health, difficulties inherent in their condition can prevent them from exercising this right. Hence this statement of principle: "Persons ought not to be disenfranchised for reasons of health" (B-155-P). In the name of equity, it was demanded that particular attention be paid to the sick (B-737-A; B-156-A). One proposal served as an effective summary in this regard: "We propose that two or three mobile polling stations be created ... to bring the voting place to those persons who for a variety of medical reasons cannot travel" (B-602-P).

Illiterate People, Homeless People and the Right to Vote

In the name of equality and fairness, many contributors requested that special attention be paid to homeless people and illiterate people. "Special efforts should also be made to address problems of registering the homeless and contacting those Canadian citizens who are unable to read or write and who may be unaware of the elections process" (B-689-P; see also B-616-A; B-418-A; B-327-A; B-484-P). Only one brief suggested denying the vote to illiterate people who do not fulfil certain conditions (B-364-P).

It was thought that the traditional interpretation of property is archaic, unnecessary and contrary to the *Canadian Charter of Rights and Freedoms*. It discriminates against homeless people. In the name of fairness, the denial of a right as fundamental as the right to vote cannot be justified in a free and democratic society. It was even held that this denial is immoral.

To make it easier for illiterate people to exercise their right to vote, the Regroupement des groupes populaires en alphabétisation du Québec (a coalition of Quebec literacy groups) made five recommendations to the Commission:

1. that the enumeration forms and notices used in an election campaign be written simply and in short sentences comprehensible to those who cannot read and write well;
2. that governments arrange for clear explanation of election procedures (federal, provincial and municipal jurisdictions) and the importance of exercising one's right to vote;
3. that authorities find unambiguous ways to associate adjectives labelling a party with its logo, for while it is known that the Liberals are red and the Conservatives blue, nothing allows a voter to associate the word "Liberal" with red or "Conservative" with blue.
4. that political parties be held ... responsible for "translating" their election platform so that it may be understood by everyone. But above all, and more realistically, that candidates be made to respond to invitations from groups to explain their election platforms, and that they clearly identify themselves in terms of the party they represent and the party in power;
5. that candidates' photographs appear on the ballot. (B-531-A)

Changes to have itinerant people treated as full-fledged citizens are also essential. Four briefs requested that all necessary measures be taken to enable people with no fixed address to get on voters lists (B-705-A; B-259-A; B-516-P; B-502-A).

Facilitating the Exercise of the Right to Vote

Some briefs dealt with several other categories of people who, for a variety of reasons, cannot exercise the right to vote. These include seasonal workers, people who understand neither official language, elderly people, new Canadians and landed immigrants, Canadians living abroad, judges and returning officers. It was thought that changes to the *Canada Elections Act* and other specific measures should help these people fulfil their civic duty.

Determining Voting Age

Several briefs expressed concern about the minimum voting age. Although some contributors believe that 18 years is an appropriate age, others wonder whether the right to vote should not be granted at the age of 17 or even 16 years. They stated these reasons for lowering the voting age:

1. the earlier maturity of the young generation;
2. its interest in important world issues; and
3. the importance of encouraging young people to participate at the earliest possible age in the democratic process where the issues affecting their future will be determined.

Another brief argued that the right to vote should instead be given to "those Canadians who are most able to vote with full knowledge of the facts and with the wisdom indispensable for an act with such heavy human and future consequences," and is not appropriate "for all citizens who have reached the age of 18 years and over." The author of this brief thinks that the age of 55 "seems to present many advantages, including among others valuing experience, full maturity, and above all age and senior citizens" (B-723-I).

By emphasizing fairness, equity, equality, responsibility, information and participation, contributors demonstrated in several briefs the pros and cons of extending or limiting the right to vote, depending on whether it is seen from an ideal or a practical perspective. The principal ethical principle at issue here is respect for the dignity of human beings, regardless of social or economic situation or of any disability. This issue does not have to do with the definition of the right to vote or with the democratic ideal itself, but with the specific conditions of its exercise in Canadian society.

REPRESENTATION

At the outset, we will present some moral issues raised in the debate on representation. We will then discuss the principal factors that must be taken into account in establishing riding boundaries, as well as the specific problems of representation encountered by Aboriginal people and by women in the entire democratic process. This section will conclude by raising the question of proportional representation which, according to many who came before the Commission, seems essential if we want to live in a true democracy.

Requirement for Full Representation in the Democratic Process

What are the moral requirements raised in the debate over representation? One contributor wrote on this subject: "It seems to me that the seriousness of the problems that our representatives have to face justifies the establishment of a more balanced and fair popular representation. National unity has everything to gain by it" (B-037-I). An organization expressed its "hope that the Commission will recommend some form of perestroika which will encourage the replacement of the representation of democracy by representative democracy" (B-309-A). Moreover, a senator did not hesitate to assert: "We do not have equal government, we have a government of inequality and privilege, and we have inequality and privilege because the existing electoral system does not promote equality" (B-368-P). This diagnosis was shared by the Taddle Creek Greens: "Our political system must be responsive. The current electoral system stifles the growth of new parties, promotes concentrated regional interests while hindering widely based national interests" (B-774-P). In the name of equality, the following is also stated: "The *Charter of Rights and Freedoms* guarantees every individual before and under the law, and each individual has the right to equal protection and equal benefit of the law without discrimination. We would argue that the principle of 'representation by population' must be addressed in changes to the *Canada Elections Act* and in the redistribution of ridings in Canada" (B-546-P). It is thus important to consider that equality of representation requires more than a simple calculation of the number of voters (B-689-P).

Establishing Constituency Boundaries

According to the Saskatchewan Association of Rural Municipalities, the issue of determination of ridings raises a number of problems. This association, along with several others, insisted that the division of ridings be established according to the following criterion: "the community of interest or community of identity" (B-565-P; B-054-P; B-511-A; B-782-A). Thus, according to the association, people who live in rural areas do not have the same concerns as people living in large urban centres: "This is logical because their social and economic systems are entirely different." Respect for democracy requires, therefore, that both these groups be represented in the House of Commons: "Both the rural and urban voter should have their own representative in the House of Commons expressing their views on their social and economic problems. An MP should not be put in the position where he could be representing major conflicting views within his own riding" (B-511-A). "Surely a new formula could be worked out using a combination of territory and population that would more equitably represent all parts of the country" (B-358-I).

Representation of Aboriginal People and Women

The problems that Aboriginal people and women encounter regarding their representation in the entire democratic process were also emphasized in briefs to the Commission. Manitoba Keewatinowi Okimakanak Inc. noted that Indians have had the right to vote since 1960, but still do not have political power: "In terms of political power, which is the essence of elections, our participation in the electoral process has not resulted in political power or for that matter in any substantial influence on Indian policy." The brief continued: "We cannot say that we have a great and rising expectation in the political process for the eventual realization of our human dignity and the full enjoyment of our treaty and aboriginal rights" (B-561-A), and appealed to the Canadian Parliament and the First Nations to find a solution that respects the needs, aspirations and rights of Aboriginal people.

Citing social justice and equity, the Fédération des femmes du Québec, supported by a number of organizations dedicated to promoting the status of women, held that sexual political interest must be acknowledged to encourage female representation: "Up to today, the principle of geographic interest has been accepted as a valid and legitimate criterion for constructing our present electoral system, each person elected representing a riding and defending the interests of this region within the political institution. Now we believe that political interest also has a sexual dimension and that, in this sense, the improvement of female political representation is an objective of social justice and equity" (B-780-A).

Proportional Representation

According to many contributors, adopting proportional representation is essential to achieving true democracy. A citizen from Calgary wrote: "Under the present system Canadians only gain good and honest representation when there is a minority government"(B-062-I). Many stated that fairness is not what motivates advocates of the status quo in our electoral system, but rather the assurance of a stable government: "Those who uphold our present system do so not on the grounds of fairness ... but rather because it is supposed to ensure stable government" (B-374-I).

Many contributors stated that respect for democracy requires proportional representation: "It appears that only Canada, the United States, and Britain remain among the democratically governed developed nations that do not have some form of proportional representation" (B-261-I).

One brief summarized the proposals supporting proportional representation fairly well, listing the principal advantages:

1. It would reflect a real cross section of public political opinion.
2. Under the present system, the theoretically possible situation of one party obtaining 51 percent of the popular vote in every constituency, thus winning all seats, and leaving 49 percent of the voting public without representation in Parliament, would make a farce out of democracy. The present situation in the New Brunswick Legislature, where there is no opposition at all, is bad enough.
3. With "representation by popular vote," more often a minority government might result. But that would bring about more consultation, compromise, etc. between various political factions and might avoid the "majority-whip" of dictatorial power, quite often mixed with arrogance.
4. More people would regain interest in the democratic process, instead of not voting at all by saying: "[my] favourite party has no chance anyway."
5. Members of Parliament should anyway not only represent their particular constituents, but should also cooperate with their fellow MPs in initiating legislation benefiting all Canadians ...
6. The formation of new political movements with country-wide acceptable platforms and goals would be encouraged. (B-298-I)

Several suggestions were made concerning proportional representation. Among these we find:

Each voter would have two ballots. On one, s/he would choose the constituency representative, the other would be the party list. To ensure an immediate move towards gender parity in the House, the names on the party list must alternate between men and women. (B-719-A)

I am proposing a dual vote on a single ballot – one for the voter's choice of candidate, the other for the voter's political party preference. That way, I feel, the scenario of any political party receiving a majority of seats by virtue of elected representatives but without gaining the country's overall majority would largely be mitigated if not eliminated.

I feel this system is more equitable in its treatment of majority parties as well as smaller parties who may "come close but no cigar" during an election, and it would provide some lively new blood in the House of Commons. Furthermore, it may help prevent polarization of parties as well as voter reaction against a good candidate who happens to be attached to an unpopular leader or party.

I also believe that this system would bring about renewed interest among the electorate and thus cause a desirable resurgence in voter turn-out, reviving the democratic process instead of undermining it. (B-715-I)

The ethical issue underlying these discussions on representation is the following: respect for democracy requires equality, equity and fairness – representing all Canadians in the entire democratic process. Hence the view of many contributors that the chance must be given to citizens who so wish to participate in political power, along with recognition of the geographic, ethnic, linguistic, racial and sexual diversity that characterizes the Canadian population.

SELECTION OF CANDIDATES

In a number of briefs, it was stressed that the Canadian Parliament does not reflect the current national mosaic. For example: "Some groups, like the poor, and aboriginal groups, are almost never represented ... The evidence is overwhelming. The House of Commons does not adequately represent the votes of political parties in elections, the regions of Canada, women, aboriginal groups, or ordinary Canadians. In short, it is an élite-operated, élite-dominated institution" (B-530-I).

In the name of democracy, people frequently insisted that the House of Commons be composed of true representatives of the population instead of being dominated, as it is currently, by an élite of privileged men. According to some, too many citizens are de facto excluded from the processes of political and legislative decision making because of their sex, skin colour, culture or standard of living. Such exclusions violate the democratic ideal:

> We assume that a democratic regime's key goal is the election of a government which, by its composition, equally represents all citizens. Because it is clearly impossible for all of us to participate directly in our nation's decision-making process, the question of who partici-

pates and how s/he is chosen becomes a vital one. If the representatives do not reflect the composition of the population at large, the interests of those who are not adequately represented will forever remain marginalized and/or trivialized. Historically, this has been the case with women, aboriginal people, other visible minorities and, in general, the poor, the ranks of whom are largely populated by the three aforementioned groups. (B-719-A)

This is the reason why it was proposed that political parties be obliged to take all steps needed to recruit candidates who are truly representative of the Canadian population, particularly the economically weakest groups: "The Royal Commission should urge political parties to more actively recruit parliamentary candidates from among low-income Canadians, to ensure that poverty concerns form part of the political platforms of the various political parties" (B-246-A).

In the debate on candidate selection, two particular issues are raised:

1. How can we encourage access to public office by all citizens regardless of their social group, race and sex?
2. What should be the requirements to run as a candidate?

Encouraging Access to Public Office by All Citizens

In several briefs, contributors insisted that ordinary citizens should have access to public office: "Ordinary citizens must always have access to standing for political office in the electoral process" (B-574-P). A resident of Toronto raised the following question: "If the majority of Canadians are middle class then the minority are the rich – why are they ruling?" (B-273-I). The Ontario Federation of Labour stated that the greatest possible access to public office must be ensured: "You must ensure that public office remains open to ordinary Canadians and does not become again what it was not long ago, the private preserve of those who can afford to run for office by virtue of their own wealth and privilege or that of their friends" (B-648-A). In his brief, one citizen reached the same conclusion: "I do not feel the present system of electing candidates is satisfactory. We should have a variety of candidates from the general public. They should not all be lawyers, business people, etc." (B-350-I). Another advised the Commission that "in a democracy such as Canada both the rich and poor should have the opportunity to serve our country as an elected representative to Parliament" (B-511-A). One brief called for some control over the nomination process for would-be candidates: "Any practice which gives a candidate an *unfair* advantage should be controlled. Our country is too important to do otherwise" (B-358-I).

Adopting a position in this debate, the National Citizens' Coalition drew the Commission's attention to the danger of arbitrarily discrediting people who have succeeded in business by claiming that they are not sensitive to the needs of the people, particularly to the less affluent. According to the Coalition, this argument disregards the history of recent social legislation:

> The premise here is that not only will money buy an election but that as a result rich MPs will pass laws harmful or not helpful to the poor. This is an argument put forth mainly by people who put their trust in extensive government intervention. They don't accept that someone who has prospered in the private sector would espouse policies which would help the poor. We believe their views are wrong and that in fact exactly the opposite is true. This argument also ignores the fact that nationally all the main elements of Canada's welfare legislation were put in place by Liberal or Conservative governments before any controls were imposed on electoral spending. (B-547-A)

There were also requests that the new *Canada Elections Act* be formulated to encourage any citizen who wishes to become a candidate, and in such a way that no person or party would be prevented from running only because certain rules were not obeyed (B-371-P). This proposal is advanced in the name of respect for democracy and sovereignty of the people: "We must not forget that in a Democracy, it is the people during an election that have the ultimate authority in determining the fate of the candidates or political party" (ibid.).

It is also necessary to eliminate "money as a significant barrier to the desire of individuals to become actively involved in politics," to "encourage access to political representation of under-represented categories of the Canadian population, such as women" (B-780-A). In fact, in the name of fairness and equity, it was very frequently requested in the briefs that women be given easier access through the candidate selection process:

> In order to ensure that women have a reasonable chance of success I believe major changes are needed particularly at the level of the candidate selection process. As it presently stands, this process will continue to shut out competent women (as well as competent men), and will never guarantee that the best candidates are nominated. If the process is fair and equal and determined ahead of time – then at least women will have the opportunity to start from the same point as everyone else, and know what is expected. (B-500-P; see also B-754-A; B-784-P)

These changes would end discrimination against women: "Women would like an opportunity to play an equal role in a more honest and open system of politics in Canada" (B-597-A).

Given that the goal is to encourage greater access to parliamentary seats, a resident of Ontario questioned the wisdom of requiring deposits from candidates:

> If the deposit was to be abolished, what effect would this have on the federal electoral system? The deposit has no real monetary function in an election – it does not serve as payment of administrative fees, nor is it necessarily expected to augment election expenses reimbursements. It exists only for its supposed deterrent effect ... Because there are many welfare recipients in Canada who may benefit from the removal of this economic obstacle to their right to be a federal candidate, the striking down of the deposit requirement is the best remedy that could be hoped for. (B-017-I)

The financial difficulties that make access to public office practically impossible for people with physical disabilities were also underscored: "The Canadian Association of the Deaf wishes to express alarm and concern at the escalating costs involved in running for political office in this country ... For the average able-bodied person, this is a very expensive gamble to undertake. For a deaf or otherwise disabled person, it is quite frankly prohibitive" (B-236-A).

Many proposals addressed candidate selection. Sometimes the authors adopted diametrically opposed positions in the name of the same values. For example, in the name of effectiveness and fairness, one brief requests that business people not be excluded from the Canadian Parliament:

> The task force was concerned that the legislative body should be able to contain men and women drawn from all sectors of the community. A legislative body that excluded persons with active and senior business experience might not be necessarily as well placed to consider the impacts of policies which may be adopted on the process of job creation and economic growth as a legislative body that contained persons of knowledge and experience who might well be able to contribute to deliberations in that direction.
>
> It is also important that members of the legislative bodies be drawn from as wide as possible a spectrum of the members of the community in order that the legislative body be truly representative ... it is unjust to bar men and women with significant economic interests

from taking part in the active life of their community simply because they have financial interests. (B-351-A)

The Parti nationaliste du Québec, on the other hand, argued that "instead of becoming more permissive, the *Canada Elections Act* should make conditions for eligibility even stricter" for people who enjoy a very high standard of living: "The 'tycoons' of industry, commerce and finance already benefit from the immense power of their capital; it is indecent to give them additional political power on a silver platter. If we are not careful, the succession to the head of the Canadian government will become the private preserve of puppets of 'corporate bums', as has been so eloquently stated by a famous Canadian politician. We want a democracy, not a plutocracy" (B-781-P).

Qualifications to Run for Office

Some briefs called for candidates to respect certain ethical requirements. Here are two opinions on this subject:

> Canadians now require their elected representatives to exhibit the most transparent openness and unfailing morality. The lure of gain is a completely human reflex, but it is incompatible with the political ideal, which must be at the service of the common good. In these circumstances, the role of the government is to discourage anything in political practice that can give rise to the discharge of public duty for personal profit. (B-217-P)

> As the money involved with governing a country has reached astronomical amounts, I think that it is imperative that a system be established whereby the Canadian public is able to monitor the political and moral ethics of their politicians. All elected politicians should be required to disclose their financial worth each year so that conflict of interest and other corruptions could be minimized. Severe fines and prison terms would be handed out to those politicians found guilty of corrupt activities. After all they are public servants who should be looking out for the best interests of the country. (B-113-I)

It was also suggested that to ensure the quality of the electoral process, "each party must provide a mechanism to inquire into the integrity of its candidate for election. If there is the slightest doubt about a candidate's integrity, it must choose another (or not have a candidate at all) [and] avoid candidates with a criminal record" (B-361-I). A member of the House of Commons proposed a fairly strict selection method: "I believe the time has come for public authority to regulate the selection of candidates representing registered political parties in order to ensure the maintenance of the integrity of the electoral process." To justify the proposal, this MP added:

> Some may argue that extension of the mandate of Elections Canada to include the nomination process is an invasion of the rights of the parties. However, the sad fact is that the record of recent abuses has necessitated some form of intervention and regulation, in much the same way it has become necessary to regulate election and leadership campaign donations. It is also worth noting that registered parties receive public funds, through rebates and tax credits and therefore their affairs should be considered within the public domain. (B-783-P)

This last stance was totally rejected by the Confederation of Regions, Manitoba party, which wrote: "Let's give the constituency or riding association of every political Party the absolute democratic right to select the member-candidate of its choice. Let's give the Party executive of every federal political Party absolute signatory rights respecting the *Canada Elections Act*. Let's return democracy to the Canadian people" (B-230-P).

Calls for strict morality did not receive the support of all contributors to the Commission. According to the British Columbia Civil Liberties Association, there is no reason to consider those who have been found guilty of corruption or illegal practices in the past to be second-class citizens and not fit to run for office. This group held that it is up to the people alone to determine their representatives: "Our system of representation is based on the principle that the people have the right to choose their own representative. While one hopes they will not often choose those guilty of such offences, surely it is the voters' right to decide who should represent them. Parliament must be wary of doing anything that interferes with this basic relationship" (B-395-A).

Finally, although contributors to this debate had conflicting positions, they agreed that the new *Canada Elections Act* must take into account the seriousness of the individual candidacy.

The debate on candidate selection, as party representatives and as MPs, has ultimately revealed the complexity of the conflict of values among equality, fairness, morality, competence and the public interest. It is difficult to express these values and at the same time respect the integrity of the democratic process.

POLITICAL PARTIES AND THEIR FINANCING

Political party financing provoked strong reactions from contributors to the Commission. There was no consensus on the rules needed to respect what are thought to be the fundamental principles of democracy.

In our study, we were first concerned with identifying the main arguments concerning the nature of political parties and their role in the democratic process. We then extracted the principal values cited to justify regulation of party financing, distinguish acceptable from unacceptable sources of financing and restrict the size of contributions.

All contributors agreed that political parties play an important role in democratic life. But how can we ensure that party financing does not prevent them from being entirely dedicated to the public interest and independent of sources of party funds? This is the main problem raised in the debate over party financing.

Role of Political Parties

According to the Institute of Political Involvement, to ensure the integrity of the party system we must respond to current severe criticism of political parties: "Strong political parties are the very basis of our democratic system of government. However, we have serious concerns about the present credibility and perceptions of the electoral system in the minds of Canadians. The integrity of the party system must be a paramount objective of those convinced of its importance" (B-550-A).

Briefs often urged the strengthening of major political parties so that they become more responsible and more representative:

> What I believe should be a focal point of your report is the need to encourage and strengthen major political parties; and not merely to throw open the political forum to any and all groups concerned solely or mainly with one issue and one point of view. One of the challenges for all truly national political parties must be to modernize, to ready themselves for new challenges – not just technically (which by and large major political parties have done) – but dynamically, so as to accept the need to become more responsible and representative.
>
> What we must work for are well-organized, inclusive, effective and representative political parties, whose membership, scope, focus and philosophy cross linguistic, cultural, ethnic and regional boundaries. Political parties have the important responsibility to reach out to help educate Canadians on the major issues of the day, and to develop the processes by which individual Canadians can influence political and legislative agendas. Political parties must fulfill their mandate and go beyond organization and fund raising to explain to

their membership, and through them to the wider Canadian public, why certain policies are good for Canada, and why they believe that to be so.

What needs to be done, and initially political parties must begin the process themselves, is to build strong political parties, strong local, regional and ultimately national centres for discussion, debate and decision making – where the microcosm of the nation can come together to build a strong political system and responsive and representative political processes.

One dramatic result of their failure is the increase of single issue groups, representing every manner and variety of causes. (B-784-P)

The submissions frequently highlighted the important role played by political parties in a democratic society. The following opinion effectively summarized the implications of this perspective:

The internal processes of political parties must conform to the public will because of their crucial role in our system of democracy. The clash of ideas and personalities, the freedom to help determine the future of one's country, the precious liberty to vote for, or against, a platform or a person, all of these are unthinkable without the assistance of political parties. Political parties are the basis of democratic government. Although they have no formal role within our Constitution, our democracy could not function without them. When elected to a majority, political parties form a government and make the State answerable to the will of the people. While in opposition, political parties attempt to express the aspirations and criticisms of the people, thereby earning the right to one day form [a] government themselves.

Given this crucial mediating role between rulers and ruled, political parties must conform to the highest democratic ideals. If the people's tools are blunted, then the house of democracy will be ill-fashioned. (B-536-P)

According to many contributors, moreover, the party system as it exists today does not correspond to the expectations of the Canadian population. A citizen from Peterborough offered this analysis:

"Party" politics, as presently practised in this country, is no longer serving the people effectively. When only 60 percent of the eligible voters cast ballots and a party is elected to govern with 40 percent of the vote, that government, in effect, represents less than one quarter of the electorate. Often capable candidates ... who are dedicated to the public good are defeated because of party affiliation, and less able people are elected for the same reason.

Voters are often confused because political parties no longer adhere to the traditional values which their names imply. Opportunism takes precedence over integrity. This applies both to parties and to individuals.

The party system is too costly in many ways. Conventions, leadership and/or policy, are expensive. The valuable thinking of individuals is lost when members must "vote the party line." Then there is the matter of patronage, when elected representatives seem to feel obligated to those who worked on their behalf as well as to those unsuccessful candidates in their own party. (B-507-I)

Political Party Financing

According to the authors of a number of briefs submitted to the Commission, political party financing raises several principal concerns:

1. the integrity and credibility of the democratic process;
2. the independence of parties as well as politicians from their backers;
3. equity and fairness for the smallest parties;
4. equal representation for regions and for Aboriginal peoples; and
5. involvement of Aboriginal peoples in party organization.

To solve these problems, some proposed an increase in control of party financing. To make political party financing more democratic, a limit of $500, $1 150, $2 000, $3 000 or $5 000 was proposed for individual and group contributions to avoid endangering democracy. The reason advanced to justify a set amount is that it is necessary to avoid the control of political parties by particular groups, "some conflict of interest problems and the risk of politicians being unduly 'controlled' by corporate, union or other special interest groups" (B-181-I). "This would prevent any candidate or party from becoming too greatly aligned with any particular interest for political contribution reasons" (B-622-A).

Several other briefs stated that limiting contributions would strengthen democratic pluralism: "This would result in increased party membership and involvement in the political process. Both are healthy features of a pluralistic democracy" (B-181-I; see also B-443-A; B-173-I). The suggestion to limit individual and group contributions is often accompanied by a suggestion to reveal the names of donors who contribute $500 or more.

Other contributors believe that exclusively popular financing is needed. According to several contributors, legislation permitting only individual contributions is needed. To justify this position, the contributors emphasized the primacy of the power of citizens and the importance of safeguarding the independence of political parties in the name of equality, equity and participation, while stressing the importance of restoring confidence in the electoral system.

This stance is justified as follows: "Popular financing encourages ... the democratization of political parties and political life in general" (B-396-A). The supporting principle is expressed in different ways: "Federal political parties should rely on only a single source of financing: their individual supporters (both the committed militant and the traditional sympathizer)" (B-781-P). "It is the individual in a democratic state who votes and, therefore, it is only the individual concerns to which parties must pay heed, to pay election expenses. Accepting funding from individuals who are citizens will cut down on the foreign influence of such controlled corporations, and unions, and enhance the principle of our democracy of individual accountability to every other individual, and vice versa" (B-307-P).

> There is no doubt that large corporations and large unions are in a position to give larger contributions than individuals. Whether large contributions have some undue influence on public policy is a matter of conjecture. However, it is true that large corporations and unions will contribute to those political parties from which they can expect the greatest return. I do not feel that the democratic process is well served by having a certain group in society being able to contribute to political parties more than any other group. In any case, political campaigns are people campaigns and I do not see why these campaigns should be financed by corporations or trade unions. Consequently, I feel that there should be a limit on the amount that can be contributed to any candidate or political party. There is also some value in having individuals (not including corporations or trade unions) be the sole contributors to candidates and political parties. (B-258-I)

> There is undue corporate involvement in our elections, and this must be curtailed as it makes mockery of the whole concept of one person, one vote. (B-575-A)

Some contributors stated that popular financing ensures better individual participation and furthers individual confidence in the democratic process. It strengthens, among other things, the integrity of the relationship between voters and candidates or parties and maintains the stability of the democratic process. These contributors believed that it allows MPs greater freedom in the development of legislation and policies.

Some submissions, however, took issue with the proposal that contributions by corporations, unions and various groups be limited or banned. They cited the following values in justifying their position: freedom of expression, effectiveness, openness and the quality of democratic life.

In one brief, a resident of Victoria said he considers control of party financing a blow to freedom of expression for Canadians (B-775-I).

The president of the Sudbury Riding Ontario Progressive Conservative Association pleaded in favour of corporate contributions. He emphasized the necessary participation of corporations and unions in the development of good legislation (B-654-P). Other contributors also supported this position.

According to those who favour group contributions, openness is of importance in party financing. It is obvious, wrote the Metropolitan Montreal Chamber of Commerce, "that only popular financing offers all the guarantees required to achieve a truly democratic system" (B-533-A). Will eliminating contributions to political parties from organizations solve all the problems? One writer disagreed:

> With regard to the exclusion of legal entities, it seems to me that such a measure would constitute more a smoke screen than a real solution to the problem of the quality of our political morals. Everyone knows that it is easy for a political party to sidestep the restriction and to indirectly obtain contributions from companies.
>
> In my opinion, the important thing is not really to prohibit corporate donations to political parties, but rather to ensure that there is true openness.
>
> I recommend, however, that [the current degree of] openness be furthered by requiring that each list of donors be produced by province and show names and addresses. (B-494-P)

There was also some indication that limiting contributions, whatever their provenance, is not a realistic option considering the exorbitant costs that political parties face in their role in the democratic process. Thus, one brief read: "Political power and money in a competitive electoral setting are necessarily related" (B-530-I). For a resident of Regina, one observation stood out: "No money, no communication, no democracy" (B-569-I).

In the name of a vigorous democracy, the head of one company justified the right of a corporation to participate actively in financing a political party. He would even make it a duty for all corporations:

> We strongly support the right of corporations to participate in the democratic process through political contributions. This is the only vehicle open to corporations. As a company we have had the privilege over the years to participate with contributions to all three major political parties. We believe it is our duty as good corporate citizens – our duty to ensure that our democratic institutions remain strong and that through our contributions we can encourage individual Canadians of any political stripe to seek office. (B-641-A)

The debate over party financing, we have observed, calls into play the quality of democratic life, which is principally centred on participation, freedom of expression, equity, equality and openness. Opinions differ not so much on the values to be promoted as on how to promote them.

INTEREST GROUPS

A debate surrounds the relevance of interest groups in the electoral process and whether their expenditure on advertising during election campaigns should be limited. We will first briefly present arguments that interest groups have their place in the political scene and then consider arguments that interest groups distort the democratic process. We will conclude this section with a discussion of a related issue, the extent of advertising spending by these groups during election campaigns.

Role of Interest Groups in Election Campaigns

A number of briefs argued in favour of total respect for freedom of expression. Freedom of expression, they wrote, goes hand in hand with the future of democracy in Canada. Here is an example:

> A federal election is vital to our democracy. It is a time to review issues and to see where others stand, to judge comments and to test the validity and strength of your convictions – whether you are a candidate or not. It is a time to listen, to attend meetings, to read about speeches, to read the views of others – and, finally, for each to exercise his or her constitutional right to vote for the party or candidate of choice to represent the elector in the House of Commons.
> The "freedom of expression" guaranteed in section 2(b) of the *Charter of Rights and Freedoms* is the freedom of all members of the community to express themselves and to learn of the views of others on matters of public interest. Without the full protection of an ample

right to be involved in political debate and in federal elections, Canada is not a democracy and its people do not have the fundamental freedom of expression that is the underpinning of all of its democratic and parliamentary institutions.

The Charter enshrines the right to vote and freedom of expression. Voting is a form of expression as well. No legislation should tinker with the rights of Canadians to express themselves at election time on the subject of the issues or the candidacy or electability of the candidates. (B-092-A)

Other arguments also support the presence of interest groups on the electoral scene. In the name of participation by each citizen in the electoral process, for example, it was argued that:

One of the greatest attributes of a democracy is that each and every citizen has an opportunity to participate in elections. If he objects to the existing government, he has every opportunity to effect change. Accordingly, there is no justification for violence or confrontation. If one can get enough people to agree with one's position, one can change the law. It is a reality, however, that it is manifestly impractical to start a new political party for every cause, and especially since most people have many causes they identify with.

The fact that third party organizations such as ours compete with the benefit of tax credits is a sign as to how out of touch some feel our political parties are from the electorate.

We object most strenuously to any attempts to legislate an end to or control funding by third party organizations.

To attempt to stifle [the participation of ordinary citizens] in the democratic process would only lead to frustration and a feeling that they are unable to participate in the electoral process. (B-114-A)

Other briefs justified interest groups as sources of information required for proper exercise of one's right to vote. They also raised themes that politicians refuse to discuss during election campaigns. It was also argued that, in the name of fundamental freedoms, interest groups must be present on the electoral scene to counter the overly significant influence of politicians and to ensure a sound and democratic debate.

Others suggested that the activities of these interest groups be regulated. Suzanne M. Birks, president of the Canadian Human Rights Foundation, stated: "The regulation of the electoral rules of financing campaigns is a means of assuring to some degree the fairness and fullness of debate" (B-558-A). The ultimate goal of this regulation is not to limit debate, but to ensure the integrity of the electoral process (ibid.). The president of the Foundation and several other contributors requested that the rules that apply to political parties be imposed on interest groups as well: "There is every reason to require that associations, individuals, businesses, commercial organizations, governments, trade unions, corporations, and unincorporated organizations who are engaged in the financing of particular platforms during a general election be subject to the same rules as those controlling the candidates and official political parties" (ibid.).

Interest Groups and the Democratic Process

Some contributors believed that the presence of interest groups distorts the democratic process. A federal MP from Ontario completely rejected the possibility of allowing interest groups, regardless of their nature, to proliferate: "What we do not need in the years ahead is a continual proliferation of special interest groups – be they religious, or corporate, or consumer, or any or all of the above, clustering and cluttering up the national agenda, trying to achieve individual piecemeal changes outside of established processes" (B-784-P).

In Quebec, the chief electoral officer wrote: "It is the people that control political power through political parties, because contributions must come from voters and not corporations." Control of political activities by political parties is threatened "if third parties are allowed to interfere." The formula of popular party financing has the advantage of "protecting the free exercise of the right to vote and, as a consequence, it ensures respect for democracy." Moreover, "the sharing of election financing by all voters to take financing out of the hands of wealthy economic powers and interest groups encourages the cleanup of electoral practices and the pluralism of ideas." He continued his argument: "In the political arena, freedom of expression must be conditional on the goal that one wishes to achieve, electing the best people possible to perform the functions of MPs and to administer public affairs." He went on to observe that "control of electoral expenditures has the goal of maintaining a certain equity between candidates in an election." According to him, it is understood that this advantage would quickly be lost if no restriction applied to third parties (B-624-I).

This conflict of values between protection of the democratic system and freedom of expression was also perceived by representatives of the Business Council for Fair Trade, which contended that the presence of interest groups in the electoral debate runs counter to equality and fairness. According to this organization, it is important to strengthen political parties to ensure a stronger and responsible democratic life. According to the Council of Canadians, protection of the democratic system, which it considered to be threatened by pressure group abuses of freedom of expression, must take priority over even freedom of expression itself.

Advertising Expenditures by Interest Groups during Election Campaigns

Interveners usually expressed one of three opinions on the sums interest groups spend on advertising during election campaigns: some briefs called for specific policies to limit expenditures, while others opposed any limitations whatsoever. A third group would ban all advertising by interest groups during election campaigns.

Some briefs held that spending by interest groups and members of interest groups affects the very foundations of the electoral system. A glaring conflict of values can be seen between the use of financial means to advance particular interests on the one hand, and the equality of citizens and freedom of speech on the other.

One brief called for control of advertising by interest groups during election campaigns: "If no controls are put on it then elections will eventually be won by those with the most money" (B-308-I). The Commission was frequently asked to recommend that the government adopt policies on advertising by these groups. According to the author of one brief: "Advocacy advertisements and commercials of condemnation should meet some standards of fairness but also spending accountability" (B-218-I). Some people requested that interest groups be authorized to spend the same or almost the same amounts as political parties, or that their spending at least be made compatible.

In contrast, to avoid undermining a freedom as fundamental as freedom of expression, an MP argued that advertising by interest groups must not be banned. Instead, we must place our trust in the intelligence of the voters, who are capable of distinguishing between what is and what is not propaganda:

> We do not ban third-party advertising, but during an electoral period we require people who had advertised with the intent to influence the electoral process to register and report their expenditures to Elections Canada. A ban of third-party advertising is really breaching a fundamental freedom, and that is the freedom of speech, and we should discourage that in a vibrant democracy. However, balanced against that is the doctrine of fairness, and I would argue that while we shouldn't stop anyone from advertising, we certainly should

monitor how much they spend so that the people can look back and see what sort of resources they have and why they are spending that money, and that these reports be published. Any ad should also indicate who is paying for it.

Voters are intelligent and sophisticated. They can see through a lot of propaganda. (B-346-P)

Finally, several people held that it is clearly necessary to ban advertising by interest groups. They believed that such advertising has a negative effect on the choice of the electorate. Others maintained that it compromises equality of opportunity between political parties. Finally, some contended that it undermines the integrity of the electoral process.

The presence of interest groups in the electoral process and the possibility of limiting restrictions on their advertising expenditure during election campaigns do indeed raise a conflict of values between freedom of expression and equality of citizens. It is, therefore, difficult to ensure a fair balance between freedom of expression, the common good and equality of participation by citizens in the electoral process. Although interest groups encourage freedom of expression in their own way, several people held that they create an inequality between citizens; some simply have more power than others to advance their viewpoints and thereby influence the vote.

REGULATING ELECTION EXPENDITURES

The problem of election expenditures is closely linked to the problem of political party financing. To ensure the democratic nature of the electoral process, we must deal with the definition, limitation and reimbursement of election expenditures.

In this section, we will first present proposed improvements to the *Canada Elections Act* that address election expenditures. We will then ask some relevant questions. Is it necessary to limit election spending by political parties? Should these expenditures be reimbursed or not? If so, to what extent?

Defining Election Expenditures

Some briefs mentioned the need for the *Canada Elections Act* to be simpler and clearer on election expenditures because "the definitions [of election expenditures] are sufficiently loose to allow for a multitude of interpretation" (B-642-P). The current confusion, it is believed, may lead people to an arbitrary decision that a candidate is dishonest. It is also recognized that ambiguities can lead to abuse, intentional or not: "The definitions of election expenditures for candidates and for political parties are vague, subject to widely differing interpretations and arbitrary in their application. This has led to confusion and the real possibility for both intentional and unintentional abuse" (B-372-P).

For this reason, the Commission was frequently asked to define election expenditure, for the sake of openness and equity.

Limiting Election Expenditures

The debate over election spending by political parties contrasted two principal trends. Some briefs lauded restrictions, while others condemned any form of restriction. There were intermediate proposals between these polar positions.

It was generally considered that in a democracy we must "prevent major backers from acquiring unwarranted power" and, as a consequence, it is necessary to "keep party expenditure, electoral or otherwise, as low as possible" (B-093-I). Similarly, it was held that "the amount of money spent by parties is detrimental to building trust between the electorate and the elected" (B-706-I).

Some briefs said that limitation of election spending is intended to ensure, without discrimination, that all candidates have the same opportunities to convey their message to the electorate. Money should not be the primary factor contributing to the election of a person, "to safeguard the principle that the person with the best ideas, not necessarily the one with the most money, is the one to be elected" (B-265-I).

At the other end of the spectrum, some saw restriction as a breach of respect for fundamental freedoms:

> Any limitation on political advertising constitutes a restriction on the fundamental freedoms of "thought, belief, opinion and expression, including freedom of the press and other media of communication" ... Any limitation on political advertising and communication is doubly odious when it seeks to restrict debate, in any way, at election time. If there is any period in a democracy when debate should be encouraged and stimulated surely it is between the announcement of an election and voting day. Yet this provision does exactly the reverse! It detracts from the electoral process by limiting free speech. It should be eliminated. (B-395-A)

Still others saw restriction as censorship of political expression: "The government has no right to interfere with the property, legally acquired, of any institution or individual in Canada, so long as the entity in question is not aggressing against the rights of others. Spending limits are a crude interference, a sort of censorship of political expression, totally out of step with Canadian political traditions" (B-405-P).

Professors from the University of Regina highlighted the apparent conflict between the different rights involved in the control of election expenditures: "In this case we must balance conflicting rights, the right to free speech, and the right to a fair electoral contest. A fair electoral contest will not occur automatically; it must involve legislation that controls financial expenditures as well as contributions" (B-530-I).

Reimbursement of Election Expenditures

Reimbursement of election expenditures also provoked debate among the groups that addressed the Commission. Some alleged that reimbursing election expenditures from public funds is a grave mistake: "No citizen should be forced to support a party or candidate which they would not do voluntarily, or be prevented from supporting the party or candidate of their choice" (B-256-P). Elsewhere, in the name of equity and the integrity of the democratic process, it was suggested that all candidates receive a sum from the government to cover some of their expenses: "The time has come for us to take measures collectively to guarantee the viability of the electoral system and protect the opportunity for all citizens to run for office" (B-741-P).

Finally, some briefs proposed regulating reimbursement of election expenditure without abolishing it.

The ethical issue in this debate concerns preserving and asserting freedom of expression, the public interest and the interests of political parties, through standards promoting honesty and integrity in the electoral process.

THE VOTERS LIST

Preparation of the voters list causes problems that several contributors to the Commission said violate fair exercise of the right to vote. First, we will discuss general remarks about the way the list is currently prepared. We will then present arguments for and against creating a permanent electoral list. Finally, we will draw attention to several key aspects of the debate concerning responsibility for registration on the voters list.

General Perceptions of the *Canada Elections Act*

Several briefs expressed the view that the traditional enumeration process no longer corresponds to current social realities:

> The present system of enumeration and revision is inefficient, cumbersome and out-dated. In the past, this system was superior due to the fact that the population was less mobile, a very large majority of

women did not work outside the home, and leisure hours were most often spent at home. (B-586-I)

The system of enumeration of voters is archaic, unreliable and inconsistent, and lends itself to serious omissions and errors ... Electoral lists are often incomplete and inaccurate. (B-585-P)

It was noted that the enumeration process should in no way violate the citizens' right to vote: "The most important and direct democratic act in which citizens partake is voting. To deny even one voter his or her primary democratic right is unacceptable and simply must not occur" (B-516-P). Contributors denounced the harm caused by the present enumeration process:

The present enumeration process is obsolete and is the source of inequities and controversy. It was meant for a time when one member of each family was usually at home, so that putting the voters list together was a simple process. Today, with two-career households, the present system is error-prone and unnecessarily lengthens election campaigns. The difficulty in finding and appointing capable enumerators is a major problem, which frequently leads to incomplete lists and the inclusion of non-citizens ... In summary, the present system lends itself to abuses, inefficiency and unnecessarily long election campaigns. (B-550-A)

In addition to the process being ill-adapted to new social realities, several contributors thought the present process deprives people of their right to vote. Moreover, the process has become too expensive and does not always foster voters' confidence in the electoral process.

Among the problems encountered in the enumeration process two areas of discrimination were mentioned: discrimination against Aboriginal people and discrimination favouring city-dwellers over country-dwellers.

The difference between urban and rural enumeration practices is often the cause not only of confusion but also of a deep sense of discrimination. According to a citizen from Ottawa: "I was astonished that no mechanism was in place for a citizen to make a declaration at the polling booth as is common in municipal elections in this province" (B-202-I). It was submitted that this feeling of discrimination is found in all areas of the country (B-543-I), and that discrimination sometimes "leads the way to dishonest practices in rural areas" (B-173-I; see also B-408-I; B-689-P; B-578-A; B-565-P; B-503-I; B-478-P; B-330-I; B-296-I; B-006-I; B-210-A; B-678-P; B-375-P; B-630-P; B-461-P; B-536-P; B-522-P).

The Commission also heard that the current enumeration process is sometimes inconvenient and even risky for people whose privacy and security could be seriously threatened.

Various proposals were made to improve voter registration:

> The present system allows only one office for the returning officer, and one sub-office ... This effectively disenfranchises people who live at a distance, and have been omitted in enumeration.
>
> We suggest that: a) there should be provision for additional sub-offices where there is a significant population centre more than 40 miles from an existing office; b) there should be wider opportunity for late registration; c) the provision for swearing in of unregistered voters should be extended from rural areas to include the advance poll. (B-254-P)

Other measures were proposed to increase the efficiency of registration and reduce the salary costs attached to enumeration.

To make the enumeration process more acceptable, an Ontario MP listed five objectives that were often cited in other briefs submitted to the Commission:

> Though the existing system has the virtue of being simple from the elector's perspective, it fails by not being accurate, accountable, economical, and shows signs of lacking in comprehensiveness. All of these conditions are the result of the door-to-door enumeration being so poor.
>
> Given that door-to-door enumeration should fall into disuse, an alternative system must be proffered. To be acceptable, the new system must succeed in five principal areas.
>
> (1) *Simplicity* An alternative system of enumeration must allow eligible voters the opportunity to enumerate themselves, or be enumerated, with as little effort as possible. No alternate system should discourage the casting of ballots by complicating the enumeration process.
>
> (2) *Universality* No group or class, whether defined by income, race, geography, or any other characteristic, should be favoured in the preparation of a voters list.
>
> (3) *Comprehensiveness* Obviously, any system designed to prepare voters lists should endeavor to include as many eligible voters as possible, and the information should be as up to date as possible.
>
> (4) *Accuracy & Accountability* The compilation of a voters list must not be dependant upon thousands of inexperienced casually

hired enumerators. Whether or not one is enumerated should not be determined by random chance, and eligible voters must know whether or not they have been enumerated, how to become enumerated, and who is accountable for their not having been enumerated.

(5) *Economy* Enumeration must be as inexpensive as possible without compromising the previous demands of an effective system. (B-021-P)

Pros and Cons of a Permanent Voters List

Some people and groups favoured a permanent voters list, principally in the name of equity, effectiveness, sound management of public funds and cooperation between the various levels of government.

In the name of equity it is becoming urgent, according to many people, to move toward a permanent electoral list by taking advantage of available technological resources. In their brief, a group of returning officers from Quebec declared that "modernization of the present system of registration and revision is needed to allow all Canadians to exercise their right to vote, the foundation of our democracy" (B-277-I).

Because of "serious gaps and inconveniences" in voter registration in the last election campaign, some contributors recommended both "a mechanism ... by which voters can register themselves personally" and "a permanent computerized electoral list" (B-277-I). They thought that these methods offer the advantages of effectiveness and low cost. One citizen justified creating a permanent computerized list in this way: "A permanent voters list will: permit flexible election timing; provide a single list for all three electoral levels, thus lowering costs, and avoiding voter confusion; permit the implementation of plebiscites with minimum costs" (B-168-I). The creation of such a list may be, according to some people, an opportunity to increase cooperation between the various levels of government (B-045-I; B-403-P; B-552-I; B-478-P; B-309-A) which could share the cost.

Some, however, adopted a "cautious" attitude toward a permanent voters list. The Progressive Conservative Association of Nova Scotia advised the Commission that it could be dangerous to use a permanent voters list without taking into account the rights and freedoms of the person (B-771-I). On this point, it recommended that the Commission ensure, through certain provisions, that such a list be used legitimately. Other briefs requested both that a permanent voters list be established and that effective means be found to maintain the flexibility necessary to revise it. The Ontario section of the New Democratic Party of Canada wrote that the permanent voters list should be created on the express condition that it would increase the number of voters (B-695-P). At first glance, this reasoning is no more obvious than the proposition that the creation of such a list will require more responsible participation by citizens.

Finally, we found several citizens opposed to the idea of a permanent list. They were not convinced that a permanent voters list would correct the problems that we wish to solve. For example, the New Democratic Party of Canada did not support the proposed permanent list because Canada's population is very mobile. It supported the idea even less if it proved to be inflexibly carried out (B-344-P). This argument was repeated fairly widely by opponents of a permanent voters list.

A Sudbury resident wrote that a permanent voters list serving all levels of government is impossible to achieve because of the considerable variations in criteria for voting eligibility (B-664-I). The New Brunswick Progressive Conservative party rejected the idea of a permanent list because of its implications for the privacy of citizens: "We are not in favour of a permanent voters list. The logistics would be too cumbersome and a permanent list has overtones of 'Big Brother'" (B-375-P).

The author of one brief wrote as follows: "I do not feel that trying to maintain a permanent voters list as current by attempting to track individuals' moves or cross referencing other databases such as drivers licences or SIN numbers is practical. Such an attempt would also open up many questions regarding use of such databases and civil libertarian concerns" (B-019-I).

Responsibility for Voter Registration

The problems raised by creating the voters list provoked one writer to suggest that "we must return to the foundation of our electoral system which rests on trust and ponder the responsibility of voter registration" (B-241-I). Whether it is decided to improve the present enumeration process or to adopt a permanent voters list, another debate arises: should citizens or elections officers be responsible for registration?

An intervener from British Columbia insisted that "changes in legislation should shift toward making the elector more responsible for ensuring that he is on the voters list. This consideration is as applicable to the current enumeration/revision process as it is to any revolutionary registration system" (B-497-I). Her call for voter responsibility is widely shared: "It should be the responsibility of each voter to put their name and correct address on a permanent list. The present enumeration process simply does not work" (B-087-I). With the goal of encouraging public responsibility, a voter registration system is also recommended: "With a registration system, those people who seriously want to vote will make the effort to register their names" (B-586-I).

Some briefs did not inevitably associate the "permanent list" with the "responsibility of ensuring one's registration on this list." Voter responsibility can be just as much a part of the present census-style system as of a new formula.

Opinions on this issue, however, were divided. Some contributors believed that voter registration should be the responsibility of the government and election officers:

> Any establishment of a permanent voters list must put the onus on the government and Elections Canada to ensure registration of voters ... We would encourage the Commission to recommend that enumerators continue to [be] responsible for the final production of voters lists in their poll and for the certifying of the eligible voters in their poll ... That certification of voters lists must remain with those people who are doing the enumeration and have met with the eligible voters in their poll. (B-546-P)

The ethical issue that emerges from the debate on the creation of a permanent voters list thus calls into question the balance between equity and responsibility. The contributors who are concerned about this problem wonder how to ensure that citizens find themselves on the voters list – hence the ethical issue – and to what extent they should be responsible for their registration on this list.

ROLE OF THE MEDIA IN THE ELECTORAL PROCESS

In this section, we address a question stemming from the debate on the role of the media in the electoral process: should their presence be regulated? We present three conflicting positions on free air time allotted to political parties, in order to set out a brief concluding account of the discussion of two other themes: broadcast debates between party leaders and election advertising.

Regulating Media Presence in the Electoral Process

Those who support mandatory regulation of media presence in the electoral process cite various values to justify their position. An Ottawa resident, for example, cited two basic principles that must be taken into account when examining the place and role of the media in election campaigns. First, there is the need to respect pluralism in Canadian society; next there is the moral and legal obligation to support media access to all involved in the electoral process in the public interest (B-347-I).

The Canadian Association of Broadcasters presented the complex position in which radio and television broadcasters find themselves during an election campaign. The association considered that when partisan messages are reported or broadcast, fairness, balance and equity as they affect the public interest are at stake (B-228-A).

Others vigorously denounced the over-large role that the media play in the electoral process, as in the following question: "Is our electoral process to be dictated by the media, or should the electoral process dictate the media coverage?" (B-574-P). According to some, the role the media play in the electoral process can be easily explained: "Newspapers and broadcasting are businesses owned by businessmen" (B-530-I).

Some briefs argued that the media presence in the electoral process should not be regulated. In the name of freedom of expression and association the National Citizens' Coalition was opposed to any regulation of the media:

> Some of those who are prepared to prohibit or limit citizens' freedom of speech or association during federal elections are apparently unwilling to do the same to the media. This poses three problems.
>
> The first is that media owned by public corporations are in fact owned by individual citizens who have freely associated together to buy shares in them. Why should most citizens' freedoms be violated when these other citizens, who happen to own a powerful media outlet, are allowed to take strong editorial stands for or against a political party or candidate?
>
> The second is the case of media privately held by either proprietors or small groups of wealthy investors. Are these citizens to be allowed to use their media to support or oppose parties or candidates when citizens of more modest means are prevented from doing so?
>
> Third, how is one to define a newspaper? Would bureaucrats be asked, for instance, to decide whether or not an NCC Election Gazette is really a newspaper?
>
> These problems can only be justly resolved, we submit, by not prohibiting or limiting citizens' freedoms of speech and association during federal elections. (B-547-A)

The Quebec Federation of Professional Journalists (QFPJ) stated that there is a "close link between freedom of information and the health of democratic life in our society." In quoting the Charter of Journalism, the

QFPJ justified its position: "Information is an essential need in an increasingly complex and pluralistic society, since it is through information that individuals can participate democratically in the life of the community ... The role of organs of information and journalists is to serve the public's right to information. They can only do this in a system that allows communication without obstructing ideas and facts" (B-583-A).

The QFPJ pleaded in favour of the responsibility of the individual in the electoral process, with a view to respecting the requirements of democracy:

> In matters of information, the role of the *Canada Elections Act* consists more of guaranteeing, in the spirit of the *Canadian Charter of Rights and Freedoms* and the Charter of Journalism, the free dissemination of information rather than of placing all sorts of restrictions on freedom of expression. These limits, if they exist, should be very exceptional.
>
> The *Canada Elections Act* will thus return to the various players in our society the responsibilities that are theirs and that the difficult exercise of democracy requires them to undertake.
>
> Citizens will be responsible for informing themselves, the media for informing them, individuals, organizations and political parties for shedding light on the debate, while themselves displaying the greatest openness. The QFPJ for its part intends to ensure that the journalistic community respects the highest standards of professional ethics in matters of information. (ibid.)

This plea in favour of the responsibility of the media in the fair treatment of information was also supported by the Association canadienne de la radio et de la télévision de langue française (B-557-A), which believed the *Broadcasting Act* constrains broadcasters to find a reasonable balance when expressing opinions on issues of public interest.

Free Political Broadcast Time

We found three conflicting positions on free broadcasting time allotted to political parties. Some contributors rejected the present system and supported a better division of available broadcasting time. Others thought, on the contrary, that there is no reason to change anything related to allocation of free broadcasting time to political parties. Finally, still others were against any regulation of media use by political parties.

Some interveners thought that current regulation infringes on freedom of expression, an essential condition of a democratic society. The Green Party of Canada (B.C. and Yukon Region), in the name of equity and the public's right to information, called for equal broadcasting time for all parties, determined by the Canadian Radio-television and Telecommunications Commission: "In order that the message from all Parties may reach the public, the *Canada Elections Act* must require, equal to all parties: free time political broadcasting, minimum free advertising time, and inclusion of all party leaders during leadership debates. To do otherwise is to fail in informing the public" (B-124-P).

In the name of the same values, another contributor offered: "Broadcasting time should be made available equally to all at a competitive rate, governed by broadcasting regulations ... The small parties may thus be able to reserve a fraction of the time offered them. Consequently, unreserved time will be made available to the other parties, again on an equal basis ... Equal availability will give all parties an equal opportunity to use the time and would ultimately give voters an equal chance to be informed" (B-404-P).

Others, however, were satisfied with current arrangements: "We see no reason to change the broadcasting time allocation rules" (B-559-A).

The Libertarian Party of Canada completely rejected the previous opposing opinions and challenged the very principle of free broadcasting time:

> The requirement for the TV networks to give free time to parties should be eliminated. Newspapers are not forced to give free advertising to parties and neither should TV networks. Any time the Libertarian Party has been eligible for and has used so-called "free time," we have avoided self-promotion and have decried the "free time" system, the usurpation of private broadcasters' property. (B-405-P)

> In the last election many private groups, both for and against free trade, showed they were able to purchase much broadcasting time with very short notice to convey a political message. Why should political parties receive special privileges? Libertarians don't believe any political party is entitled to any free time. Furthermore, limits on the amount of time that any group is allowed to purchase is an infringement on the right to free speech. All political groups (including parties) should be free to purchase all the broadcast time they can afford. (B-397-P)

Leaders Debates and Election Advertising

Several contributors emphasized the constructive role of election campaign debates between party leaders. Some drew particular attention to the benefit of the circulation of ideas; others believed that such debates enlighten the electorate: "Leaders' debates provide a tool for the educated electorate to base part of their decision on, and [are] a useful part of the Federal election campaign" (B-364-P). Along these lines, a professor from the Université de Montréal proposed: "So that election campaigns better serve the interests of voters ... televised debates should be institutionalized and electoral law should set the terms" (B-692-I).

In some briefs, contributors wrote that, in the name of the public's right to information, "a stop must be put to the arbitrary nature of the decisions by television and radio broadcasters who judge on the electorate's behalf whether a political party is in the public interest" (B-781-P). The Parti nationaliste du Québec requested legislation governing regional debates to respect the interests of Canadians (ibid.).

These proposals did not meet with the approval of all contributors. According to the Quebec Federation of Professional Journalists, the broadcast debate is "a potentially crucial moment for public information during election campaigns" (B-583-A). For the sake of freedom of information, it is important to leave the responsibility for organizing these debates to the media. It was thought, moreover, that in the name of this same right "the media should have the freedom to invite any party leader they wish to any debate or interview, since the obligation to keep the public well informed is ultimately their responsibility" (B-488-I). The Canadian Association of Broadcasters argued: "The CAB firmly believes that there should be no obligation on the part of broadcasters to cover debates. Likewise, it should be left to the discretion of the broadcast licensees whether or not to televise a debate or to rebroadcast it at another time" (B-228-A). The Canadian Broadcasting Corporation also held that subjecting debates to legislation would violate freedom of expression (B-726-A).

The use of advertising during elections is also a general concern. Some contributors insisted on the importance of encouraging greater responsibility on the part of the candidates and parties in the use of advertising. Others called for equal treatment for all parties. The Reform Party of Canada criticized the use of public funds by the party in power to promote its policies because it considered this behaviour partisan, leading to a form of patronage. With the support of some other contributors, this political party proposed that certain forms of government advertising favourable to the party in power be prohibited during an election campaign (B-660-P). However, while some contributors would like to see the use and content of advertisements regulated in the name of democracy, others see these measures as an infringement on fundamental freedoms, citing the same values (B-376-A).

The participation of the media in election campaigns raises a debate between media owners and professionals on the one hand and groups and individuals who worry about media influence on the other. What is the media's responsibility to the public interest in the electoral process? The suggestion of controlling media activities raises another ethical question: In a democratic society, can one limit, and to what extent can one limit, freedom of the press, which cannot be dissociated from freedom of expression?

OPINION POLLS DURING AN ELECTION PERIOD

The use of opinion polls during elections raises a number of questions. What purpose do they serve? Why should we approve their use or ban them? Should they be regulated or should we trust the scientific and ethical responsibility of the pollsters? If they should be regulated, how should it be done? How should opinion polls in the election period be viewed? Are they tools indispensable to the public's right to information, or are they disruptive influences undermining the integrity of the electoral process? These were the main concerns about polls found in briefs presented to the Commission.

First, we will briefly raise the issue of how useful opinion polls are during an election, from the perspective of those who support them. We will then present the main criteria suggested to ensure the integrity of the electoral process. Finally, we will specify the main arguments put forward by those opposed to the use of opinion polls during election campaigns.

According to a number of contributors to the Commission, opinion polls do not damage the integrity of the electoral process: "Public opinion polling in connection with the electoral process is a legitimate political, sociological and journalistic pursuit and ... it would be wrong to ban the practice and wrong to prohibit the publication of poll results" (B-726-A). One brief claimed that "polling is a natural extension of our democratic institutions" (B-619-A).

The majority of contributors defending this position considered opinion polls a means of encouraging dissemination of information. One brief argued: "Poll results constitute an important element of the overall body of information upon which the electorate bases its decisions. There has always been a natural and justifiable public interest in which party or idea meets with the widest favour and support. Through polling and the reporting and analysis of poll results, the media reflect that interest" (B-726-A).

The fundamental value cited by proponents of this position is the public's right to information, a right that guarantees a healthy democracy:

Clearly those who support the regulation of the reporting of opinion polls feel that the results of such polls are more dangerous to the health of Canadian democracy than other statistics and that Canadians must be especially protected from them. This feeling is no basis for the restriction of freedom of the press ...

Polls will continue to be conducted and their results known to politicians, journalists, and those they talk to. There is no reason to give such individuals privileged access to information about the views of the ordinary Canadians while limiting the access of the voters. Such a double standard is undesirable in a democracy. (B-376-A)

Although they did not demand that opinion polls be banned, some people regarded polls as "self-fulfilling prophecies" (B-689-P). It is important, therefore, to seek a balance in exercising control over them: "Obviously a balance between the legitimate rights of free speech and undue influence of polls needs to be struck" (ibid.).

To ensure that polls perform their role in the electoral process, some briefs called on pollsters and the media to develop a sharper sense of ethics, and to concern themselves with scientific quality. It was also proposed that citizens be taught to develop a critical attitude toward polls. As well, specific proposals were offered concerning the use of polls during an election campaign.

In defence of these first two positions, the following values were cited: the right to information, freedom of speech and the public's right to reliable and good information.

Finally, some briefs argued that the use of polls during an election campaign is unacceptable, and they must be banned. Five briefs (B-377-I; B-757-P; B-602-P; B-420-P; B-575-A) proposed that the results of a poll should not be announced during an election campaign because they are disruptive: "an undue and disturbing influence on the electoral process" (B-575-A). They were sometimes deemed to draw the public's attention away from real problems: "They distract attention from issues the election is designed to resolve" (B-159-A). It was also thought that polls exert undue influence on a segment of the voting public: "Public opinion polls serve no useful purpose other than to unduly influence a segment of the voting public and possibly create an illogical stampede in favour of one party or another" (B-511-A).

It was also claimed that they are used to mislead voters: "All polling of public opinion relating to an election should be prohibited during an electoral campaign, whether or not the results are published. The present situation of unlimited polling gives too much advantage to money, and it makes it too easy for a candidate or a party to present a false face to the public" (B-275-P).

Finally, some contributors maintained that it is not the responsibility of pollsters or the media to determine the mood, needs or desires of the electorate: "Although it is argued that polls only reflect opinion, there is a great deal of evidence that polls in fact guide and lead opinion. It should be the responsibility of the parties and the candidates participating in an election to determine the mood, needs and wishes of the electorate, not the pollsters" (B-471-P).

Discussions about the relevance or irrelevance of publishing opinion polls during an election campaign enabled us to note a major ethical issue in the realization of the right to information – a value recognized as fundamental to democracy – and of the integrity of the electoral process that ensures the quality of democratic life.

THE ELECTION CAMPAIGN AND THE CONDUCT OF THE VOTE

Under this heading are assembled several points on aspects of the electoral process. These include nomination of returning officers, the length of election campaigns, holding of elections on set dates, the choice of election days, balloting, proxy voting and the sale of alcohol on election day.

At the heart of the debate surrounding these questions we have identified diverse values, including equity, neutrality, credibility, participation and religious freedom, that contributors say must be taken into account in a democratic system.

Appointment of Returning Officers

A citizen from Winnipeg insisted on the importance of selecting returning officers carefully: "The Returning Officer is the most visible election official during an election and must be perceived by voters, candidates and political parties as a representative of an electoral system that is fair and impartial" (B-699-I). One brief said that an impartial electoral system requires impartial elections officers (B-210-A).

Other contributors would prefer the appointment of these officials to be depoliticized to ensure their neutrality and credibility (B-208-I). It was also suggested that the chief electoral officer be appointed impartially after consultation with political parties: "The *Canada Elections Act* [should] provide that, no later than ninety days before the Chief Electoral Officer reaches retirement, the Speaker consult with each party that polled fifteen percent or more in the immediate past election and that the name of a consensually emerging person be then placed, in a resolution, before the House of Commons" (B-680-I).

Moreover, it was proposed that "the power to name returning officers [be] transferred to the Chief Electoral Officers" (B-208-I). It was also proposed that returning officers and assistant returning officers be nominated through a public competition under the auspices of the chief electoral officer (B-241-I).

In the interest of impartiality, the author of another brief stated that "deputy returning officers and clerks ... should be recommended and appointed via the same procedure currently in use for enumerators and revising agents" (B-158-I). It was requested that "the nomination of enumerators [also be] depoliticized" (B-208-I) and that it be ensured that they receive all necessary training (B-785-A).

Length of the Election Campaign

In briefs submitted to the Commission, there were three proposals on the length of election campaigns. Some suggested that it be reduced, others would like nothing to be changed, and others proposed that it be lengthened.

A number of briefs claimed that election campaigns are "too long" (B-459-P). It was observed that campaigns could be shortened by at least 10 days through the creation of permanent voters lists. "It would be an overall saving," it was added (B-173-I). The length of election campaigns ought to be brought down to two (B-051-I) or three weeks (B-095-P) or to four or five weeks, as is the case in most Western democracies (B-588-I). One brief suggested shortening the election period to 30 days. A shorter election campaign would have the following three benefits: it would be less expensive, less exhausting and would encourage greater participation.

By contrast, the Reform Party of Canada advanced three reasons to maintain the current length of election campaigns. It said that shorter campaigns would not encourage dialogue between candidates and the electorate, that they would disadvantage voters in rural areas, and that they would not enable the population to participate (B-660-P).

The residents of northern areas did not want election campaigns shortened at all. The Western Arctic New Democrats wrote: "Although election campaigns may seem over-protracted in some parts of Canada, the difficulties of transportation and communication in remote ridings compel us to object to any proposal to shorten the election period" (B-670-P). The Yellowknife Chamber of Commerce wrote that election campaigns should actually be lengthened in consideration of the particular conditions of northern regions (B-708-A).

Fixed Dates for Elections

The authors of some briefs believed that holding an election on an established date every four years would encourage voter responsibility (B-343-I; B-529-I; B-151-I) and would make the election process "much simpler" (B-125-I). It was stated that this new provision would eliminate uncertainty: "This would be a great help to candidates, workers and the general public, taking away the uncertainty of the Election Call" (B-370-I). It was said as well that holding an election on a set date would prevent the party in power from manipulating public opinion (B-335-I).

Election Day
To encourage greater participation, it was frequently suggested that elections take place on Sundays (B-717-I; B-567-P; B-241-I). Several briefs shared the view that "it would be much easier for people to vote on a Sunday and [that] would make organizing the election easier" (B-488-P; B-173-I; B-533-I; B-460-P). One association wrote that the selection of Sunday as election day would make it possible to reduce voting time (B-671-P).

Others who were against Sunday elections held that this proposal violates religious values: "We believe this to be a day set aside for spiritual activity, and not physical, secular, or civil activities when not a necessity. Our desire is not to impose our views on others, but we feel that our government too is accounted to God, and it is our duty to point out this responsibility. We believe, with reference to God's commandment to ... 'keep the Lord's Day holy' that we cannot mock God and prosper (2 Chron. 24:20)" (B-798-A).

The Pentecostal Assemblies of Canada echoed these arguments, adding that holding an election on a Sunday would also violate family values (B-476-A).

In the name of respect for religious freedom, the Commission was also asked not to recommend that voting take place on a day affecting the religious practices of any group in society.

The Ballot
Some contributors thought that the ballot, in its current form, restricts voter choice. For this reason, a new way was suggested to express disagreement with the candidates on the ballot rather than spoiling the ballot or choosing not to vote at all: "Providing a 'none of the above' option on all ballots to select members of the House of Commons could provide an opportunity for dissenting voters to be recorded and not be mistaken or dismissed as illiterate or apathetic" (B-422-I). Many contributors made this suggestion (B-484-P; B-593-I; B-765-I; B-700-P; B-405-P; B-016-I; B-244-I; B-553-I; B-207-I; B-489-I).

Voting by Proxy
The conditions for proxy voting, as currently stipulated in the *Canada Elections Act*, do not always encourage participation. For this reason, the

Commission was asked to consider changes in approach: "These alternatives ensure that citizens have a greater opportunity to vote and, not only that, ensure as well that the individual has the opportunity to cast his or her own vote personally which ... is the essence of our democratic system" (B-466-A).

We encountered three positions on this subject. Some contributors suggested increasing the number of categories of persons eligible to vote by proxy, and enabling students and people with disabilities to benefit more easily from this right. Others would like the vote by proxy to be accessible to all: "It is interesting to note that municipal elections have no stipulations regarding who can vote by proxy as long as they are duly on the voters list" (B-010-I). Finally one brief recommended that proxy voting be abolished outright "because it gives a different person the right to vote" (B-241-I).

Alcohol Sales on Election Day

A number of associations and groups of people (B-148-I; B-340-I; B-568-A; B-238-A; B-713-A; B-154-A) requested that provisions relating to the sale of alcohol be removed from the *Canada Elections Act*. Some briefs asserted that these provisions are too expensive for industries and governments, while others saw the prohibition of the sale of alcohol as an anachronism that should be removed.

By contrast, one brief preferred the status quo: "We strongly recommend pubs remain closed until after polls close" (B-559-A). Another brief justified prohibition in this way: "Voting is taken seriously by people in Canada. Therefore, it is logical to prohibit sale of liquor in any outlet or retail establishment until after the polls close. Such legislation speaks for most electors" (B-529-I).

The Royal Canadian Legion of Cape Breton County suggested that the current Act be revised to make it even stricter:

> We suggest that the use of the term "liquor" is not inclusive enough. The term MAS [mood-altering substances] is more appropriate in this age.
>
> It is our belief that all sales of liquor on election days should be in a controlled environment; that is, that no political biases be exhibited or expressed in any tavern or public place where sales of liquor take place.
>
> We suggest that any person who attempts to influence any voter in their franchise by offer of gifts or sales of any mood-altering substance should, on being charged and found guilty, be disenfranchised for life. (B-701-A)

POLL CLOSING TIMES AND THE DISCLOSURE OF ELECTION RESULTS

Canada is a huge country. From Newfoundland to British Columbia, there are six time zones. There is a concern, particularly in the western provinces, with the problem of disclosure of the election results in the East when one part of the electorate, in the West, has not yet finished voting.

Briefs to the Commission presented two conflicting positions on this issue. As far as freedom of expression was concerned, the first held that fairness and equity require greater consideration for each citizen. All voters, proponents held, must be conscious of being active participants in the final decision.

The second position held that early disclosure of election results does not really pose a problem. In the name of democracy, proponents claimed that such a procedure does not prevent any member of the electorate from deciding his or her vote freely and in full awareness. The electorate of the West is influenced little or not at all by the disclosure of the results in the East.

Those who found early disclosure of election results unacceptable said that it is important to place respect for the voter ahead of the interests of broadcasters. They even wrote that this situation does nothing for national unity (B-511-A) and poses serious questions concerning membership in Canadian confederation (B-283-I). According to many (B-574-P; B-148-I; B-687-P; B-689-P; B-283-I; B-734-I; B-567-P; B-500-P; B-671-P; B-773-I; B-167-P; B-700-P), all polls must open and close at the same time. Others suggested that elections be held according to a schedule specific to each region (B-759-A; B-651-P; B-293-I; B-670-P; B-226-A; B-421-I), so as not "either to encourage or discourage one from voting" (B-717-I). This method would contribute to a stronger sense of belonging among eligible voters: "It would give Canadians a sense of 'oneness' knowing that we are all voting at the same time from Vancouver Island to Newfoundland" (B-550-A).

A Trois-Rivières returning officer wondered whether an "embargo" should be placed on results from the East to avoid influencing the voters in the West, or polls should be closed later in the East (B-125-I). Others suggested that votes be counted only after polls are closed in the West (B-418-A; B-228-A; B-421-A; B-320-I; B-420-P; B-602-P; B-579-I; B-218-I).

Those who accepted early disclosure pointed to the positive aspects. They maintained that it does not affect the final result. According to a citizen from the Prairies, revealing election results from the East can even encourage greater exercise of democratic freedom:

> Premature broadcasting of results ... would influence those who have not yet voted and could influence the outcome of an election ...

> Isn't that what a vote is supposed to do? ... Influence the outcome of an election? If a voter sees a trend developing and wishes to try and alter that trend by voting a particular way, isn't that the right of the individual? How can it be reasoned in a democratic country that an act of government may prevent some individuals from casting their ballot in a particular way because they don't have the information available? (B-584-I)

A representative of the Thompson [Manitoba] Chamber of Commerce stated that one cannot go against technological developments: "In a society of growing technology, we do not think prohibition of premature disclosure is practical" (B-559-A).

The issues surrounding the closing of the polls and disclosure of election results bring into play fundamental values such as freedom of expression, fairness, equity and respect for citizens.

CONCLUSION

Ethicological analysis of briefs submitted to the Commission revealed several major ethical issues. Each is an essential feature of the various problems identified by individuals, groups or associations that came before the Commission to express their opinions on the reform of the *Canada Elections Act* and party financing. Let us re-examine each of these issues before offering a diagrammatic summary of our findings.

The principal ethical issue identified in the debate on reform of the *Canada Elections Act* shaped the process leading to this conclusion. The issue is: How can we encourage more equitable participation by all citizens in the entire electoral process?

Different perceptions of democracy provide the backdrop for the debate on reform of the *Canada Elections Act*. We isolated a two-pronged question: How can we realize the planned democratic ideal in law and practice? And, even more important, how can we implement this ideal so the entire Canadian population can see themselves as participants in it? This dual line of questioning led us to the discovery of two major ethical issues: To encourage the most equitable participation possible in the electoral process, how do we articulate the following moral values: freedom, fairness and respect for differences? What legislation can respond in a socially constructive way to the imperatives of these moral values to ensure the integrity of the Canadian democratic system?

An important ethical issue, respect for the dignity of human beings, regardless of social or economic situation or any disability, emerged when we dealt with the question of the right to vote. This issue is not so much a question of principle as of the concrete exercise of this right considered essential to a democratic system.

The ethical issue underlying discussions on representation can be expressed as a respect for democracy requiring equality, equity and fairness as foundations for representation of all Canadians in the entire democratic process. Thus, many people were preoccupied with giving equal chances to citizens who wish to participate in political power, along with recognition of the geographic, ethnic, linguistic, racial and sexual diversity that characterizes the Canadian population.

The debate over selecting candidates, either as party representatives or as MPs, reveals the complexity of the conflict of values among equality, fairness, morality, competence and the public interest. We have shown the difficulty of expressing these values and at the same time respecting the integrity of the democratic process.

Political parties play an important role in democratic life. How do we ensure that their sources of financing do not prevent them from operating independently and in the public interest? We have demonstrated that party financing calls into play the quality of democratic life, which is principally centred on participation, freedom of expression, equity, equality and openness.

The presence of interest groups in the electoral process and the possibility of restricting their advertising expenditure during election campaigns raise a conflict of values between freedom of expression and the equality of citizens. Thus it is difficult to ensure a fair balance between freedom of expression, the common good and equality of participation by the citizens in the electoral process. Although interest groups have their own ways of encouraging freedom of expression, a number of people said they create inequality between citizens, as they give some people more power than others to communicate their viewpoints and influence the vote.

Control of election expenditure was also discussed in briefs submitted to the Commission. The ethical issue focuses on preserving and asserting freedom of expression, in the public interest and the interests of political parties, through standards promoting the honesty and integrity of the electoral process.

Another ethical concern emerges from the debate over preparation of a permanent voters list. This issue calls into question the balance between equity and responsibility. The contributors to the Commission who dealt with this problem wonder how to ensure that citizens find themselves on the voters list – hence the ethical issue – and to what extent they should be responsible for their registration on this list.

The participation of the media in election campaigns raises a debate that brings into conflict the media owners and professionals on the one hand and the various people or groups of people who worry about media influence on the other. What are the media's responsibilities to the public interest in the electoral process? The suggestion of controlling media activities raises another ethical question: In a democratic society, can one limit freedom of the press? If so, to what extent? These questions cannot be dissociated from the fundamental issue of freedom of expression.

Discussions concerning the relevance of publishing opinion polls during an election campaign enabled us to discover another ethical issue in the realization of the right to information and of the integrity of the electoral process that ensures the quality of democratic life.

A discussion of a variety of points – the nomination of returning officers, the length of election campaigns, set dates for holding elections, the choice of election days, ballots, proxy voting and the sale of alcohol on election day – enabled us to identify certain values, such as equity, neutrality, credibility, participation and religious freedom, that contributors to the Commission say must be taken into account in a democratic society.

According to some contributors, the issues surrounding the time to close the polls on election day and the disclosure of election results bring into play freedom of expression, fairness, equity and respect for citizens.

The diagram opposite, figure 1.1, gives an overview of the major ethical issue brought forward at the start of this conclusion: How can we encourage more equitable participation by all citizens in the entire electoral process? It brings to light the four perspectives or aspects of any ethical issue: the practical, regulatory, axiological and justificatory.

With this ethicological analysis complete, ethicists should enter the debate on the democratic ideal, the values supporting the ideal and the standards it requires, so that the letter and spirit of the legislation and the organization of the electoral process will truly reflect the expectations of the Canadian public.

We hope that this study will help inspire the Commission in its deliberations. It should enable the Commission to identify the principal values most important to Canadians and to frame its recommendations in the spirit of these values. We like to think that this study also has the merit of showing that it is possible to call for different rules and standards in the name of the same values. The Commission's challenge is to delineate effectively the concept of democracy that it favours from the concepts proposed in the briefs. The Commission must also identify clearly the supporting values when proposing changes to the *Canada Elections Act*. Furthermore, it is the Commission's responsibility to be

65
ETHICS AND REFORM OF THE ELECTIONS ACT

Figure 1.1
Principal ethical issue: how can we encourage more equitable participation in the electoral process by all citizens?

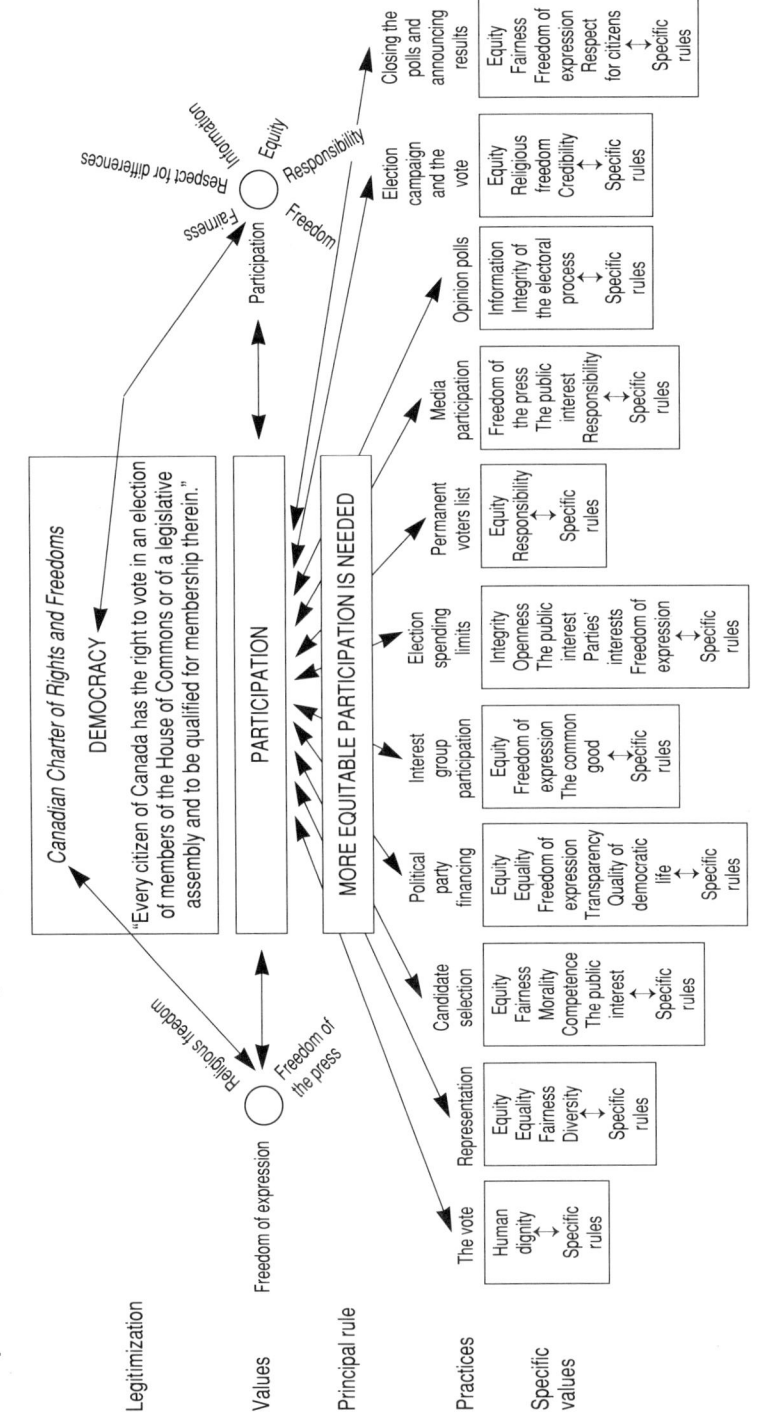

clear and open in the recommendations it addresses to the government so that the new *Canada Elections Act* can ensure more equitable participation by all citizens in the entire electoral process, the principal ethical issue discovered in this analysis.

APPENDIX
LIST OF BRIEFS USED

B-006-I	Anastase Koutroulides
B-010-I	Scott D. Mills
B-016-I	Carmel Gaffiero
B-017-I	Joseph A. Crouchman
B-018-I	William Archie Baldwin
B-019-I	J.W. Dawson
B-021-P	Don Blenkarn, MP, Mississauga South
B-037-I	Phillippe Duport
B-045-I	Robert S.D. Chown
B-051-I	W.J. Weir
B-054-P	Ross Belsher, MP, Fraser Valley East
B-062-I	R.E. Wolf
B-074-I	Klaus H.E. Priebe
B-087-I	Sandra Wilson, Returning Officer, Saint-Henri–Westmount
B-092-A	Canadian Daily Newspaper Publishers Association
B-093-I	Sylvain Auclair, Green Party of Canada candidate, Rosemont
B-095-P	Elizabeth Rhodes
B-113-I	Glenn Cunningham
B-114-A	Saskatchewan Pro-Life Association
B-124-P	Green Party of Canada, British Columbia and Yukon Region
B-125-I	Paul Charest, Returning Officer, Trois-Rivières
B-148-I	Geoffrey B. Capp
B-151-I	Jo-Anne L'Heureux-Giguère
B-154-A	Association des propriétaires de tavernes et brasseries du Québec inc.
B-155-P	Arnold Malone, MP, Crowfoot
B-156-A	General Hospital (Grey Nuns) of Edmonton
B-158-I	Jacques Charpentier, Returning Officer, Louis-Hébert
B-159-A	Canadian Home and School and Parent–Teacher Federation
B-167-P	Rita Ubriaco
B-168-I	Peter Bulkowski
B-173-I	André Marois, Returning Officer, Mégantic–Compton–Stanstead
B-181-I	David Finnis
B-202-I	John D.R. Ferguson
B-203-I	M. Day
B-207-I	Prudence M.A. Packwood, Returning Officer, Ottawa West

Ethics and Reform of the Elections Act

B-208-I	Laurier Lévesque, président d'élection, Madawaska–Victoria
B-210-A	REAL Women
B-217-P	François Gérin, MP, Mégantic–Compton–Stanstead
B-218-I	Ken Jamieson
B-224-A	Ted Kotyk, editor, *The Insider*, Stony Mountain Penitentiary newspaper
B-226-A	Canadian Labour Congress
B-228-A	Canadian Association of Broadcasters
B-229-I	Edward Earl Taylor
B-230-P	Fred P. Debrecen, Leader, Confederation of Regions, Manitoba Party
B-236-A	Canadian Association of the Deaf
B-238-A	Association of Canadian Distillers
B-239-P	Claudy Mailly, former MP, Gatineau–La Lièvre
B-241-I	Suzanne Carrière, Returning Officer, Hull–Aylmer
B-244-I	Ken McRae
B-246-A	Metro Tenants Legal Services
B-254-P	Prince George–Peace River Progressive Conservative Riding Association
B-256-P	John Clarke, Libertarian candidate, Vancouver South
B-258-I	B.G. Nayman
B-259-A	Coalition of Provincial Organizations of the Handicapped
B-261-I	J.C. Bohlen
B-265-I	Gary R. Hughes
B-267-P	John Harvard, MP, Winnipeg–St. James
B-273-I	Rebecca Adsett-Macintyre
B-275-P	Rachel Thomson
B-277-I	Céline Bernier, Returning Officer, Saint-Laurent–Cartierville, Henriette Guérin, Returning Officer, Outremont, Jocelyne Lavoie, Returning Officer, Laval, Jean-François Longpré, Returning Officer, Duvernay
B-283-I	Paul J. Lewans
B-293-I	Terry G. Wilson
B-296-I	Michael Spencer
B-298-I	Siegfried Osterwoldt
B-307-P	Ronald Cook
B-308-I	Francine Dick
B-309-A	Concerned Citizens for Civic Affairs in North York Inc.
B-320-I	Fred G. Marsh
B-327-A	Victoria Civil Liberties Association
B-330-I	Guy Tessier, Returning Officer, Portneuf
B-331-P	Don Valley East, Don Valley West, Rosedale, St. Paul's and Scarborough Centre Federal Progressive Conservative Associations
B-335-I	Terry Dral
B-340-I	Barbara A. Craven, Returning Officer, Saanich–Gulf Islands

B-342-I	Douglas Chalmers
B-343-I	Marguerite Balshaw
B-344-P	New Democratic Party of Canada
B-346-P	Scott Thorkelson, MP, Edmonton–Strathcona
B-347-I	Robert M. Roth, Research and Teaching Assistant, Carleton University School of Journalism
B-350-I	H.J. Lafferty
B-351-A	Vancouver Board of Trade
B-352-I	Judith Anderson
B-358-I	Frances G. McKean
B-361-I	Jean-Thomas Dumart
B-364-P	G. Cameron Donald
B-366-P	Len Hopkins, MP, Renfrew–Nipissing–Pembroke
B-368-P	Senator Len Marchand, Kamloops–Cariboo
B-370-I	Cecil E. MacPhail
B-371-P	Scott Adams
B-372-P	Willowdale New Democratic Party Federal Constituency Association
B-374-I	Christopher Levenson
B-375-A	Progressive Conservative Party of New Brunswick
B-376-A	British Columbia Civil Liberties Association
B-377-I	Jerry E. Herman
B-395-A	British Columbia Civil Liberties Association
B-396-A	La Confédération des syndicats nationaux
B-397-P	Greater Vancouver Libertarian Association
B-403-P	Surrey–White Rock Progressive Conservative Association
B-404-P	Christian Heritage Party of Canada
B-405-P	Libertarian Party of Canada
B-408-I	Al Dahlo, Returning Officer, North Vancouver
B-418-A	British Columbia Federation of Labour
B-419-P	Green Party of Canada
B-420-P	Saanich–Gulf Islands Federal Liberal Association
B-421-A	British Columbia Association of Broadcasters
B-422-I	David Crawford
B-423-A	Federated Anti-Poverty Groups of British Columbia
B-437-I	Mohammad Boroudjerdi
B-443-A	Forum des citoyens âgés de Montréal
B-459-P	New Brunswick Liberal Association
B-460-P	Prince Edward Island New Democrats
B-461-P	Harry H. Cook
B-466-A	Progressive Conservative Riding Associations of Prince Edward Island
B-469-I	Jay Millen, for eight returning officers, Capilano–Howe Sound
B-471-P	Vancouver Island Progressive Conservative Riding Associations
B-475-A	Association des centres d'accueil du Québec

B-476-A	Pentecostal Assemblies of Canada
B-478-P	David Walker, MP, Winnipeg North Centre
B-484-P	Saskatoon–Dundurn and Saskatoon–Humboldt Progressive Conservative Associations
B-488-P	Jean-Pierre Roy
B-489-I	Richard Peever
B-493-I	Betty Eckgren
B-494-P	Raymond Garneau
B-496-I	Carolle Simard, Professor, Université du Québec à Montréal
B-497-I	Dianna Brown
B-498-A	Elizabeth Fry Society of Saskatchewan
B-500-P	Marie Marchand
B-502-A	Saskatchewan Voice of the Handicapped, Saskatoon Chapter
B-503-I	Frank Quennell
B-507-I	Robert M. Wigle
B-511-A	Saskatchewan Association of Rural Municipalities
B-513-A	Centre psychiatrique de Roberval–L'Envol
B-516-P	Rey Pagtakhan, MP, Winnipeg North
B-520-I	Dennis Pilon
B-522-P	Garnet M. Bloomfield, former MP
B-529-I	Ed Whelan
B-530-I	Howard Leeson, Chair, Association of Professors, University of Regina
B-531-A	Regroupement des groupes populaires en alphabétisation du Québec
B-533-A	La Chambre de commerce du Montréal métropolitain
B-535-A	Elizabeth Fry Society of Ottawa
B-536-P	Chris Axworthy, MP, Saskatoon–Clark's Crossing
B-543-I	Laurie Clarke, Returning Officer, Kamloops
B-544-I	Terry R. Stratton
B-546-P	Carleton–Gloucester NDP Riding Association
B-547-A	National Citizens' Coalition
B-550-A	Institute for Political Involvement
B-552-I	Eleanor L. Hadley
B-553-I	D. Kirk
B-557-A	Association canadienne de la radio et de la télévision de langue française
B-558-A	Canadian Human Rights Foundation
B-559-A	Thompson [Manitoba] Chamber of Commerce
B-561-A	Manitoba Keewatinowi Okimakanak Inc.
B-565-P	Leona Mayer
B-567-P	Regina–Wascana Progressive Conservative Association
B-568-A	Canadian Association of Liquor Jurisdictions
B-569-I	Keith Lampard
B-572-A	Assembly of First Nations, Manitoba Region
B-574-P	Saskatoon–Dundurn Liberal Association

B-575-A   Citizens Concerned About Free Trade, National Office, Saskatoon
B-578-A   Manitoba Anti-Poverty Organization, Inc.
B-579-I   Howard Johnston
B-583-A   Fédération professionnelle des journalistes du Québec
B-584-I   M. Flegal
B-585-P   Saint-Henri–Westmount Liberal Association
B-586-I   Shirley McNair, Returning Officer, London West, and Donna Kleiman, Assistant Returning Officer, London West
B-588-I   Vincent Lemieux, Département de science politique, Université Laval
B-593-I   Graeme Decarie, History Department, Concordia University
B-597-A   Committee for '94
B-602-P   Kamloops Liberal Association
B-607-A   University of Western Ontario, University Students' Council
B-616-A   Learning Disabilities Association of the Yukon Territory
B-619-A   Environics Research Group Ltd.
B-622-A   Reformed Christian Business and Professional Organization
B-624-I   Pierre F. Côté, QC, Directeur général des élections du Québec
B-630-P   London West New Democratic Party Riding Association
B-641-A   Wardrop Engineering, Inc.
B-642-P   Graham McDonald, President, Yukon New Democrats
B-648-A   Ontario Federation of Labour
B-651-P   Communist Party of Canada
B-653-A   Laurentian University Students' General Association
B-654-P   Sudbury Riding Ontario Progressive Conservative Association
B-660-P   Reform Party of Canada
B-664-I   Ellen Kerr, Chief Electoral Officer and City Clerk, Sudbury
B-666-A   Galvanic Analytical Systems Ltd.
B-670-P   Western Arctic New Democrats
B-671-P   Confederation of Regions Party
B-672-P   Lethbridge Federal New Democrats
B-676-I   Eric P. Groody
B-678-P   Edmonton East New Democratic Party Federal Constituency Association
B-680-I   Frederick C. Engelmann, Professor Emeritus of Political Science, University of Alberta
B-687-P   Vince Croswell
B-689-P   Yukon Liberal Association
B-692-I   Denis Monière, directeur de la faculté des arts et des sciences, Université de Montréal
B-695-P   Ontario Section of the New Democratic Party of Canada
B-699-I   Richard D. Balasko
B-700-P   Gregory H. Vezina, Registered Agent, Green Party of Canada
B-701-A   Royal Canadian Legion in the Industrial Area of Cape Breton County

B-705-A	Alberta Federation of Labour
B-706-I	Douglas Barrett
B-708-A	Yellowknife Chamber of Commerce
B-713-A	Canadian Restaurant and Foodservices Association
B-715-I	Heldor Schafer
B-717-I	Ted Murphy and Rénald Guay
B-719-A	Saskatchewan Action Committee on the Status of Women
B-723-I	Joseph Côté
B-726-A	Canadian Broadcasting Corporation
B-734-I	A.J. Moreau
B-737-A	Saint Mary's Hospital, New Westminster, BC
B-741-P	L'Association du NPD, Hull–Aylmer
B-742-P	Hon. Robert Kaplan, PC, QC, MP, York Centre
B-751-A	Canadian Bar Association
B-754-A	Nova Scotia Advisory Council on the Status of Women
B-757-P	Garfield Warren, MHA, Torngat Mountains, Newfoundland House of Assembly
B-759-A	Randy Simms
B-765-I	Dave Roe
B-769-A	Native Council of Nova Scotia
B-771-I	Progressive Conservative Association of Nova Scotia
B-773-I	James E. Burnett
B-774-P	Taddle Creek Greens of Toronto
B-775-I	Michael Wheatly
B-780-A	Fédération des femmes du Québec
B-781-P	Parti nationaliste du Québec
B-782-A	Native Council of Canada
B-783-P	Albina Guarnieri, MP, Mississauga East
B-784-P	Maureen A. McTeer
B-785-A	Canadian Ethnocultural Council
B-798-A	P. Koppert, Canadian Lord's Day Association, Norwich

ABBREVIATIONS

c.	chapter
R.S.C.	Revised Statutes of Canada
s(s).	section(s)

REFERENCES

This study was completed in January 1991.

In this study, quoted material that originated in French has been translated into English.

Canada. *Broadcasting Act*, R.S.C. 1985, c. B-9.

———. *Canada Elections Act*, R.S.C. 1985, c. E-2.

———. *Canadian Charter of Rights and Freedoms*. Part I of the *Constitution Act 1982*, being Schedule B of the *Canada Act 1982* (U.K.), 1982, c. 11, s. 3.

United Nations. 1948. *Universal Declaration of Human Rights*. Document No. A/810. 10 December.

2

PUBLIC SECTOR ETHICS

Vincent Lemieux

IN THIS STUDY we propose a new way of seeing public sector ethics as distinguished from private sector ethics. From this perspective, we provide a preliminary description of patronage, corruption and conflict of interest. This description is then compared with that given by participants in politics. To establish this comparison, data from a study of Canadian provincial election campaigns have been used. In the last part, after distinguishing the secondary dimension of public sector ethics from the primary dimension, we will see how it is possible to control political conduct and party financing in the name of this ethics. Finally, several recommendations intended for the Commission will conclude this study.

A CONCEPT OF PUBLIC SECTOR ETHICS

Many authors have examined political or public sector ethics. Few, however, have done so using a conceptual framework that allows comparison with private sector ethics, or that provides specific criteria for evaluating the practices grouped together under the terms patronage, corruption and conflict of interest. Although the relative nature of the conceptual framework proposed in this study cannot be ignored, we think that it allows us to tackle problems related to public sector ethics in a new way and one that is more systematic than traditional approaches.

The Three Types of Transactions

The point of departure, the conceptual framework, is the important distinction established by Polanyi (1944) between the three types of transactions involving resources: reciprocity, market exchange and redistribution. Redistribution will be considered in its broad sense, which includes not only the redistribution of wealth, but also all government regulatory activities. For this reason we will call it "political redistribution." Societies of the past can be characterized by the relative importance placed on these three types of transactions. It can be argued, however, that in today's society, these types coexist and constitute the principal routes through which resources flow between participants.

These three types of transactions are organized into separate systems, each with its own rules and incentives. The rules for reciprocity are informal, and the incentives for participants rest primarily on the relationship they maintain or develop with each other. The rules for market exchange are more formal, and the incentives motivating participants are concerned with efficiency: obtaining for a given cost the greatest possible benefit, or obtaining for the lowest possible cost a given benefit. The rules of political redistribution are also formalized through laws, regulations or other official decisions. It is more difficult to identify the incentives, however, because political redistribution, as it is understood in today's society, extends into many domains, claiming, moreover, to correct deficiencies in reciprocity and market exchange.

Expanding on the meaning of a term put forward by Hirschman (1970), one could say that the incentives for participants in political redistribution, whether they hold the power to govern or are subject to it, lie in the political "voice" they can obtain or retain through this process. Thus, those who govern, and those who aspire to govern, seek to obtain or to retain a "voice" that ensures them positions of authority, while those who are governed seek to obtain or to retain a "voice" that ensures political redistribution will be to their benefit or at least not to their detriment.

These distinctions between reciprocity, market exchange and political redistribution are clearly analytical. In an actual transaction, the three types are frequently mixed. At times, efficiency is a consideration in reciprocity: the gift I give to someone who gave me a gift should be no more costly than the gift I received. Conversely, reciprocity is a consideration in market exchange: I will continue to buy an item from a vendor I like, even though the price is higher than elsewhere. In political redistribution, there are considerations of reciprocity and market exchange. Thus, patronage consists essentially of introducing into political redistribution those transactions that meet the requirements of reciprocity, while current attempts to make political redistribution more efficient are aimed at subjecting it to the rules of market exchange.

The Ethics of Political Redistribution
In the view adopted here public sector ethics has similarities to political redistribution, while private sector ethics follows reciprocity or

market exchange more closely. How can we define public sector ethics accurately while acknowledging that the incentives motivating participants are the political "voices" they seek to obtain or to retain, and that these incentives have their own value, just as do those associated with reciprocity and market exchange?

Our proposed definition seeks not only to affirm this distinction, but also to acknowledge the relationship with other types of transactions. Public sector or political redistribution ethics may be defined as the science or the art of conduct, particularly by those in power, that aims not to impose restrictions on competition among participants or on their responsibility to the public to seek solutions to the shortcomings of reciprocity or market exchange transactions.

This definition requires further explanation:

1. First, public sector ethics is referred to as a science or an art to emphasize that there is both a science and an art of ethics. In this study, the quest is to develop the science of public sector ethics, but this also involves the art of behaviour, which may or may not be illuminated by science.
2. Next, it is cautiously suggested that behaviour that complies with public sector ethics must, at the very least, aim to restrict neither the competition between participants nor their responsibility to the public. This does not mean, of course, that such behaviour does not also seek to ensure or even to develop competition and responsibility.
3. The behaviour that has important consequences for competition and responsibility is above all that of the political authorities (Gibbons 1976), principally of the government and those associated with it. This does not mean that the behaviour of other political players, public servants and interest groups is not also important from an ethical standpoint. However, the conduct of those who control political redistribution seems more significant to us.
4. The term "voice" rather than the term "power" is used to emphasize the distinction between political power as it relates to economic power and to power in general, which is not limited to political activity. The notion of "voice," borrowed from Hirschman (1970), has the advantage of referring to both the means available to political players when decisions are being voted on and the means used during discussions and debates before a vote. "Voice" also refers generally to the means used to obtain favourable political decisions when they are reached other

than by a vote. [The expression "voix" in French has connotations of both "voice" and "voting." Thus the notion encompasses both the means of decision and the process for making decisions. – ED.]

5. The term "political redistribution" is employed to emphasize that the political system redistributes much more than wealth. It also seeks to regulate "public" situations that give rise, or are likely to give rise, to problems in society. This regulation can be achieved by redistributing wealth, but also through other types of intervention that come under the general heading of political redistribution.

6. The problem situations are related principally in our opinion to deficiencies in market exchange or reciprocity-based transactions. Commenting on these shortcomings is clearly part of the political game. Something may be gained by hiding them or, on the contrary, by exaggerating them. In other words, the failures of these transactions are matters for debate in the political system of "voice," not objective phenomena. In the same way, the remedies for these deficiencies can be diverse, ranging from substituting political redistribution for the other two types of transactions, as in state socialism, to correcting the most obvious deficiencies, as in more liberal systems of government.

7. Finally, emphasis is placed on the relationship between our definition of ethics and the famous distinction drawn by Weber (1959) between the ethics of conviction and the ethics of responsibility. This distinction refers to the two political principles identified in public sector ethics. It should be observed that these principles are also found in Schattschneider's definition of democracy (1960). To use Clark and Wilson's (1961) typology of the three types of incentives, the ethics of conviction are based on a belief in a cause, on the prospect of material gain or on a sense of solidarity with allies in a cause. If the ethics of conviction are not tempered by the ethics of responsibility, however, the principles governing political redistribution may be at risk. The defence of a cause, motivated by the prospect of material gain or a feeling of solidarity, never unites more than a portion of the public – one group of players against other groups. Those who assert their "voice" in the political redistribution process are responsible not only to their own partisans, but also to the public as a whole. Unlike market exchange or reciprocity, political redistribution operates in an arena that includes all segments of society; it is also responsible for holding them together.

PUBLIC SECTOR AND PRIVATE SECTOR ETHICS

It is generally accepted that political redistribution must not be a substitute for reciprocity or market exchange transactions, but rather be a remedy for their shortcomings, with all the ambiguity that implies. Similarly, reciprocity and market exchange need not contradict the logic of the political redistribution process, that is, jeopardize the competitive, responsible system based on "voice."

There is a private sector ethic whose object is reciprocity and market exchange. The predominance of market exchange and the problems associated with it are no doubt why private sector ethics are generally equated with "business" ethics. In this study, the ethics of reciprocity is also included in private sector ethics. The major principles underlying the ethics of reciprocity will therefore be taken up before the discussion turns to market exchange or business ethics.

The Ethics of Reciprocity

Mauss (1950), in his famous essay on giving, defined the three obligations underlying reciprocity: the obligation to give, the obligation to receive and the obligation to repay. For example, couples are compelled to extend dinner invitations to their friends from time to time. Such invitations must be accepted and subsequently repaid with a return invitation. As Mauss observed, a link is created or maintained. Today it would be termed a "personalized" link, as opposed to a relationship based on the demands of market exchange or political redistribution.

The personal nature of the link in reciprocity or in giving is expressed also by the greater importance accorded the relationship, compared to that of the things exchanged (Hyde 1979). Giving differs in this from market exchange, where participants do not seek so much to maintain an often ephemeral relationship as to gain benefits at the lowest possible cost.

Market Exchange Ethics

To use Simon's (1957) distinction, market exchange ethics involve behaviour designed to ensure, through the interplay of supply and demand, that each of the parties to an exchange is reasonably satisfied. Since impediments to a fair balance are more likely to occur on the supply side than on the demand side, behaviour that leads to a monopoly, a cartel or collusion is considered contrary to this ethic. Shoplifting by consumers is an example of behaviour contrary to the market exchange ethic, because it deprives merchants of benefits to which they are entitled.

It is, however, important to note the increased value placed on market exchange in the 1980s as a means of social organization, in reaction to perceived abuses in the political redistribution process. This trend was accompanied by an expansion of business ethics to include a social dimension. (See Velasquez 1982 and De George 1990 for a general overview of business ethics.) In the United States, the desire to expand the scope of business ethics began in the 1970s, with the post-Watergate revelations of fraudulent practices in the private sector and the formation of groups concerned with corporate social responsibility (consumers, environmentalists, peace activists). Many companies adopted codes of ethics, and the teaching of business ethics became common in business schools (see, for example, Mahoney 1990).

The traditional concept of private sector ethics has been attacked by the proponents of a social role for business, as well as by critics of the market exchange system. The latter emphasize the imperfections of markets, which are not as competitive as traditionalists hold. The marketplace would be incapable, for example, of providing a decent life for the unemployed, for persons with disabilities or for other marginalized members of society. The proponents of corporate social responsibility also point out that not all the means used to ensure efficiency are socially beneficial. Certain practices are fraudulent: misleading advertising, fraud, bribes, tax evasion. Other practices, such as the manufacture of hazardous products, pollution and resource depletion, have even more negative consequences for society because of their far-reaching effects.

Implicitly or explicitly, these ethical considerations concerning the market system refer back to the political redistribution system. The question is whether to oppose it, emphasize its limitations or demonstrate that regulation of the economic system cannot be achieved without intervention by the political system. These two systems are closely intertwined, as an examination of some common practices in political redistribution will show.

PATRONAGE, CORRUPTION AND CONFLICT OF INTEREST

Patronage, corruption and conflict of interest are generally considered to be contrary to public sector ethics, although certain questions remain about the extent to which they are in fact contrary. Thus, "bad patronage" is considered contrary to public sector ethics, but "good patronage" is not. "Small-scale" or petty patronage is a less serious breach than "large-scale" patronage. The distinction between corrupt and non-corrupt practices is not always clear. After all, some accusations of conflict of interest draw vehement protests from those accused that the alleged conflict is in fact non-existent.

The proposed definitions of public sector ethics, the ethics of reciprocity and market exchange ethics should give us a better perspective of these issues.

The study could also have included fraud, since this is generally defined as any activity contrary to the standard rules of the game (Bailey 1971). It is intended to skew competition and responsibility in a political system based on "voice." Fraud is not included because it is behaviour that is relatively clearly contrary to public sector ethics. It may, however, be referred to on occasion.

Patronage

Of the three types of transactions, it is the practice of political patronage that has given rise to the greatest number of studies. (For general studies on this topic, see Lemieux 1977; Schmidt et al. 1977; Eisenstadt and Roniger 1984.)

Political patronage is a complex type of transaction that follows the dictates of reciprocity, market exchange and political redistribution. In other words, it is a practice that simultaneously involves linkage, efficiency and political "voice." Patronage is often, moreover, defined in these terms. It is an exchange of goods or services between a "patron" and a client that conforms to the principle of reciprocity. It increases, or at least maintains, the "voice" of each: that of the patron against rivals and that of the client against the authorities who would otherwise hold sway over the client.

For example, through a patron, a client obtains a public service job in exchange for party work. A market exchange has taken place in this transaction: employment is received for work done. There is also reciprocity, assuming that the two parties to the exchange know each other well and are cultivating an enduring link. Finally, there is political redistribution, in that patrons, by making their voice heard by the authority distributing the jobs, enable clients to obtain positions they would not otherwise have obtained. In return, the client's voice is joined with others to improve or to maintain the patron's and the party's voice in political redistribution.

According to the definition of public sector ethics given above, political patronage is acceptable only if it both compensates for deficiencies in reciprocity or market exchange and does not restrict the competitive, responsible nature of the voice-based system of political redistribution.

Because market deficiency is a relative concept, its measurement is controversial. It is clear, however, at least in the most extreme cases, that some patronage practices are geared more specifically than others to compensating for market deficiencies. For example, in some cases (Vastel 1989), federal programs of development assistance to local community groups appear to have led to patronage on the part of both provincial and federal legislators. They have directed subsidies to small firms whose executives are either rewarded thereby or are expected to reciprocate the favour at a future date. Such subsidies appear better suited to correcting the effects of market deficiencies than those that are, for example, awarded to established firms owned by political organizers as a reward for work at election time or for their substantial contributions to the party's campaign coffers.

To the extent that large-scale patronage, in which sizable sums of money are at stake, is gaining ground relative to petty patronage (Noel 1987; Simpson 1988; Lemieux 1990), it can be assumed that this trend is more advantageous to well-off players than to those less equipped for markets that work against them. These cases must be distinguished from those where senior positions in government agencies or party organizations are awarded by patronage as a reward for services rendered, or to ensure that services rendered will adhere to the party line. This "entourage patronage" (Noel 1990) serves not so much to make up for market deficiencies as to select individuals who have already proved themselves, or could prove themselves, in these markets. Unlike the preceding examples, however, entourage patronage at least has the merit of not using the political redistribution process to reinforce the market position of individuals who are already able to take care of themselves.

Political redistribution can rarely recover reciprocities lost to society; it is better suited to improving the efficiency of market exchange. The compensatory nature of political redistribution consists generally of substituting mediation for reciprocity in situations where people who cannot, or can no longer, engage in reciprocity are taken in charge by a state agency with which they have a more or less decisive voice. For example, people who have lost the capacity to live independently and can no longer count on their relatives are assisted by governmental or quasi-governmental services.

Political patronage is used most often to consolidate existing reciprocal links between patrons and clients, rather than to compensate for the disappearance of these links. This runs counter to the increasing bureaucracy of political redistribution, in which arm's-length third parties take charge of relationships that people would prefer to keep between themselves (Lemieux 1971). If patronage is justified in relation to the deficiencies of reciprocal transactions, it is because patronage helps to bolster this type of transaction against the encroachment of transactions through the political redistribution system.

A critical question arises, however: assuming that political patronage offers solutions to deficiencies in reciprocity or market exchange, does it not also interfere with competition and responsibility in political redistribution?

The same question could equally be raised concerning the internal operation of party organizations. In other words, does political patronage promote democracy within the party? This issue will not be considered here, the focus being on the political system. Let us note, however, as Noel (1990) does, that "party entourage patronage," along with other factors, no doubt contributes to the centralization of political parties and thus to restrictions on internal democracy, that is, on competition and responsibility in party operations.

In practising political patronage, the governing party inhibits the competitive, responsible nature of the political redistribution system. It uses public funds, provided to the state by citizens, to grant favours, often hidden from the public eye, to its supporters or to those it wishes to convert to its cause. The opposition party or parties often lack a comparable "voice" in the discretionary decisions of the political redistribution system, which aggravates their position of weakness. From this perspective, political patronage is contrary to public sector ethics as defined for the purposes of this study.

Two additional considerations must be brought to bear, however, in assessing more correctly the consequences of political patronage for the competitive, responsible voice-based system of political redistribution.

First, it must be recognized that despite the parties' protests while in opposition, once in power, they are quick to accept practices that offer them advantages, or that, if they have never been in power, they hope will offer them advantages in the future. This is somewhat the same attitude as is aroused by the majority election system: while in opposition, a party suffers from it, once in power, benefits from it.

Second, this acceptance contains the seeds of its own destruction. Actions by federal and provincial governments against patronage have increased and have been widely publicized since the 1960s, so well that the electorate is now much more sensitive than in the past to government public morality. A government that transgresses is more likely to suffer electoral consequences than was the case a few decades ago.

Corruption

Although opinion polls and speeches may not differentiate between corruption and patronage, the two should not be confused. They overlap only partially, and from the perspective of public sector ethics, corruption differs from patronage.

Corruption consists of behaviour contrary to the standards or rules of political redistribution, through which the corrupter obtains from the person being corrupted a benefit that the corrupter would not otherwise obtain. (See Scott 1972; Heidenheimer et al. 1989; and Gibbons and Rowat 1976 on the subject of corruption.) As Friedrich (1972, 127) has observed, the advantage may be a material one, but it may also consist of a promotion, an award or other inducement.

Corruption may occur within a patronage relationship, but in many cases the person who corrupts and the person corrupted are not united by such a link. The transaction between them does not adhere to the principle of reciprocity: for example, the manager of a department or independent agency may make a decision favourable to someone after having been "bought" by this person. This decision might occur in a patronage situation as only one of many transactions between two individuals who know each other well, but it might also consist of a market exchange with no further consequences. The existence of a patronage link often encourages corruption, but corruption can occur without any prior tie of reciprocity linkage and without any lasting relationship between the corrupter and the person corrupted. Corruption, like patronage, is contrary to public sector ethics in that it violates a standard or rule intended to ensure competition among, and responsibility of, the "voices" in political redistribution.

Conflict of Interest

Conflict of interest, as commonly defined, differs from corruption in terms of its position in the transaction systems that interest us.

Conflict of interest consists of using the political redistribution system to gain benefits in the market exchange system. (On this subject, see in particular Peters and Welch 1978; Atkinson and Mancuso 1985.) A Conservative minister from Quebec, for example, arranged to have one of his organizers, a friend, lend him money to sort out problems in his personal life. This was apparently in exchange for contracts with the minister's department, which were awarded without tender. Not only is such behaviour contrary to public sector ethics because it restricts political competition, it is also contrary to business ethics, at least under today's broad definition. Current business ethics do not permit subversion of the competitive voice-based system to obtain market advantages that would not otherwise have been obtained.

PARTICIPANTS' PERCEPTIONS

According to the proposed definition, patronage, corruption and conflict of interest are contrary to public sector ethics. One may wonder whether

Canadians perceive these phenomena in the same way. Blais and Gidengil's 1991 review for the Commission shows that by the late 1980s, Canadians' perceptions were rather negative.

In a 1988 Environics poll, 38 percent of those interviewed believed that corruption in government circles was a very serious problem, while 45 percent said that it was a fairly serious problem. In an Environics poll taken the year before, 45 percent of Canadians expressed the view that corruption was a very serious problem.

Similarly, in the 1988 Environics poll, half the Canadians interviewed considered that the scandals afflicting the Conservative government were everyday phenomena. In 1987, at the time of the Oerlikon affair involving a minister, 56 percent of those polled shared this opinion.

Respondents in that survey thought that the Conservative government was somewhat more corrupt than the previous Liberal government. An Angus Reid poll conducted at the beginning of 1988, however, showed that 70 percent of those questioned thought that the extent of scandals and immoral conduct would not change, no matter what government was in power. In 1987, another Angus Reid poll showed that 67 percent of Canadians believed that there was no difference between the parties in terms of scandal or corruption. Thus, when asked which party was least likely to resort to job patronage, two out of five Canadians lacked confidence in any party, while 36 percent leaned toward the New Democrats, 12 percent toward the Liberals and 9 percent toward the Conservatives.

A Gallup poll in early November 1990 showed that almost two Canadians in three believed that political favouritism and corruption were on the rise in Ottawa. This figure was markedly higher than the results of the two preceding Gallup polls taken on this topic in 1986 and 1988.

Abuses of Political Patronage

These survey data give only a general indication of people's attitudes toward public morality of political personalities. Research in this area provides more precise illustrations. In our own research, we observed that most abuses of political patronage reported by our informants consisted of violations of the standard rules of reciprocity by one of the parties, especially by the "patron" (Lemieux 1971; Lemieux and Hudon 1975).

The first type of perceived abuse occurs when a patron restricts transactions to certain clients. It involves nepotism, which limits the prerogative to relatives, or favouritism, which limits it to certain privileged individuals, while reciprocity, where it exists, must be contagious, and extend to larger networks of clients.

Our informants also denounced bribery ("greasing someone's palm"), which sins against reciprocity because one of the parties in the relationship, usually the client, receives more than is due. The patron thus creates an obligation that the client cannot repay. The effect is to reinforce the domination of the client by the patron, in a way that has more to do with gaining political "voice" than with maintaining links between players. When patrons "grease their own palms" by keeping resources that should be provided to clients, market exchange triumphs over reciprocity.

Finally, it was also emphasized that the patron must not blackmail or threaten the client, that is, force the client to enter into, or to remain in, a patronage relationship. Such an excess also runs counter to reciprocity, in that it imposes the requirements of "voice" or those of efficiency.

According to information gathered in this field, patronage should encourage reciprocity or maintain it against an encroaching bureaucracy, which is often incapable of correcting market deficiencies.

Public Morality Issues in Provincial Election Campaigns

In the absence of specific data on Canadian perceptions of how behaviour conforms to or conflicts with public sector ethics, data were compiled on issues related to public morality, raised during election campaigns. This made it possible to identify the types of cases of patronage, corruption, conflict of interest or fraud that have been debated publicly.

The results of a research project supported by the Social Sciences and Humanities Research Council of Canada were used for that purpose. This research focused on election campaigns, particularly on issues that were the subject of debate among the parties.

The sources used in the research included, in addition to daily newspapers, scholarly works about parties and elections, as well as biographies and memoirs of political personalities. The daily newspaper coverage spanned the period from the day an election was called to election day. The issues grid used was designed by Budge and Fairlie (1983). One of their 14 categories of issues concerns the performance and the circumstances of the government, and includes cases of fraud, corruption, patronage and conflict of interest.

Obviously, cases involving public morality that prompt debate provide only indirect information concerning the perceptions of political participants. Such cases are usually raised by opposition parties in the hope that voters will react negatively toward the governing party. It is not possible, however, to measure the effect of these revelations on the electorate. To maximize the validity of the study, however, only cases that received intensive media coverage during an election campaign were considered. The media themselves no doubt believed that these cases were likely to draw the electorate's attention because they involved breaches of public morality.

The analysis of these cases is presented by province, moving from west to east, noting the players involved. The point of departure is the year 1950, and only those cases involving specific persons are discussed; general accusations were ignored.

British Columbia

During the 1956 campaign, the minister of lands and forests was accused of issuing logging licences to large companies in exchange for favours, among them personal loans to the minister. This case involved patronage, corruption and conflict of interest.

At the time of the 1966 election, the chairman of the Purchasing Commission had to resign, having been accused of corruption in the exercise of his functions. There was also a case of fraud involving someone close to the premier who allegedly forged the premier's signature to obtain Canadian citizenship for one of his friends.

During the 1969 campaign, a minister was accused of conflict of interest as a result of using a government plane for personal purposes. The sons of the same minister were also accused of profiting from the sale of land intended for highway construction. This also constituted a case of conflict of interest.

The 1983 election campaign was marked by several "scandals," notably a case of fraud stemming from the preceding election campaign. Another conflict of interest case involved the premier's brother.

Conflict of interest cases involving ministers were raised during the 1986 election campaign: investments in forestry companies that had obtained logging licences over the objections of environmentalists; transactions with financial institutions in which the government had deposited money; and so on. The premier's wife was even accused of profiting from a rezoning of agricultural land by realizing huge earnings on land she owned. Corruption and conflict of interest were alleged in this case.

Alberta

At issue in the 1955 election campaign were the resignations of two members of the legislature found in conflict of interest for renting a building they owned to the government. The opposition also accused the government of giving loans more readily to companies that it dealt with, leading to suspicions of patronage.

Accusations by the opposition of conflict of interest were central to the 1967 election campaign. Two government ministers were accused of participating in businesses and land speculation that allegedly placed them in a conflict of interest.

In 1979, the premier was accused of having accepted free flights since 1971 on aircraft belonging to two different companies. Some regarded this as a conflict of interest, but the premier eventually repaid a sum of money corresponding to the value of these "gifts."

In 1982, the opposition raised the case of two ministers in conflict of interest: one for using his department's resources for personal gain, the other for realizing a profit on the sale to the government of land he owned.

Saskatchewan

Saskatchewan differs from the other provinces in that, according to our sources, breaches of public morality did not play an important part in the election campaigns between 1950 and 1990. In 1956, however, the premier was obliged to defend two public servants who were accused of attending political meetings.

It is possible, however, that this situation can be explained in part by the lack of a Saskatchewan daily paper in the libraries where our assistants worked.

Manitoba

The only cases involving conflicts with public morality were raised at the time of the 1981 election. One member of the government was accused of involvement in drug trafficking. Another was suspected of conflict of interest because he owned land at the site selected for the new location of a large company.

Ontario

In Ontario, on the other hand, issues of public morality were raised during a number of elections, starting in 1955.

In that year, the minister of highways was forced to resign after six employees in his department were found guilty of conspiring to defraud the government. The system of awarding contracts without an invitation to tender was also at issue because of the patronage opportunities it afforded.

In the 1959 election campaign, the Conservative premier had to defend himself following the resignations of three of his ministers who had ignored the premier's directive prohibiting ministers from owning shares in a natural gas company the government had purchased.

In 1963, the opposition's campaign theme was "A scandal a day." The principal cases involved a minister without portfolio, the chief commissioner of the Liquor Control Board of Ontario (LCBO) and his wife. The latter was alleged to have been involved in businesses selling alcohol, which is prohibited for board members and employees, while the minister was alleged to have had new products placed on the LCBO list in exchange for personal favours and contributions to the party.

Another case involved a candidate, the former mayor of a city that had been the subject of a government inquiry following problems stemming from mismanagement. The opposition accused the government of soft-pedalling the report on the city's administration to protect the former mayor.

Other cases involved organized crime. Government employees were accused of being involved in illegal betting. More generally, the government was accused of being lax in dealing with organized crime, the existence of which was well established.

In 1975, the premier and one of his ministers were accused of conflict of interest for using government airplanes for private purposes.

Several other cases have been mentioned, concerning privileged information that those close to ministers were said to have obtained in order to make business deals in operations that depended on decisions made by the government. The minister of agriculture was alleged to have received money from his own ministry for improvements to his farm. An advertising firm with close ties to the Conservatives was alleged to have obtained government contracts worth several million dollars.

During the 1977 election campaign, a hazardous waste disposal firm was said to have benefited from a government decision a few months after donating $35 000 to the Conservative party. A contract awarded to Hydro-Québec was also said to have involved political influence.

In 1981, a former minister was accused of using his influence to help a trust company obtain a federal charter in 1974 when he was in charge of regulating trust companies on behalf of the province.

During the 1985 campaign, the opposition raised several presumed cases of patronage involving the hiring of individuals or the implementation of government programs. Liquor Licence Board inspectors allegedly pressed licence holders to contribute to the coffers of the party in power.

In 1987, attacks were made on two ministers, one who had neglected to declare his interest in a mining company and one because her husband had received government assistance for his business.

Quebec

In 1952, the opposition attacked two ministers who were alleged to have made a profit on transactions involving Crown lands.

In 1956, the leader of the opposition denounced the excessive favours granted to a U.S. iron mining company operating in the northern part of the province. The usual accusations of patronage were repeated, involving contracts awarded without tender and the allocation of liquor licences. Election fraud was also alleged.

During the 1960 election campaign, the affair known as the "natural gas" scandal received the heaviest media coverage. Ministers were accused of selling the natural gas distribution network belonging to Hydro-Québec to a private company in which the ministers held shares. A case of the government paying a voter $3 200 for changing party allegiance was also raised.

In 1962, despite the fact that a new party was in power, the attack on the former government's practices continued following the appearance of the first instalment of a report by a commission of inquiry into these practices. At the end of the campaign, the opposition party was accused of fraud for falsifying voters' certificates.

This issue was raised again during the 1966 election campaign by the party that had been accused of the same thing in 1962. The party now in opposition claimed that this was a manoeuvre by the government to discredit it.

In 1976, the government was faced with several accusations involving public morality: the granting of contracts to lawyers, accountants and engineers with party connections; Loto-Québec distribution agents collecting unjustified revenues; and leading Liberal members of firms doing profitable business with the provincial liquor board.

In 1989, the treasurer of the governing party was the object of several opposition attacks. He was suspected of having pressured the farmlands protection board to rezone farmlands belonging to him, which netted him a large profit. He was also accused of operating a vast patronage network that was allegedly bending the rules for awarding contracts to favour friends of the government. A minister was also accused of having violated government directives aimed at preventing conflicts of interest.

New Brunswick

During the 1974 election campaign, several accusations were made against the party in power. A minister was in a conflict of interest because a company he owned was alleged to have done business with the government. A transportation company with close government ties was alleged to have obtained an exclusive contract with the New Brunswick Liquor Licensing Board. A minister was accused of granting liquor licences in return for contributions to the party. A former party fund raiser was alleged to have obtained a sinecure in the public service and was accused of inordinate patronage and corruption. Another minister and former party leader was accused of awarding contracts without tender in exchange for election contributions.

Some of these cases resurfaced in 1978, along with new ones, but opposition attacks were neutralized by the report of a commission of inquiry, which cleared the government of the charges against it.

The case involving the former party fund raiser resurfaced when he was finally found guilty of corrupting a public servant. Members of the government were not prosecuted, although they were shown to have had knowledge of the accused's practices.

Nova Scotia

In 1953, in addition to general accusations of patronage against the government, ministers were accused of conflict of interest for having an interest in firms doing business with the government.

In 1956, seven individuals involved in government alcohol purchases were accused of receiving pay-offs from the companies whose products were purchased.

During the 1967 campaign, the opposition alleged that voters would accept money or alcohol on election day, and would sell their votes in this way to the highest bidder.

At the beginning of the 1974 campaign, a series of articles by a former party organizer embarrassed the two major parties, raising the issues of election fraud and patronage.

In 1984, the provincial solicitor general was accused of hindering an RCMP investigation of certain cabinet members' expense accounts. The RCMP claimed, however, that there was no such investigation.

In 1988, the opposition exploited the case of a government member found guilty of election expense fraud and expelled from the party. There was also the issue of a former minister who had filed false expense accounts during his tenure as minister, and who, as in the preceding case, was expelled from the party. Another former minister was obliged to resign after admitting that several banks had forgiven his debts when he entered the cabinet. Other ministers likewise resigned, but for various reasons, not all of which had to do with public morality. A lawyer, a friend of the premier, was accused of receiving excessive fees for government work. The premier responded by establishing a code of ethics for members of the government.

Prince Edward Island

In 1955, the opposition levelled accusations against the premier's brother, alleging that the construction company with which he was associated was benefiting from government largesse.

During the 1974 election campaign, allegations were made that land belonging to government party supporters had been purchased by the government at a high price.

In 1986, it was claimed that the premier, while on vacation in Florida, had received the hospitality of a businessman from whom the government had purchased a bankrupt hotel. This was seen as a conflict of interest situation.

In 1989, an issue was made of the case of 122 former public servants who complained before the provincial Human Rights Commission that they had lost their jobs following a change of government.

Newfoundland

The 1951 election was marked by an important case of election fraud: a large number of voters in an opposition stronghold complained that their names did not appear on the voters list.

In 1956, the opposition could have exploited the case of a former senior public servant, with ties to the party in power, who had been accused of using government funds he administered for personal gain. He had also pocketed funds intended for the party's election coffers. Despite the media revelations, however, the case did not become a campaign issue.

The 1959 election gave rise to renewed accusations of election fraud. The election results were changed after a recount.

In 1975, elections in three ridings were nullified, leading to by-elections. Once again, during the by-elections, the opposition knew about, but refused to exploit, a number of cases of patronage.

Conclusions about the Campaign Issues

Clearly, certain regional differences exist in the cases involving conflicts with public morality that have become issues in provincial election campaigns since the 1950s. In Saskatchewan and Manitoba, if such cases occurred they were not raised during election campaigns, even if opposition parties and journalists knew about them. In Newfoundland, most of the cases involved voting fraud, although other cases involving public immorality could have been exploited.

Certain patterns emerged in the cases surveyed. First, those targeted were frequently ministers, the premier, or members of their families or entourages (see Greene 1990, 233). This confirms what was suggested in the definition of public sector ethics, namely that breaches of these ethics are more likely to implicate those in power than other participants in the public sector.

Second, the most common accusations against ministers and their entourages were of conflict of interest rather than fraud, patronage or corruption, although these were not entirely excluded. Thus, those in power were particularly criticized for receiving personal gain from their behaviour rather than for political activities where the gains sought were of a public rather than a private order.

Third, no matter what form immoral conduct took, it was principally excessive gains that were denounced. This may in fact have been a media phenomenon: just as there is a greater chance of creating news by accusing a minister rather than a backbencher, there are also more opportunities to create news if the benefits from immoral practices appear to be excessive rather than modest.

THE PRACTICAL IMPLICATIONS OF PUBLIC SECTOR ETHICS

Our definition of public sector ethics postulated that political redistribution was supposed to remedy market exchange and reciprocity deficiencies. We noted that the word "remedy" must be understood in the broadest sense, ranging from substitution pure and simple, as in state socialism, to correction of the most blatant faults, following more liberal political systems.

The Secondary Dimension of Public Sector Ethics

The secondary dimension of public sector ethics is thus the component relating to remedies for deficiencies of the market and reciprocity. From this perspective, conflicts of interest above all, but also most cases of corruption and patronage, are reprehensible, as most political participants recognize quite readily.

Cases of conflict of interest are the clearest because they usually involve individuals who are successful in the market exchange system, or who have been successful but now find themselves in difficulty (bankruptcy, personal debts) because of their own mistakes or normal market forces. When they use their "voice" in the political redistribution system they do so not to correct market exchange deficiencies but to maintain or even improve their privileged position in the market exchange system. However, what is a profitable situation for some people may lead to failures suffered by others, a situation the political system should correct.

In cases of corruption or patronage, it is not always so clear that the behaviour of participants is contrary to public sector ethics, at least in terms of this secondary dimension. Let us consider, for example, a case of "small-scale" patronage, coupled with corruption. By bribing a public servant, a patron or party supporter obtains a modest public service position for a client. It may be argued that by acting in this manner, the patron is remedying a market deficiency, assuming that the client would not have succeeded in finding a private sector job. To justify this practice further, it might even be said that it permits the preservation of a certain reciprocity in human relations from an ever more invasive bureaucracy.

It is significant that these cases of "small-scale" patronage are not debated to any great extent during election campaigns, although they may be included in broader accusations of patronage. Instead, it is cases of "large-scale" patronage that tend to be raised because, as in most cases of conflict of interest, clients who benefit from these practices, far from being disadvantaged in the market exchange system, usually enjoy an excellent position in it. Large-scale patronage improves this position still further, and when the resulting gains do not remain purely private, they are reinvested in the system of "voice" through which political redistribution occurs. In this respect, there is a difference in terms of conflict of interest between the client who obtains the money required to pay off personal debts and the client who obtains a lucrative contract, and reinvests part of the profits in the party's election coffers.

If large-scale rather than small-scale patronage transgresses against the secondary dimension of public sector ethics, both types transgress against its primary dimension – safeguarding competition and responsibility in the political redistribution system.

The Primary Dimension of Public Sector Ethics

Even if it does not involve conflict of interest, political patronage is contrary to public sector ethics when it gives the government an unfair competitive advantage relative to other parties without the public's awareness of the behaviour that confers these advantages.

Not all patronage practices are to be condemned from this standpoint. When a minister has public funds available to set up an office and hires friends or supporters as a reward for services rendered, or in hopes of obtaining personal or party services from them, the minister is practising political patronage. But this is not contrary to public sector ethics as we have defined them. On the other hand, when a politician holds or converts many voters to the cause through "petty patronage," or lines the party's coffers with contributions from clients in exchange for considerable benefits, the competitive, responsible system of "voice" in political redistribution is affected. Thus, at least under our definition of the term, some patronage is contrary to public sector ethics and some is not.

The parties and the other political players are aware of this distinction. Patronage that is not contrary to public sector ethics is generally practised in the full light of day. Patronage that undermines competition and responsibility is considered contrary to public sector ethics, judging by the efforts made to conceal it from public view.

Our political culture has evolved in this respect, to the point where the potential for patronage has been restricted by means of a steadily increasing number of rules designed to maintain competition and responsibility in awarding jobs, contracts and other public benefits. Before such rules existed, patronage – particularly "petty patronage" – was not considered contrary to accepted standards of political behaviour. Now that rules abound, the public judges patronage much more harshly, especially when it is accompanied by the excesses we have highlighted, for example, nepotism, graft, blackmail or conflict of interest. We should not underestimate, however, the extent to which committed party supporters (although their numbers are on the decline) accept patronage as a privilege from which the parties benefit in turn.

These reflections on the secondary and primary dimensions of public sector ethics lead to a few suggestions for making the conduct of politicians, and especially the financing of political parties, more consistent with public sector ethics as defined in this study.

Public Sector Ethics and Politicians' Conduct

There are three ways of looking at controlling politicians' conduct to make it conform more closely to public sector ethics in which the values of competition and responsibility are central.

The first is to rely on written regulations intended to limit, if not eliminate, fraudulent practices, patronage, corruption and conflicts of interest.

The *Canada Elections Act* and provincial election laws include measures to prevent fraud. This is an area in which fraudulent practices are easy enough to identify and one that has preoccupied legislators for many years.

By contrast, it is harder and more controversial to define what constitutes patronage and corruption. These are the activities that royal commissions and task forces are formed to examine. Regulations have been established to award contracts, purchases and public sector jobs so as to avoid the restraint of competition and responsibility that are built into practices of patronage and corruption. Although these regulations are fairly effective, it is always possible to get around them or even simply to claim that the conduct in question is not really patronage or corruption.

Recently, political authorities have concentrated their efforts on clarifying the meaning of conflict of interest, specifically because many cases of public immorality have become issues during elections and at other times have constituted conflict of interest situations, as brought out in the preceding section.

In a recent article on the subject, Greene (1990) noted that, as well as in the federal government, six provinces (Newfoundland, Prince Edward Island, Nova Scotia, New Brunswick, Ontario and Manitoba) have adopted conflict of interest legislation. In the other provinces as well, except for Quebec, certain legislative measures exist to handle conflicts of interest. In Quebec, there are only directives issued by the premier, but, as Greene notes, they rank among the strictest in Canada.

In three provinces, the laws state that ministers, members of the legislature and their spouses are forbidden to practise nepotism, that is, patronage toward their relatives. This legislation aims essentially to prevent the people cited from deriving private gain, in the market exchange system, through their participation in political redistribution. The measures taken are diverse, including disclosure of assets and private interests, prohibition of the use of privileged information and withdrawal from political decision making when private interests are concerned.

These rules of ethics have not prevented new conflict of interest cases from breaking out in public. Nevertheless, they have the merit of attacking the important loopholes in public sector ethics, such as the use of influential voices in political redistribution, not to make up for market failures but rather to improve a position in the market exchange system.

Along with regulations adopted by legislatures and governments, codes of ethics or duty that parties could adopt constitute a second way of controlling conduct contrary to the values of competition and responsibility.

The Royal Commission on Electoral Reform and Party Financing could suggest that the federal parties include in their by-laws a declaration of principle whereby they refuse to become involved in practices of patronage and corruption that, when they form a government, confer an undue political advantage, and allow them to shirk their responsibility to the public. This declaration would have to be written as precisely as possible, with reference to the most common types of patronage and corruption known to and practised recently by politicians.

From the moment at least one of the major federal parties adopts it, the others will come under heavy pressure to adopt it as well.

Finally, besides official regulations and self-discipline, there is another way to control political conduct deemed contrary to public sector ethics. Public vigilance, especially by the information media, whose task is to enlighten, constitutes an important controlling factor. Given the often sensational nature of cases of fraud, patronage, corruption and conflict of interest committed by leading politicians such as premiers, ministers and their entourages, the media are inclined to inform the public about it. This is true only if they do not become so closely linked to the governing party that they no longer exercise their watchdog function. That remains entirely hypothetical, however, considering how the media have operated in recent years.

Bringing to the light of day conduct that does not conform to public sector ethics has certainly embarrassed politicians, and has probably made them more prudent, if not less immoral. When revealed to the public by the media or opposition parties, patronage, corruption and conflict of interest produce effects contrary to what was intended. Instead of improving the political position of the governing party, they help erode it. This possibility ought to encourage politicians to choose self-discipline instead of running the risk of self-destruction. One can hope that conduct that does not conform to public sector ethics will eventually end by itself.

Public Sector Ethics and Party Financing

Other measures, this time concerning party financing, could alleviate the negative sentiments many Canadians feel toward the scandals and the immoral conduct in government. Along with several other factors, this negative attitude undermines the legitimacy of political redistribution in Canada.

Party financing certainly constitutes an important area for action in seeking to restore this legitimacy. At the federal level, reforms of the 1970s can be considered positive from the standpoint of responsibility in that the names of those individuals and groups who contribute an amount of $100 or more annually to a political party are now made public. The reforms are of more questionable value for competition, however, because they do not limit the total contribution to the parties. In Quebec, contributions are limited to $3 000 per party per year, and only individuals (i.e., voters) can provide money to parties or candidates.

Given our definition of public sector ethics, it is not so much the source as the size of contributions that should be regulated. The survey of provincial cases of public immorality showed that both individuals and groups benefited improperly from public decisions, whether for private gain or to obtain benefits that would be reinvested in whole or in part in the political fray. Moreover, the distinction between individuals and groups (physical and legal entities) is frequently arbitrary, as demonstrated by the cases studied. There is also nothing to prevent a group from contributing to a party under the guise of individual contributions, as is said to be happening in Quebec under party orders.

This is why we propose to limit the annual contribution to a political party by groups or individuals, with the aim of strengthening and safeguarding competition among the various voices in the political redistribution system and the legitimacy of this system in people's minds. We do not believe that this ceiling will impair the parties' capacity to raise funds. Some believe that the parties already have too much money, which would become more apparent if the length of election campaigns were limited (Kent 1988).

In our view, this proposal should also apply to election spending by "third parties," groups or organizations that purchase advertising clearly favourable to the position of one political party, as occurred on the subject of free trade during the 1988 federal campaign. Quebec's election law, which also applies to legal entities, is very strict in this area. Even if legal entities were allowed to contribute to political parties, it is not clear how they could be authorized to do indirectly what they could not do directly, i.e., to contribute more than a legislated sum to a political party.

Some might argue that this restriction jeopardizes freedom of expression, but in the circumstances, this is a rather hollow argument. Freedom of expression depends in fact on a political system that remains competitive. This is why it is important to limit this freedom when it takes the form of financial contributions that are liable to skew the competitive nature of the system of "voice" or diminish its legitimacy in the eyes of the public. Those who support a position put forward by one of the parties would still remain free to express themselves in favour of the issue. In promoting this cause, they would be prohibited only from spending funds that exceed the allowable annual limit on donations to a political party.

As for the partial reimbursement of candidates' election expenses, we wonder about the regulation requiring a candidate to receive at least 15 percent of the vote to get the right of reimbursement. Why 15 percent instead of 20 percent, which is the rule in Quebec? And what justifies granting a candidate who gets 15.1 percent of the vote a privilege denied to a candidate who gets 14.9 percent? Obviously, this rule assures reimbursement to the larger parties in almost all ridings while the smaller parties are unable to take advantage of the same right.

This rule makes some parties "more equal" than others in electoral competition. Certain candidates can allow themselves to spend to the allowable ceiling, knowing that half their expenses will be reimbursed. Candidates for "less equal" parties, on the other hand, know that they will not be reimbursed unless they reach the fateful threshold of 15 percent. As they generally have less money to start with than candidates from the larger parties, the 15 percent rule tends to accentuate the inequality rather than correct it.

We could adopt a more equitable way of doing things that is very simple to apply. The amount of campaign expenditure to be reimbursed to candidates would be pegged to the number of voters enumerated in a riding. Across Canada as a whole, this amount could be more or less equivalent to the amount reimbursed after the 1988 election. The proportion of reimbursement each candidate would receive would be equal to his or her share of the vote. For example, if three parties get 50 percent, 40 percent and 10 percent of the vote respectively, they would get the same proportions of the reimbursement for that riding.

In Quebec, a similar rule was adopted for the distribution of the annual subsidy for party organizational and operating expenses. A global amount to be divided up is decided on, and the parties receive the proportion of that amount that corresponds to the proportion of the vote they received in the last election.

RECOMMENDATIONS

Accordingly, we recommend:

1. That the Commission encourage the federal government to strengthen not only the regulations on conflicts of interest, but also the regulations concerning purchases, contracts and public service jobs, to assure greater political equity between parties and greater responsibility to the public on their part.
2. That a declaration of principle be drawn up, and federal parties be encouraged to include it in their by-laws, stating that they refuse to be involved in practices of patronage and corruption that give them an undue advantage in political competition or allow them to evade their responsibility to the public.
3. That, to safeguard the competitive nature of the political system in practice and in perception, a limit be placed on the total annual contribution that can be made to a political party, and that this

limit apply to "third parties," groups or organizations that, during an election campaign or at any other time, fund advertising that favours a particular party.
4. That from now on, the partial reimbursement of candidates' election expenses be based on the percentage of votes they receive, not the arbitrary threshold of 15 percent.

ABBREVIATIONS

R.S.C.   Revised Statutes of Canada
S.Q.   Statutes of Quebec

REFERENCES

Atkinson, M.M., and M. Mancuso. 1985. "Do We Need a Code of Conduct for Politicians?" *Canadian Journal of Political Science* 18:459–80.

Bailey, F.G. 1971. *Les règles du jeu politique*. Paris: Presses universitaires de France.

Blais, A., and E. Gidengil. 1991. *Representative Democracy: The Views of Canadians*. Vol. 17 of the research studies of the Royal Commission on Electoral Reform and Party Financing. Ottawa and Toronto: RCERPF/Dundurn.

Budge, I., and D.J. Fairlie. 1983. *Explaining and Predicting Elections*. London: George Allen and Unwin.

Canada. *Canada Elections Act*, R.S.C. 1985, c. E-2.

Clark, P.B., and J.Q. Wilson. 1961. "Incentive Systems: A Theory of Organizations." *Administrative Science Quarterly* 6:129–66.

De George, R.T. 1990. *Business Ethics*. New York: Macmillan.

Eisenstadt, S.N., and L. Roniger. 1984. *Patrons, Clients and Friends*. Cambridge: Cambridge University Press.

Friedrich, C.J. 1972. *The Pathology of Politics*. New York: Harper and Row.

Gibbons, K.M. 1976. "The Study of Political Corruption." In *Political Corruption in Canada*, ed. K.M. Gibbons and D.C. Rowat. Toronto: McClelland and Stewart.

Gibbons, K.M., and D.C. Rowat, eds. 1976. *Political Corruption in Canada*. Toronto: McClelland and Stewart.

Greene, I. 1990. "Conflict of Interest and the Canadian Constitution." *Canadian Journal of Political Science* 23:233–56.

Heidenheimer, A., M. Johnston and V.T. Levine, eds. 1989. *Political Corruption: A Handbook*. New Brunswick: Transaction Books.

Hirschman, A.O. 1970. *Exit, Voice and Loyalty*. Cambridge: Harvard University Press.

Hyde, L. 1979. *The Gift*. New York: Vintage Books.

Kent, T. 1988. "Now Is the Time for All Good Persons to Come to the Aid of the Parties." *Policy Options* (October): 3–5.

Lemieux, V. 1971. *Parenté et politique*. Quebec: Les Presses de l'Université Laval.

———. 1977. *Le patronage politique*. Quebec: Les Presses de l'Université Laval.

———. 1990. "Les nouvelles formes du patronage." Paper presented at a seminar in memory of K.Z. Paltiel at Carleton University.

Lemieux, V., and R. Hudon. 1975. *Patronage et politique au Québec: 1944–1972*. Sillery: Boréal Express.

Mahoney, J. 1990. *Teaching Business Ethics in the UK, Europe and the USA*. London: Athlone Press.

Mauss, M. 1950. "Essai sur le don." In M. Mauss, *Sociologie et anthropologie*. Paris: Presses universitaires de France.

Noel, S.J.R. 1987. "Dividing the Spoils: The Old and New Rules of Patronage in Canadian Politics." *Journal of Canadian Studies* 22 (2): 72–95.

———. 1990. "From Parties to Symbols and Entourages: The Changing Uses of Political Patronage in Canada." Paper presented at a seminar in memory of K.Z. Paltiel at Carleton University.

Peters, J.G., and S. Welch. 1978. "Political Corruption in America." *American Political Science Review* 72:974–84.

Polanyi, K. 1944. *The Great Transformation*. New York: Rinehart.

Quebec. *Election Act*. S.Q. 1989, c. 1.

Schattschneider, E.E. 1960. *The Semisovereign People*. New York: Holt, Rinehart and Winston.

Schmidt, S.W., L. Guasti, C.H. Lande and J.C. Scott. 1977. *Friends, Followers and Factions: A Reader in Political Clientelism*. Berkeley: University of California Press.

Scott, J.C. 1972. *Comparative Political Corruption*. Englewood Cliffs: Prentice-Hall.

Simon, H.A. 1957. *Administrative Behavior*. New York: Macmillan.

Simpson, J. 1988. *Spoils of Power: The Politics of Patronage*. Toronto: Collins.

Vastel, Michel. 1989. "Le PQ et le PLQ dans la guerre du 'petit patronage'." *Le Devoir*, 27 May.

Velasquez, M.G. 1982. *Business Ethics – Concepts and Cases*. Englewood Cliffs: Prentice-Hall.

Weber, M. 1959. *Le savant et le politique*. Paris: Plon.

3

ALLEGATIONS OF UNDUE INFLUENCE IN CANADIAN POLITICS

Ian Greene

ONE OF THE obvious tasks faced by a royal commission charged with recommending improvements to the federal electoral and party-finance rules is to determine whether the current rules permit undue influence and, if so, to suggest procedures designed to curtail it. But what is undue influence in the electoral process? One approach to answering this question is to analyse media stories related to the subject of undue influence, and then use this analysis to develop a definition and recommendations for reform. The assumption behind this approach is that the media stories reflect the concerns of Canadians about undue influence in the electoral process.

The study begins with a review of newspaper stories related to undue influence from January 1979 to March 1990.[1] The stories are divided into 10 categories according to subject-matter, and are summarized in appendices A to J. The concerns raised by each of the categories are analysed and this analysis guides the construction of a definition of undue influence and recommendations for limiting it. These recommendations take into account what is legally possible given recent court decisions on the *Canadian Charter of Rights and Freedoms*.

METHODOLOGY

All classifications in the *Canadian News Index* from January 1979 to March 1990 that appeared to include stories on undue influence were reviewed. The *Canadian News Index* classifications included:

- Canada – elections
- Elections for each province

- Patronage
- Each large national party (Progressive Conservative, Liberal, NDP, Parti québécois)
- Campaign funds

The research probably missed some media stories related to undue influence either because the stories were not picked up by the *Canadian News Index* or because the titles of the news stories did not clearly relate to the topic. It should also be kept in mind that few reporters have time to engage in "investigative reporting" regarding undue influence. The stories they print are, for the most part, the ones that they encounter by chance and that they are able to confirm with at least two reliable sources. The stories reviewed in this paper, therefore, likely represent only a fraction of the incidents of what could be considered as undue influence in the electoral process. However, assuming that there was no systematic bias in the stories missed – and this assumption seems to be a reasonable one – the items included in this analysis provide an accurate indication of the issues related to undue influence which Canadian newspapers consider newsworthy. And because newspapers print what they believe their subscribers are most interested in reading, the analysis provides an indicator of the kinds of issues related to undue influence that Canadians are most concerned about. One hundred and thirty stories from the *Canadian News Index* were located. The stories were then analysed and sorted into the 10 categories shown in appendices A to J. The total number of entries in these classifications is 140, since several stories dealt with issues in more than one of the ten categories. The subject-matter of the stories is summarized in a different way in figure 3.K1 and tables 3.K1 and 3.K2 in appendix K. The total number of items presented there is 165, as the stories were broken down according to whether they dealt with the federal, provincial or municipal governments, and several stories concerned more than one government.

As figure 3.K1 in appendix K shows, the number of allegations of undue influence increased substantially during the 11-year period under scrutiny. Table 3.K2 indicates that the increases occurred at every level of government.

The summarized stories in appendices A to J are presented in descending order, from most recent to least recent, with one exception. In appendix B, which deals with violations of electoral laws, there were a number of stories in 1989 which concerned the Patricia Starr affair in Ontario; the relation of these stories to each other is easier to grasp when presented in chronological order.

THE MEANING OF UNDUE INFLUENCE

Before developing a definition of undue influence which is guided by the issues raised in newspaper reports, it is necessary to consider to what extent the reports about undue influence may simply represent a "media phenomenon." During the last decade, the number of newspaper reports related to the financing of elections and undue influence in election campaigns has risen dramatically (as indicated by figure 3.K1 in appendix K) from a handful of stories each year in the early 1980s to several dozen per year in the late 1980s.[2] One of the factors which may account for this trend is a self-generated tendency in the media to give greater attention to stories on undue influence. There is a possibility that journalists may have discovered that such stories "make good copy" and enhance their professional stature. However, since there is no evidence which suggests that journalists might be more aware of such possibilities today than they were 10 or 20 years ago, it is necessary to search for other explanations. The following three appear to be the most plausible ones:

- A tendency for the public to place greater stress on social equality as a result of the human-rights movement which has affected all of the western democracies since the early 1960s. Undue influence, such as special favours for donors to political parties, violates the principle of social equality which implies that all citizens have a right to treatment as equals (Greene 1990, 245). Hence, such practices, often tolerated when social equality was a less important value, are now widely condemned.
- Reaction to the "Watergate" scandal in the United States. According to Kenneth Kernaghan, this event raised demands in the United States and Canada that higher ethical standards should be set for politicians (Kernaghan 1974, 531).
- A trend toward the increasing regulation of electoral activities through limits placed on spending and disclosure requirements. When new rules are created, some are inevitably broken. When this happens, it is usually reported by the media.

If the third explanation were the most important, there would be substantially more items reported in appendix B, which lists reports of violations of laws regarding election contributions or spending limits. Although the Watergate scandal has undoubtedly had a major impact, it is unlikely that this event alone could explain all of the heightened interest in political ethics. Of these three explanations, the first – social equality – may be the most important because it can explain why people were so much more outraged by the Watergate scandal than by political ethics scandals in earlier eras.

It is evident that social equality is a more important value today than it was several decades ago. For example, a recent survey found that 72 percent of Canadians disagreed with the statement, "some people are better than others" (Russell et al. 1987); it is not likely that such a high proportion would have expressed this opinion 20 or 30 years ago. The greater stress on equality has not only led to more stringent equality guarantees in the *Canadian Charter of Rights and Freedoms* and the provincial human-rights codes, but has also resulted in higher standards in codes of ethics for public officials – such as the rules prohibiting conflicts of interest (Greene 1990, 242) – and will probably increase the demand for stricter rules promoting the equality principle as it relates to the electoral system and party financing.

As a result of this trend in the evolution of social values, it can safely be concluded that the increase in the rate of reporting incidents of undue influence reflects a real public concern with this subject, and is not simply a media-generated phenomenon. Newspaper stories may therefore be considered as a useful indicator of what Canadians perceive as undue influence in the electoral process.

The stories on undue influence are divided into 10 categories as follows:

1. Relation between a donation to a party or candidate and a favour, contract, or grant provided to the donor (51 stories, or 55 items when broken down according to level of government)
2. Violations of laws regarding election contributions or spending limits (30 stories, or 41 items when broken down according to level of government)
3. Donations to candidates and parties made public as required by law (17 stories, or 19 items when broken down according to level of government)
4. Weak laws regarding election contributions or spending (14 stories, or 17 items when broken down according to level of government)
5. Outside interference in election campaigns (9 stories, or 13 items when broken down according to level of government)
6. Fund-raising for leadership candidates or senior party officials criticized (7 stories, or 8 items when broken down according to level of government)
7. Campaign contributions used in questionable ways (4 stories)

8. Friends of government party (especially campaign workers) get favours, but no allegation involving money (4 stories)
  9. Ethics of relying on a few large donors or accepting money from donors who violate party principles (3 stories)
  10. Pressure on an electoral-boundary commission by a politician (1 story)

Because of the concentration of stories in the first category, it would appear that undue influence in the electoral process is primarily associated with a relation between a donation to a party or candidate and a public office favour (such as a contract or grant) provided to the donor by the party or candidate. As well, we can say that it refers to the violation of laws regarding election contributions spending, "outside" influence in the electoral process (such as federal parties receiving financial or advertising support from U.S. companies), inadequate controls on the financing of the parties' leadership conventions, the misuse of campaign funds, the government party providing special favours to campaign workers, concerns about too much reliance on major donors, and interference with the impartiality of electoral-boundary commissions.

A working definition of undue influence could therefore be "an attempt, whether actually realized or not, to influence a candidate or party in relation to the electoral process in a way which violates the principle that all citizens have a right to be treated as equals in the design and operation of the administrative and policy processes in government."[3] Violations of the equality principle in the electoral process include attempts to influence government policy or practice through doing favours for the candidate, the candidate's party, or the candidate's family and friends (especially favours involving money). Narrow or concentrated interests (such as large corporations, large unions or well-financed public-interest groups) which seek to limit the influence of a broader range of opinion, or forces from outside the electoral jurisdiction which try to influence an election result, are also perceived as seeking undue influence.

Only a few of the allegations of undue influence are such that they can be proven in a court of law. There have been some convictions, however. For example, Conservative MP Michel Gravel was convicted of influence-peddling charges in 1988 (appendix A, no. 24); Conservative party organizer Pierre Blouin was convicted of influence peddling in 1986 (appendix A, no. 33); Liberal fund-raisers J.G. Simpson, Charles MacFadden and Irvine Barrow were convicted of conspiracy to peddle influence in Nova Scotia in 1982 and 1983 (appendix A, no. 46); two of Energy Minister Marcel Masse's campaign workers and Lavalin Inc. were convicted of violating the federal election-spending laws in 1986 (appendix B, nos. 18, 19); and Conservative candidate Armand Lefebvre was convicted of campaign fraud (appendix B, no. 24).

There are several reasons why only a few of the allegations of undue influence eventually translate into convictions. First, some practices which may be regarded by members of the public as constituting undue influence are not illegal. For example, paid lobbyists sometimes advise businesses seeking government contracts or more favourable government regulations to make "strategic donations" to parties or candidates (appendix A, no. 5). Party fund-raisers sometimes target companies receiving government grants or contracts, or which are the recipients of favourable government policies, for fund-raising campaigns (appendix A, nos. 6, 7, 25, 30, 34, 38). Some companies receiving government grants or contracts, or which are or hope to be the recipients of favourable government policies, make generous donations to the party in power (appendix A, nos. 1–4, 8–16, 23, 26–32, 35–37, 39, 42, 43, 48). Some fund-raisers openly advocate giving money to a party or a candidate because of a financial favour already provided by the party in power to a particular group (appendix A, nos. 44, 45, 48).

Second, unless those making donations to a party are willing to admit that they are doing so with the expectation of a later favour or with an explicit promise of one, which they rarely do except when the party does not deliver (as in the Blouin case, appendix A, no. 33), the actual buying of favours is often impossible to prove beyond a reasonable doubt (appendix A, nos. 3, 33, 47, 51).

Third, the decision-making process with regard to the awarding of government contracts is sometimes secret, and in some cases tenders are not called for or are very limited (appendix A, nos. 11, 26, 35, 37, 40, 41).

Fourth, in some instances, those responsible for pursuing prosecutions decide that it is simply not worthwhile to prosecute, either because a candidate has died or was defeated (appendix B, no. 28), or for discretionary reasons related to the public interest (appendix B, no. 18).

Most allegations of undue influence, therefore, are in a grey area, outside the realm of legal sanctions but within the realm of what many Canadians would describe as objectionable practices. As a result, there is a need to update the approach to regulating undue influence. The recommendations developed in this paper will be guided by a closer examination of Canadians' perceptions of undue influence as reflected by newspaper reports. Each of the 10 categories into which the newspaper reports are divided will be considered in turn. Because the first category is the largest (and most troublesome), most of the analysis will be devoted to it.[4]

PERCEPTIONS OF UNDUE INFLUENCE

1. Relation between Donation to Party or Candidate and Favour, Contract or Grant to Donor (33 Percent of 165 Items)

A third of the 165 items – 55, or 33 percent – fell into the first category. Twenty-nine items, just over half, concerned federal politicians. The category included the following kinds of allegations:

- Companies receiving government grants tend to do favours for government politicians, such as contributing to their election funds.
- The government party targets those companies receiving grants as potential donors.
- A company receiving a government grant or contract is expected to donate a specific percentage of it, usually 5 percent, to the party in power, a practice known as "tollgating."
- Executives of companies receiving government grants or contracts act as the chief fund-raisers for the government party.
- Companies or individuals who donate to the government party get or expect favours (such as grants, contracts, favourable application of regulations or jobs).
- The government gives grants or contracts predominantly to those making contributions to the government party.

The Overall Picture regarding Political Donations
Canadian political parties depend on a large number of donations from diverse sources. In 1986, for example, W.T. Stanbury shows that the federal Liberal and Progressive Conservative parties received about half of their donations from individuals, while the NDP received about a third from this source.[5] About 35 000 individuals contributed to the Liberal party in that year, 53 000 to the Conservatives, and 90 000 to the NDP. The average donation ranged from $56 per person for the NDP to $149 and $163 for the Conservatives and Liberals respectively. Forty-six individuals contributed more than $2 000 to the Conservatives and 64 to the Liberals; in 1985, 10 individuals contributed more than $2 000 to the NDP. These $2 000-plus donations, between 1983 and 1986, accounted for between 2 and 10 percent of individual donations to the Liberals and Conservatives (Stanbury 1989, 360–65).[6]

Contributions from corporations accounted for about 45 percent of the donations received by the federal Liberals and Conservatives, while the NDP received about the same proportion of its funds from provincial party organizations. Eight percent of the NDP's donations came from unions, and only 1 percent came from corporations (Stanbury 1989, 360–65).[7]

The Liberal party received about 6 000 corporate donations in 1986, with an average of nearly $800 per donation; the Conservatives received twice the number of corporate donations, averaging almost $600 per donation. Both the Conservative and the Liberal parties received about 100 corporate donations of over $10 000 in 1986, and the average large donation was roughly $25 000 for both parties. The large donations accounted for between 16 percent and 30 percent of the total corporate donations to the Conservative party between 1983 and 1986, and between 25 percent and 45 percent of the total corporate donations to the Liberal party. The largest single donations ranged from $50 000 to $150 000 between these years. About half of the corporations which made large donations to the Conservatives also contributed to the Liberals. Canadian Pacific, for example, usually gave both parties about $50 000 per year (Stanbury 1989, 365–71).

Not all large corporations make political contributions. In fact, only about a quarter of the top 100 financial enterprises in Canada made contributions either to the Liberal or Conservative party between 1983 and 1986. Half of the top 25 life insurance companies made political contributions during the time period, as did about 80 percent of the 15 largest investment dealers. Of the 30 largest oil companies in Canada, 8 gave $10 000 or more to the Liberals, and 13 made similar large contributions to the Conservatives. However, Imperial Oil, Texaco, Shell, Dome, Amoco and Mobil did not make any political contributions over $10 000 (Stanbury 1989, 365–71). Stanbury found that interest groups, such as professional associations, trade associations, and ethnic groups, did not tend to make significant contributions to political parties (ibid., 373–75).

What is suggested by these statistics is that the vast majority of donations to the three large national parties are small enough that they could not be expected to result in undue influence. Moreover, the great majority of individuals and corporations apparently feel that they can achieve their economic goals without making political donations at all. It is possible, however, that some of the larger individual and corporate donations may be associated with undue influence. As Stanbury (1989, 378–79) observes:

It is hard to believe that when a corporation gives $50 000 or more to one or more of the main parties they do so with no expectation of return. Campaign contributions express the giver's identification with the recipient's cause ... In other words, campaign contributions, particularly if they are large, secret and variable and where they are given and received with influence in mind, lie in the morally fuzzy domain in which it is difficult to distinguish gifts from tacit bribes.

All parties say they refuse all contributions "with strings attached." Yet, the Liberals and Tories appear to be offering "paid access opportunities," and many practitioners and students of political finance say, without embarrassment, that large contributions do provide access to top political decision makers. The exchange of large contributions for access is a potentially serious threat to democratic principles for at least two reasons. First, the best way to exercise influence is to have access ... Second, special access connotes the chance to have one's problems considered in a way which does not follow normal channels. Even if special access only provides the lobbyist with the opportunity to "sensitize" the decision maker to subsequent formal communications open to all, a substantial advantage has been gained.

Newspaper Stories about Trading Political Donations for Public-Office Favours

Stanbury's fears about the impact of some large donations on the political process can be explored through a study of the newspaper stories on the relation between political donations and favours to donors.[8] There are three stories that report on proven cases of undue influence, where donations to a political party are actually traded for a public-office favour:

- A Drummondville businessman gave $50 000 to Conservative party fund-raiser Pierre Blouin explicitly in exchange for a $1-million contract. In the end, however, the contract was given to another businessman with connections to the Conservative party. Blouin was convicted of influence peddling (appendix A, no. 33).
- J.G. Simpson, Charles MacFadden and Senator Irvine Barrow were convicted of conspiracy to peddle influence in 1983. They raised $593 000 for the Liberal party by pretending to have influence on the provincial government (appendix A, nos. 46, 47).
- A heavy-equipment contractor said that in 1971 he agreed to pay the Nova Scotia Liberal party 3 percent of his sales to the Nova Scotia Liberal government. A Toronto contracting firm's president

said that he was asked to give to the Liberal party 3–5 percent of his fees from government contracts (appendix A, no. 47).

All the other stories concern a situation in which an individual or a company made a donation of at least $500 to the government party or a government candidate, and received a public-office favour either before or after the donation. There is no proven relation between the favour and the donation – the problem is that the close proximity of the two events raises the question of whether there might be a connection. The following are examples of these stories:

- David Lam and his wife gave $17 000 to the PC Canada Fund in 1988; Mr. Lam was appointed lieutenant governor of British Columbia by the Conservative prime minister (appendix A, no. 1).
- Fraser Surrey Docks contributed $11 000 to nine federal Conservative candidates in 1988. R.J. Smith, president of the company, is chairman of the Pacific Pilotage Authority (a federal appointment) (appendix A, no. 2).
- Fraser River Dredge and Pile Driving gave $2 500 each to four federal Conservative candidates, $250 to another candidate, and $1 000 to the PC Canada Fund in 1988; it won a $13-million dredging contract (appendix A, no. 2).
- Two companies that donated $33 000 to the Ontario Liberal party received a $5-million government paving contract from the Liberal government (appendix A, no. 11).
- Clearwater Fine Foods of Halifax contributed $2 000 to the 1988 campaign of federal fisheries minister Tom Siddon in Vancouver. Siddon later made an administrative decision that allowed the company to keep its fishing licences even though it is partly owned by a British company (appendix A, no. 15).
- Peter Pocklington's Gainer's meat-packing company gave $3 550 to the Alberta Conservative party; it also received $71 million from the government for various expansions. Another Pocklington company, Palm Dairies, gave $4 600 to the provincial Conservatives; it received a multi-million dollar line of credit from the Alberta Treasury (appendix A, no. 16).
- Don Cormie, head of the Principal Group, gave $20 000 to the 1985 leadership campaign of Don Getty, as well as $15 000 to Joe Clark. Alberta's Conservative government was criticized in the Code inquiry for failing to take action earlier against the now-

bankrupt subsidiaries of the Principal Group (appendix A, nos. 10, 22, 23).
- Bombardier contributed $21 188 to the federal Conservative party in 1986; it received a contract for the maintenance of CF-18 fighter planes (appendix A, no. 30).
- Oerlikon contributed $3 000 to the federal Conservatives; it received $678 million in federal contracts. Deidra Clayton of Oerlikon, a Swiss-owned company, said that Oerlikon was led to believe that firms receiving government contracts in Canada were expected to make donations to the political party in office. She had been approached by Conservative party fund-raisers (appendix A, no. 30).
- Magna International Inc. donated $2 000 to Sinclair Stevens's campaign in 1984. Around that time, Magna was negotiating with Stevens for government grants and tax breaks. The company eventually got $64.2 million in direct federal money, including $49.2 million in industry department funds personally approved by Stevens. Magna did not make a donation to Stevens's opponent (appendix A, no. 37).
- The federal Department of Supply and Services awarded a $60-million advertising contract to Media Canada in 1984. Peter Swain, a long-time Conservative, was invited to join the Media Canada bid, but he refused because part of the firm's 3 percent commission would be turned over to the Conservative party for "educational purposes." Swain said that this was "unacceptable" (appendix A, no. 41).
- *Le Devoir* discovered that 54 companies hired by a federal Crown corporation responsible for the Old Port project in Quebec City donated more than $140 000 to the Liberal party, which controlled the federal government until 1984. The federal funding for the project amounted to $155 million over five years; $90 million was spent without any control by Parliament. Each of the companies donated an average of just over $1 000 during each of three years (appendix A, no. 43).

The Relation between Conflicts of Interest and Political Donations
There is a similarity between conflicts of interest and political donations connected with public-office favours. A conflict of interest, according to the approach of Mr. Justice W.D. Parker, is a situation in which a public official has knowledge of a private economic interest that might appear to influence the exercise of his or her public duties and responsibilities (Canada, Commission of Inquiry 1987, 29). One of the

important current issues in the literature on conflict of interest in Canada is whether situations related to political patronage, such as donations to political parties associated with public-office favours, should be considered as conflicts of interest (Greene 1990, 253–56).

The purpose of the rules against conflicts of interest is to promote impartial decision making under the law. Further to the equality principle, no public officials should receive special economic or personal benefits through exploiting their public decision-making powers. As the rules against conflicts of interest have evolved over the past two decades, it has become accepted that it is as important to avoid the *appearance* of a conflict of interest as to avoid real conflict-of-interest situations. Otherwise, the integrity of the political system will be widely questioned, and this could threaten the legitimacy of the political system in the eyes of the public.

To claim that conflicts of interest include links between political contributions and public-office favours is to argue that, under certain circumstances, political donations could interfere with impartial decision making as much as a direct financial benefit to a public official could. To phrase this issue differently, is it possible that a cabinet minister could be swayed as much by an economic benefit to his or her party as by a personal economic benefit? It would be difficult to answer this question in the negative. Politicians generally care a great deal about whether they win their seats. The closer the election race, and the more imminent the voting day, the more likely it is that a candidate would value a contribution to the election fund as much as a personal economic benefit. A good argument could be made that, when a candidate has knowledge of a party or campaign contribution that might appear to influence the exercise of his or her public duties and responsibilities, this situation is as serious as other conflicts of interest.

Politicians sometimes claim that they have no knowledge of who contributes to their election funds (appendix A, no. 49). Even if we take such claims at face value, however, undue influence could still occur. The politician's chief campaign workers know who made contributions and the amounts of the contributions, and these people often have the power to provide access to those with influence – a problem identified by Stanbury in the quote above. I had personal experiences with such situations during a year that I spent as assistant to a cabinet minister in Alberta in the early 1970s. Occasionally I would receive a telephone call from one of the minister's campaign workers; I would be asked to talk to one of the minister's constituents about a problem he or she was having with the bureaucracy. I would agree to make the appointment. Just before the campaign worker hung up, I would be told that the constituent in question gave generously to the minister's riding association. I would tell the campaign worker that such information would make absolutely no difference, but I was annoyed at having been given the information about the contribution. Would I be blamed if the constituent stopped giving to the riding association? Could I treat the constituent as I would any other constituent, knowing that my approach might affect my job – a job dependent on the minister's discretion?

If the concept of conflict of interest is considered to include relations between political contributions and public-office favours, then many of the situations listed above would be considered as conflicts of interest. None of these, however, are currently regulated by any conflict-of-interest rules. To avoid such conflicts of interest, two different approaches could be adopted:

- No elected public official whose party benefits from large campaign contributions and who has knowledge of such contributions may make decisions affecting the persons responsible for these contributions. Such decisions would have to be made by non-elected officials. This is the approach referred to in the literature on conflicts of interest as "recusal."
- Individuals or corporations who have dealings with the government should be prohibited from making contributions which could be considered large enough to have a bearing on the impartiality of decision making affecting that individual or corporation.

The first approach is not an effective one in an electoral system such as the federal one in Canada in which the names of all individuals or organizations donating at least $100 are publicly disclosed. Claims by public officials that they do not know who contributed to the party will not be credible; therefore, no elected politician (and no person serving at the pleasure of an elected politician) would be able to participate in decision making affecting large publicly listed donors to the government party or a government candidate. The effect of such an approach would be to transfer from elected politicians to public servants with tenure the responsibility for making discretionary decisions such as the awarding of contracts and grants. Elected politicians would not be likely to respond positively, however, to such a major diminution of their decision-making powers.

This leaves the second approach as the only feasible one: placing limits on the total amounts contributed by individuals and corporations.

The Level at Which Limits to Campaign Contributions Should Be Set

In setting a limit to campaign contributions, the question of how large a donation is considered by the public as large enough to affect a politician's decision making becomes critical. According to the stories summarized in appendix A, it would appear that individual or corporate donations of one or two thousand dollars or more per year are certainly considered large enough to affect public-office decision making; annual donations of $500 or more are sometimes considered large enough to cause undue influence. The lower the limit, the fewer will be the allegations of undue influence, and therefore the greater will be the perception that politicians are honest and impartial. But the lower the limit, the more effort the parties will have to devote to fund-raising.

According to Stanbury, only between 2 and 10 percent of the individual donations to the Liberal and Conservative parties (and individual donations accounted for about half of these parties' funds) were given in amounts above $2 000, and between a sixth and a third of the total corporate donations were in amounts above $10 000 (Stanbury 1989, 360–75). It therefore appears that, if individual and corporate donations were limited to $2 000 and $10 000 respectively per year, the total amount of funding received by these two parties would be reduced only by 10–20 percent. Increasing the number of individual and corporate donors to maintain the same level of income would require only a modest effort for the parties, and the pay-off for them might be a larger body of committed supporters since financial contributions tend to increase commitment.

If the contribution limits were set somewhat lower – say $500 per year for both individuals and corporations – the effect on the fund-raising activities of the parties would be more than incidental. (There appear to be no allegations of a relation between political donations and public-office favours regarding contributions of less than $500.) A rough guess based on Stanbury's data would be that a limit of $500 per year on all donations would probably cut the Conservative and Liberal coffers by 20–40 percent. Therefore, if a limit on donations as low as $500 were to be implemented, it would probably have to be phased in over a period of years.

It appears that placing a limit on yearly contributions would affect the NDP in about the same way that it would affect the Conservative and Liberal parties. Between 1974 and 1979 (which was the last year that the NDP did not rely on funds from provincial party organizations), the NDP received between 9 and 37 percent of its funds from trade unions (Stanbury 1989, 359–60).[9]

A compromise solution would be to place a limit of about $3 000 per year on all donations – individual, corporate and union – which would probably leave all three parties with 80–90 percent of their current funding sources intact.[10] As long as the legislation was framed in such a way as to prevent loopholes, the number of allegations of undue influence relating to political donations should drop dramatically. If a party wished, it could set a maximum limit below the statutory requirement; if the self-imposed limit was $500, the party would be likely to avoid entirely allegations of undue influence related to donations.

It should be noted that other jurisdictions have experimented with limiting contributions to political parties and campaigns, although not to the extent recommended in this study. In the United States in 1974, a $1 000 limit was set on individual contributions to federal candidates, as well as an overall annual limit of $25 000 to all candidates, parties and public action committees. In 1976 the limit was changed to a maximum of $5 000 to a public action committee and $20 000 to the national committee of a political party. In Quebec, the maximum allowable contribution to political parties in a year is $3 000, and only individuals may make contributions.[11] As well, during the 1988 federal election campaign, all Conservative candidates in Quebec agreed to accept individual contributions only; corporate or union contributions were rejected (Ontario, Commission on Election Finances 1988, 122; Quebec, *Election Act*).

In Ontario, the maximum contribution allowable to a riding association in a non-election year is currently $750, with a maximum aggregate of $3 000 to riding associations of the same party. In addition, a maximum gift of $750 may be given to a candidate during an election period (with a maximum of $3 000 to all candidates of the same party). A maximum of $4 000 annually may be given to a political party, but an additional $4 000 may be given during a campaign period. (Individuals, corporations and unions are treated similarly under Ontario's rules.) Although limits to campaign contributions appear to be a step in the right direction to limit undue influence, Ontario's rules do not appear to go very far toward preventing conflicts of interest relating to political contributions. During an election year, for example, a corporation could give $8 000 to a political party and an additional $3 000 to riding associations; the president of the corporation could do the same. A donation of $22 000 could represent a substantial tacit bribe for a public-office favour.

Objections to Limits on the Amount of Donations
It may be argued that there is no need to limit the size of donations because, in a system in which those making donations of $100 or more

are publicly listed, disclosure will ensure that donations are not traded for public-office favours. In other words, the names of large donors will be reported by journalists, and these journalists can also be expected to report the public-office favours received by the donors. Politicians awarding such public-office favours will realize that they may have to defend the impartiality of their decision making; the potential public embarrassment that may result if they cannot successfully defend themselves will deter them from giving special favours to large donors. Indeed, as appendix C shows, newspapers do report the names of large donors to political parties, and appendix A demonstrates that public-office favours received by donors are also reported very often.

However, there are at least two reasons why relying exclusively on public disclosure and media reporting to prevent conflicts of interest associated with campaign funding is inadequate. First, disclosure by itself does not prevent a conflict of interest. It must be accompanied by a requirement that elected politicians withdraw (or "recuse") from decision-making situations involving large donors, and current federal regulations do not require such action.[12] Without the recusal requirement, disclosure represents a somewhat empty gesture. And a recusal requirement is unlikely to come about given the impact it would have on restricting the scope of the decision-making powers of elected politicians.

Second, relying on the media to report possible associations between large donors and public office has at least two disadvantages. First, as noted above, the relation between the two is often difficult to prove even in a court of law, and reporters certainly do not have the investigative powers of the police. Second, reporting all large donors and the public-office favours they have received tars both the innocent and the guilty with the same brush – the suspicion of trading public-office favours for political donations.

It would appear that the usual objections to placing limits on campaign contributions are not very convincing.

Political Contributions from Unions

Unions sometimes make political contributions, most often to the New Democratic Party and its candidates. A common way for unions to generate operating funds is through a legally sanctioned system known as the "check-off," by which union dues are automatically deducted from the salaries of all members of a bargaining unit represented by that particular union, whether or not the members of the bargaining unit are union members.

There are some who feel that union funds collected through the check-off ought not to be spent on political contributions, because such contributions associate members of the bargaining unit who have chosen not to join the union with the union's political views. In 1986, Merv Lavigne, a college teacher in Ontario, sought a court declaration that union political contributions financed through the check-off violate "freedom of association" as protected by section 2(*d*) of the *Canadian Charter of Rights and Freedoms*. Although Lavigne achieved a partial victory at the trial court level, he lost both in the Ontario Court of Appeal and in the Supreme Court of Canada. In June 1991, the majority on the Supreme Court held that the forced payment of union dues by all members of the bargaining unit does not result in a violation of section 2(*d*), even if the union spends part of the dues on political donations. They concluded that Lavigne's refusal to join the union disassociated him from the political stance of the union, and he was in no way forced to accept the union's political position (*Lavigne* 1991).

This decision leaves Canadian unions free to make political contributions as they deem appropriate, although there is at present no legal impediment to legislatures limiting or prohibiting political contributions from unions and corporations, as the Quebec National Assembly has done.

2. Violations of Laws regarding Election Contributions or Spending Limits (25 Percent of 165 Items)

Other than the Patti Starr affair, most of the allegations in this category involved failure to disclose contributions to parties or exceeding statutory spending limits during campaigns. The category also included allegations of illegal contributions to parties (such as contributions from charities in the Starr affair), and two instances in 1983 in which Crown corporations made contributions to the party in power. The number of news items was unusually high in 1989 because of the Starr affair.

Given the number of federal, provincial and municipal candidates for elected office, and the extent of the regulation of election financing and spending at all levels of government, it is perhaps surprising that there are not more reports of actual or alleged breaches of the rules. The conclusion that can be drawn here is that parties and candidates do not usually have much difficulty in complying with the current rules.

The Starr affair is a special case which requires comment. Early in 1989 it came to the attention of the media that Ms. Starr's charitable organization, the Toronto section of the National Council of Jewish Women, had made substantial donations to a number of federal, provincial and municipal candidates. According to newspaper reports, the organization (which ran a non-profit housing project) used up to $150 000 of its funds to make strategic donations to candidates and politicians who were (or could be, if elected) in positions to make decisions beneficial to the charity and the developers associated with it. The money came from provincial sales tax rebates (which should have been passed on to its tenants) and "consulting fees" charged to a local development company. Many of the contributions did not exceed single donations of $500, but were made on numerous occasions so that the totals to individual candidates and parties became substantial. As well, the donations were often made at strategic moments to increase their impact. A provincial inquiry into the affair was discontinued after a court ruling that the terms of the inquiry exceeded provincial jurisdiction and jeopardized the rights of those being investigated. However, a police investigation led to charges being laid against Ms. Starr. Between March and June of 1991, she was convicted of eight breaches of the Ontario *Election Finances Act* and two breaches of the *Criminal Code* (criminal breach of trust and fraud) (*Globe and Mail,* 22 March 1991, A4; 19 April 1991, A6; and 28 June 1991, A8).

So far, the lesson from this affair is that donations as small as $500 can, if given repeatedly and at strategic times, constitute attempts to secure undue influence, and that for some, such forms of influence are not considered to be an abuse of the political process. Ms. Starr claimed that the political contributions from her charity were not "sleazy," "sinister" or "political" (appendix B, no. 8). This affair suggests that action is needed both to limit the opportunity for undue influence, and to promote a better understanding of why undue influence is unethical. If each political party adopted a code of ethics, this approach might help to promote not only greater public understanding of why undue influence is unethical, but also a better understanding of the nature of undue influence.

3. Donations to Candidates and Parties Made Public as Required by Law (11 Percent of 165 Items)

These items include media reports of donors to federal, provincial or municipal parties or candidates in those jurisdictions where disclosure of donations is required. Items in this category do not contain allegations of undue influence per se, although the stories sometimes imply that the large donors to parties and candidates may be making the donations because of the expectation of favours at a later time. The stories sometimes include interviews with politicians or political analysts who speculate about why certain companies or individuals would make large donations to a particular party.

This item is included in the analysis because it turned up frequently in the stories reported in the *Canadian News Index* under the headings examined. It provides a means of comparing the more or less "neutral" stories related to election financing (11 percent of the total number) with the other stories which involved actual allegations of undue influence. As tables 3.K1 and 3.K2 in appendix K show, the incidence of this kind of news story has remained fairly constant since 1980.

4. Weak Laws regarding Election Contributions or Spending (10 Percent of 165 Items)

There are several stories which criticize parties for avoiding laws relating to election contributions through fund-raising dinners or events at which funds are collected anonymously through "passing the hat." The important lesson here is that, if limits are set on the amount which can be donated to federal political parties from single sources, care must be taken to ensure that donations made through fund-raising dinners are properly recorded and that no anonymous donations through passing the hat be allowed.

A related issue is whether those paying several hundred dollars to attend a fund-raising dinner should, as part of the package, be given special access to cabinet ministers or other influential officials. It would seem that, by applying the equality principle, the answer would depend on how the ministers treat guests at such dinners. If ministers are present simply to provide guests with a glimpse of themselves in person, to give speeches and shake hands, no harm is done. If they make themselves available to discuss government business so that patrons at the dinners are given privileged access, then the equality principle is violated. This is a matter which might be better handled through a code of ethics for political parties than through laws controlling election contributions.

There is also criticism of governments for announcing new programs during an election campaign, or for spending government money on an advertising campaign that is ostensibly to inform the public about government programs but is really intended to boost the image of the government party. The first weaknesses could be dealt with by banning the announcement of new government spending programs after an election has been called. The second might be handled most appropriately either through a code of ethics for political parties, or through a system whereby an all-party committee would be required to approve (or at least report on) the appropriateness of government advertising campaigns.

Another loophole in the federal laws which requires attention is that there is no provision to force parties to return contributions which have been collected in violation of the law (appendix D, no. 3).

5. Outside Interference in Election Campaigns (8 Percent of 165 Items)

"Outside interference" includes instances of the federal government announcing a new federal program or project in a particular province during the provincial election campaign; contributions by U.S. companies to Canadian political parties (especially federal parties); the financing of municipal candidates by federal or provincial parties; and the financing of provincial candidates by federal parties.

If we apply the equality principle to these situations, it follows that all citizens of a particular jurisdiction ought to be shown "equal concern and respect" (Dworkin 1985) in their desire to participate in the electoral process and to influence the results of the election. It may be argued that the funding of parties from sources outside the jurisdiction may interfere with this principle because outside intervention in the form of financial support for a party or its platform could give that party an unfair advantage. (For example, there was much criticism of U.S.-owned companies advertising in favour of free trade during the 1988 federal election campaign.) Although this particular interpretation of equality may have merit, it could also be argued that the citizens of a particular jurisdiction obviously have connections with persons outside the jurisdiction, that in order to make informed choices citizens have a right to know the views of "outsiders" and that the opinions of "outsiders" are sometimes most appropriately expressed by a domestic political party, which naturally accepts financial assistance for getting the message across. This is an issue that deserves more attention, in particular from the political parties, which may wish to consider limiting or rejecting contributions from outside sources. In any case, if a limit is placed on electoral contributions from any source, such a provision would be likely to ensure that contributions from outside the jurisdiction would rarely be substantial enough to result in a perception of undue influence. Similarly, if limits are placed on campaign advertising by interest groups not affiliated with political parties, such provisions would be likely to have the added effect of ensuring that foreign advertising is not pervasive enough to be perceived as undue influence.

When federal parties make contributions to provincial or municipal parties or candidates, are they engaging in undue influence by interfering with the equal right of those in smaller jurisdictions to determine who their provincial or municipal politicians should be? A case could be made that such contributions should be limited, but whether they can be limited most effectively through federal legislation, codes of ethics for federal political parties, or provincial regulations is a question that should be left to the judgement of the policy makers.

6. Fund-raising for Leadership Candidates or Senior Party Officials (5 Percent of 165 Items)

There are several stories which suggest that the failure to include leadership contests in laws governing election contributions constitutes a major flaw in the system of regulating political donations. These stories imply that the current federal system requiring the public disclosure of contributors to the federal parties is hollow if the party leaders receive their major financial contributions from donors to their leadership campaigns, whose names are kept secret.

This problem could be tackled by extending the federal election contribution rules to include party leadership campaigns, by codes of ethics for political parties or by a combination of both. This issue is so important, however, that it would seem wise to ensure that donors to leadership campaigns come under the umbrella of federal laws governing donations to political parties in general.

There were also stories in this category which criticized the raising of funds to supplement the party leader's salary, or to provide retirement benefits to a leader or senior party official. There is no doubt that such fund-raising activities should be regulated in the same way as other donations to political parties. The possibility of such donations leading to a conflict-of-interest situation is perhaps even greater than with pure contributions to political parties, because contributions are being made that will provide a direct benefit to a politician.

7. Campaign Contributions Used in Questionable Ways (2 Percent of 165 Items)

This category includes stories about politicians using campaign contributions for activities not related to a party purpose or an election campaign.

There are two ways in which such problems could be controlled. The first is to ensure that the law permits parties to spend their funds only on party promotion, party advertising, and campaign-related activities. When Canadians make tax-deductible donations to political parties, they assume that their donations will be used for a party activity and not to provide special benefits to party officials. The second is to provide stricter safeguards to ensure that donations to political parties are always properly recorded and deposited in the party's or the candidate's official account. One way to ensure the latter would be to require that all donors be issued both an "unofficial" receipt for their contribution from a party worker, and an "official" receipt from the party's or riding association's treasurer. Donors who do not receive the official receipt can be expected to make further enquiries.

8. Friends of the Government Party Get Favours, but No Allegation Involving Money (2 Percent of 165 Items)

In these items, the government is alleged to have rewarded its friends and party workers through grants, contracts or jobs, but there is no suggestion that those getting the special favours have made financial contributions to the party. They have instead made contributions of other kinds in terms of their time and energy devoted to a campaign – contributions as important to candidates as funds.

One way of dealing with this problem would be to require public disclosure of the names of all campaign workers contributing, for example, more than 10 hours of work to the party, with the hope that the media will investigate the possibility of special favours being given to such persons. But for the reasons already discussed under category 2, such an approach is likely to be only partly effective. This is an issue which is perhaps more appropriately dealt with through a code of ethics for political parties.

9. Ethics of Relying on a Few Large Donors or Accepting Money from Donors Who Violate Party Principles (2 Percent of 165 Items)

The problem of parties relying too heavily on large donors has already been dealt with under category 1. The issue of whether a party of principle should accept donations from corporations whose philosophy it disagrees with is an internal party matter.

10. Pressure on an Electoral Boundary Commission by a Politician (1 Percent of 165 Items)

There was only one instance of this kind of allegation; it occurred in British Columbia in 1980. This item illustrates how the ethical concerns of Canadians with regard to election issues have shifted from matters such as gerrymandering – which was apparently a common concern a century ago – to the relation between party donations and political favours, a relationship which was accepted as normal in the political process in Canada's early years.

RECOMMENDATIONS AND CONCLUSION

The purpose of rules to prevent undue influence in the electoral process is to ensure respect for the principle of equality, which is arguably the central constitutional precept in liberal democracies. From the perspective of newspaper stories on undue influence during the past decade in Canada, we could say that undue influence is an attempt, whether realized or not, to influence a candidate or party in relation to the electoral process in a way that violates the principle that all citizens have a right to be treated as equals.

The central concern of Canadians regarding undue influence, if newspaper reports are an accurate indication of that concern, is that no one should receive special favours from the government in return for making campaign contributions or for working on the government party's campaign. This study adopts the position that an association between a political contribution and a public-office favour is a conflict of interest. To prevent such conflicts of interest, *it is recommended that a limit of $3 000 per year or less be placed on contributions from a single source to any political party (including donations made to the national party and to riding associations).* (There would be no reason to limit *total* contributions to $3 000; if an individual, corporation or union wished to donate $3 000 to each of the three major parties, for example, they should be allowed to do so.)

The contribution limit should be constructed so as to plug, in advance, potential loopholes. For example, a person who owns five companies should not be allowed to order a donation from each of his or her companies plus an individual donation, for a total donation of $18 000. Each of these $3 000 donations should be considered as emanating from the same source. All donations should be recorded; anonymous donations through "passing the hat" at political meetings should be banned. Donations through fund-raising dinners must be included in the $3 000 maximum donation from a single source. And donations to special funds to supplement a party official's salary should be clearly identified as such and donations to such funds should be included in the total donation to the party.

If an association between a political contribution and a public-office favour is considered to be a conflict of interest, then care must be taken to ensure that the provisions for preventing undue influence in federal election campaigns dovetail with the federal conflict-of-interest rules. Conflict-of-interest legislation was introduced into the House of Commons in February 1988, but the draft legislation was allowed to die at the completion of the session of Parliament. The legislation was reintroduced essentially in the same form in November 1989. In most respects it is a strong piece of legislation, but it contains a loophole which exempts gifts from parties to MPs and cabinet ministers from the conflict-of-interest rules. This exemption is unique in the conflict-of-interest rules in Canadian jurisdictions except for New Brunswick.[13] If the recommendations in this study are to dovetail with the federal conflict-of-interest rules, it is essential that this loophole be removed before the legislation is passed. Otherwise, there will be no disincentive in the federal conflict-of-interest rules for donors to the government party to trade party contributions for personal favours. (These transactions would still be illegal under the *Criminal Code*, as they always have been, but, as noted above, evidence acceptable in a court of law to prove the existence of such acts is exceedingly difficult to collect. It is therefore important that the conflict-of-interest rules include adequate safeguards against this practice.)

Although those responsible for fund-raising from each of the parties can be expected to object strenuously to placing yearly limits of $3 000 on contributions from single sources, the objective is a manageable one because the three major parties already collect the bulk of their funds from individual donors who give less than $2 000 annually. A limit of $3 000 would leave all three major federal parties with 80 percent or more of their current funding sources intact. In the long run, ending the parties' reliance on large donors will encourage each party to build up a larger base of committed supporters, something which will no doubt strengthen their organizations. Consideration could even be given to setting an *initial* limit of $3 000 on single source donations, while reducing the limit by $500 per year until a limit of between $500 and $1 000 is reached. The lower the limit, the fewer will be the actual or perceived occurrences of undue influence, and the more credible and legitimate will be the political system in the eyes of the Canadian public.

Even if a maximum yearly political contribution is legislated, the names of donors giving $100 or more should continue to be made public in order to discourage persons from trying to circumvent the single source rule. These lists of donors should be made easier to analyse by the political parties, either by presenting the lists in alphabetical order, or by making them available in an electronic format. The latter would simplify analysis by journalists and academics.

Limiting political donations from single sources to a maximum of $3 000 or less should free public officeholders from any sense, conscious or unconscious, that they are obliged to provide favours to donors in order to maintain their ability to get elected. However, it is clear, because of the number of incidents of proven or suspected undue influence, that steps should be taken to promote greater public awareness of what undue influence is, and why it is unacceptable in the Canadian political system. One method for implementing this objective would be to *encourage each of the political parties to develop a code of ethics* which would commit the party to taking appropriate steps to discourage undue influence. Such a code could also commit the party to promoting impartial decision making under the law when it is in government so that, for example, public-office favours to campaign workers would be considered unethical.

Because the political system should promote a competition between political parties which is as fair as possible, the party in power should refrain from using the machinery of government for partisan political purposes. For example, some Canadians feel that the government party attempts to exercise undue influence by announcing major spending programs (as opposed to promises to implement new programs if elected) during an election campaign. Such announcements may be considered as attempts to bribe the electorate. Therefore, *it is recommended that rules be instituted to prevent the announcement of new spending programs during the campaign period.* Another way in which the party in power sometimes takes advantage of the machinery of government for its own purposes is to launch an extensive campaign to advertise government programs shortly before an election is announced – a thinly veiled manoeuvre to use taxpayers' money to advertise the success of the government party. *It is recommended that requests for the expenditure of funds for government advertising programs be submitted to an all-party committee of the House of Commons, and that this committee be given substantial powers regarding the approval of such advertising programs.*

If Canadian political parties obtain significant funding from foreign sources, or if foreign-owned companies advertise for or against the policies of the parties during an election campaign, some may consider such activities to be undue influence because they interfere with the equal right of individual Canadian voters to determine their own future. A limit on all individual campaign contributions, however, may have the effect of preventing any significant campaign funding from foreign sources. Similarly, if limits are placed on campaign advertising by all interest groups not affiliated with political parties, such provisions would be likely to have the added effect of ensuring that foreign advertising is not pervasive enough to be perceived as undue influence.

Because the winners of party leadership campaigns are likely to feel as indebted to those financing these campaigns as to those financing the party's election campaign, *it is recommended that donors to leadership campaigns come under the same umbrella of rules as those governing donations to political parties in general.* In other words, a $3 000 limit should be placed on donations to leadership campaigns, and all donors of amounts of over $100 should be publicly listed. Because leadership conventions are relatively infrequent occurrences, there is no harm in allowing such donations to be in addition to donations made to political parties.

Some concern has been expressed about the misuse of funds by political parties. Two problems have been identified. The first is that tax-deductible donations are made for the purpose of promoting a party or assisting with a campaign, and then used for other purposes such as providing gifts to leading members of the party. *It is recommended that the law permit parties to spend tax-deductible funds only for party promotion, party advertising and campaign-related activities.* If a party wishes to establish a fund to provide benefits to officials of the party, a separate fund should be established, the names of donors making contributions of over $100 should be made public, and if the fund is for an official who has influence over potential public-office favours, the donation should be included in calculating the yearly limit of $3 000.

The second is that sometimes money collected for a political party allegedly ends up in the pockets of party officials rather than in the party's bank account. *It is recommended that stricter safeguards be devised to ensure that donations to political parties are always properly recorded and deposited in the party's or the candidate's official account.* One way to ensure this would be to require that all donors be issued both an "unofficial" receipt for their contribution from a party worker, and an "official" receipt from the party's or riding association's treasurer.

Finally, there have been allegations that persons who contribute their time to the election campaign of the government party are given public-office favours in return. The names of all campaign workers contributing, for example, more than 10 hours of work to the party could be made public with the hope that the media will investigate the possibility of special favours being given to such persons. But for the reasons already discussed under category 2, this approach is likely to be only partly effective. As a result, *preventing conflicts of interest involving party workers is an issue that is perhaps more appropriately dealt with through a code of ethics for political parties.*

As a postscript, it should be noted that one reason why the laws governing election contributions in Canada are not as effective as they could be is that such laws are different for the federal, provincial and municipal jurisdictions. A more uniform set of rules could alleviate much of the current confusion about election contributions, and would help to promote a general ethical standard for elections. Although the Royal Commission on Electoral Reform and Party Financing has a mandate to consider only the federal rules, it would be useful for the commission to recommend that discussions be held with representatives of the provincial governments with a view to standardizing election contribution laws across the country.

APPENDIX A
Category 1: Relation between Donation to Party or Candidate and Favour, Contract or Grant to Donor

1. Vancouver *Sun*, 31 March 1990 ("Big Business and the Tories"). During the 1988 election campaign, British Columbia corporations tended to give large donations to federal Conservative cabinet ministers with industry-related portfolios. The Conservatives collected $1.7 million in British Columbia, 53 percent of which came from corporations. The party spent only $1.25 million, leaving $450 000 for the next election. Among the top donors were David Lam and his wife, who gave $17 000 to the Progressive Conservative Canada Fund. Subsequently, he was appointed lieutenant governor of the province. Gerry St. Germain, the federal Forestry minister, conducted British Columbia's richest campaign, raising $123 427. It was the third-richest campaign in Canada, and one of nine to collect more than $100 000. (He ended up with a surplus of $78 372.) In spite of this, St. Germain was defeated by Joy Langan, who had the 16th poorest-funded NDP campaign. She raised $44 392 and spent $33 832.

    Teck Corp., a giant mining corporation, gave $18 500 to nine Conservative candidates, including $4 500 to St. Germain. Teck also donated $27 630 to the PC Canada Fund, but only $10 000 to the Liberals. In addition, the head of Teck, Norm Keevil, gave $2 000 to St. Germain, and Moli Energy, owned by Teck, gave him $1 500. Cominco Ltd., of which Keevil is chairman, gave $1 000 each to St. Germain and several other Conservative candidates, and $26 731 to the PC Canada Fund. The Liberals got $10 000 from Cominco. Fletcher Challenge, a forestry company, gave $30 000 to the PC Canada Fund, $4 000 to St. Germain, and nothing to the Liberals. Other forestry companies making large donations to St. Germain were Canadian Forest Products (which also gave $26 653 to the PC Canada Fund), Terminal Forest Products, and Doman Industries (which also gave $15 000 to the PC Canada Fund).

2. Vancouver *Sun*, 31 March 1990 ("Some Donors do Business with Feds"). At least two dozen businesses or individuals who contributed to the federal Conservative party in British Columbia during the 1988 election either do business with the government or sit on federal boards or commissions. For example, Fraser Surrey Docks contributed $11 000 to nine Conservative candidates. R.J. Smith, president of the company, is chairman of the federal Pacific Pilotage Authority. Wendy McDonald was appointed chairman of the Pacific Region Council by Tom Siddon, and contributed $1 600 each to Siddon and two other Conservative candidates. Hugo Eppich was appointed to the National Research Council; his company gave $5 000 to Tom Siddon. Hector Perry, chairman of the Vancouver Port Corp., gave $2 148 to the PC Canada Fund. Fraser River Dredge and Pile Driving won a $13-million dredging contract, and gave $2 500 each to four Conservative candidates, $250 to another candidate and $1 000 to the PC Canada Fund.

Moli Energy held defence contracts and received federal loan guarantees and grants worth millions. Before going into receivership, it contributed $1 500 to a Conservative candidate, and its parent company gave $18 500 to nine Conservative candidates.

3. *Globe and Mail*, 13 March 1990 ("Tory MP Decries Large Corporate Donations"). Conservative MP François Gérin, at the first public hearings of the Royal Commission on Electoral Reform and Party Financing, said that "the large engineering firm that makes a political contribution of $100 000 takes it for granted there will be contracts afterwards." He said that limits to corporate donations are fiercely resisted by PC Canada Fund officials, and that "raising funds exclusively from individual citizens will limit the clout in party circles of the professional bagmen who are real political parasites with a disproportionate influence on parties ... It will give political parties back to their members and those who vote for them."

4. Montreal *Gazette*, 10 February 1990 ("Desmarais Seeks Political Capital from Power Links"). Paul Desmarais, chief executive officer of Power Corp., cultivates connections with those with political power, regardless of their party, and makes substantial donations to the Liberal and Conservative parties. According to John Rae, the corporation's vice-president, "the reason people give to politics isn't a quid pro quo. The system needs people who can participate in it without having to worry if they can meet their election expenses." But a prominent Montreal Conservative said that "these guys [such as Desmarais] have tentacles in all the political parties. This country is so small and economic power is so concentrated, it is simply unavoidable." Stephen Langdon, NDP MP, said that the most important pay-off from political connections is what governments *don't* do. "They [companies that contributed to the parties] know they're not going to be targeted in a tough way in tax reform, or that they're not going to lose government aid when they need it."

5. *Globe and Mail*, 3 December 1989 ("Lobbyist Advised Developer to Donate to Liberal Ridings"). Ivan Fleischmann, acting as a lobbyist for Huang and Danczkay Ltd., a Toronto development company, advised the company to make strategic donations to Ontario Liberal candidates and to Toronto municipal politicians. The firm donated $500 each to three Liberal candidates, and $1 000 to the Ontario Liberal party. (Municipal election donations do not have to be disclosed.) Toronto City Council had previously halted work on a condominium project which Huang and Danczkay had been building on Toronto's waterfront because of complaints about the height and ratio of floor space to site area.

6. *Globe and Mail*, 29 November 1989 ("Tories Proposed Favours List, Papers Suggest"). A federal Conservative party official prepared a memo for a high-level, five-member committee of the PC Canada Fund chaired by Peter Clark, brother of Joe Clark. The memo suggested that the party's list

of corporate donors should include information about "government contracts, grants or policy issues that profit the firm." Nicholas Locke, executive director of the PC Canada Fund, said that the recommendation that such records be kept was not implemented.

7. *Globe and Mail*, 21 November 1989 ("Tory Memo Advises Favours for Donors"). A PC Canada Fund official prepared a memo recommending that those who contribute more than $5 000 to the fund be given insider information. Major U.S. firms would be among the targets. The executive director of the fund said that this policy was never implemented.

8. *Globe and Mail*, 9 August 1989 ("Public Financing Urged to Trim Developers' Role in Municipal Politics"). At least 75 percent of declared financial contributions of $100 or more given to elected municipal politicians in Metro Toronto and the four regions surrounding it in the November 1988 election campaign came from developers, contractors, lawyers, real-estate brokers and construction supply firms. The City of Toronto was the only municipality in the Greater Toronto Area which was not controlled by developer-backed candidates. Candidates are allowed to pocket surplus election contributions. Possible antidotes to this concentration of influence include requiring candidates to file a preliminary list of financial backers one month before the election, and banning donations to candidates after the election.

9. *Globe and Mail*, 8 August 1989 ("Toronto Developers Main Bankrollers of Civic Campaigns"). Similar to above article. It was noted that in Scarborough, Vaughan, Richmond Hill, Markham and Mississauga, the development industry provided more than 80 percent of the campaign funds of elected municipal politicians.

10. *Winnipeg Free Press*, 3 August 1989 ("NDP Queries Cormie Donation"). NDP members of the Alberta legislature wondered whether the large donations made by Don Cormie, head of the Principal Group, to the provincial Conservative party explained why the government did not take action earlier against two Principal subsidiaries which eventually went bankrupt. (For more details, see appendix A, no. 23.)

11. *Toronto Star*, 22 June 1989 ("Firms Got Contract after Donating Cash to Liberals, Rae Says"). Bob Rae pointed out that two companies that donated $33 000 to the Ontario Liberal party received a $5-million government paving contract. Companies that did not donate to the Liberal party either did not get contracts or received only small contracts. Premier Peterson said that the allegation was "smear and innuendo." Peterson said that he did not know of the companies which got the large paving contracts.

12. *Calgary Herald*, 21 June 1989 ("Oilpatch Helped Fuel Orman's $100 000 Race"). Alberta's energy minister raised $100 000 in campaign contributions, mostly from donations from oil companies. NDP leader Ray Martin said that this constituted a conflict of interest.

13. *Toronto Star*, 21 June 1989 ("Pieces Begin to Fit in the Patti Starr Puzzle"). The Toronto section of the National Council of Jewish Women received a provincial sales tax rebate for a non-profit housing project. The money – about $250 000 – was supposed to be used to reduce rents, but instead it was used to make contributions to the Liberal and Conservative parties and their candidates.

14. *Toronto Star*, 17 June 1989 ("Starr's Slush Fund for Politicians: Where the Money Came from"). Similar to above.

15. *Toronto Star*, 19 April 1989 ("Fish Firm Contributed to Siddon Campaign"). Clearwater Fine Foods of Halifax, Nova Scotia contributed $2 000 to federal Fisheries Minister Tom Siddon's 1988 campaign in British Columbia. Clearwater is partly owned by a British company, but must be "Canadian-controlled" to keep its fishing licences. Siddon made an administrative decision that the company is "Canadian-controlled" so that it could keep its licences.

16. *Calgary Herald*, 6 April 1989 ("Oilers Helped Fuel Tory Machine"). Gainers, Peter Pocklington's meatpacking company, gave $3 550 to the Alberta Conservative party, and received $71 million from the government for various expansions. Palm Dairies, also owned by Pocklington, gave $4 600 to the provincial Conservative party, and received a multi-million dollar line of credit from the Alberta Treasury. Another Pocklington business, the Edmonton Oilers, gave $4 050 to the provincial Conservative party.

17. *Toronto Star*, 23 November 1988 ("PM Denies Owing Debt to Business for His Win"). Mulroney acknowledged that the support of the corporate sector and of the Quebec Liberal Premier Robert Bourassa was helpful in his election victory. However, he said that he doesn't owe anyone any "Christmas presents." He said that "certain people tend to believe that intervention by small and medium-sized business in a campaign like this is anti-constitutional. On the contrary ... that's democracy."

18. *Globe and Mail*, 3 October 1988 ("Policies Turning off Donations from Companies, Liberal Says"). Corporations are reluctant to donate money to the Ontario Liberal party because they disagree with its environmental policies and its support of pay equity, according to the party's treasurer.

19. *Globe and Mail*, 21 September 1988 ("Hosek Denies Donors Influenced Decision"). Chaviva Hošek received half of her campaign funds from sources associated with the building and development industry. Opposition members alleged that it was because the development industry was opposed to the policies of John Sewell, chairman of the Metro Toronto Housing Authority, that Ms. Hošek decided not to reappoint Mr. Sewell as chairman of the agency. They claimed that, because Ms. Hošek was beholden to the development industry, her decision about Mr. Sewell put her in a conflict of interest.

20. *Globe and Mail*, 20 September 1988 ("Peterson Attacks 'Innuendo' about Contributions to Hosek"). With regard to the above story, Premier Peterson said that "it's the cheapest, easiest charge – conflict of interest – for anybody to make. It's just innuendo, and completely unsubstantiated. It's shoddy."

21. Montreal *Gazette*, 17 September 1988 ("Banks' Favours to Politicians Raise Question of Conflict"). Banks sometimes write off loans to politicians and the article implies that they may expect favours in return. For example, in 1980 four chartered banks wrote off slightly more than $100 000 in loans to Nova Scotia cabinet minister Roland Thornhill. Although the RCMP had decided to lay charges against the banks and Thornhill, the Nova Scotia attorney general, Harry How, decided not to proceed with the prosecutions. In 1982 the Bank of Montreal wrote off $550 000 in loans to federal Liberal cabinet minister Bryce Mackasey. Part of the write-off was considered as a payment to a numbered company to lobby for federal government contracts. In 1984 the Bank of Montreal forgave most of a debt of $410 000 to Lee Richardson, who at the time was deputy chief of staff to Prime Minister Brian Mulroney. Banks had lent Joe Dutton, executive secretary to former Alberta premier Peter Lougheed, money to play the stock market. Dutton lost $1.5 million, and declared personal bankruptcy. Donald Blenkarn, chairman of the House of Commons Finance Committee, said that it would be almost impossible to prove whether such loans are granted and then written off in return for a favour. The answer, he said, is to disclose such information. Disclosure, however, may not stop gifts in return for political favours. "I guess the question is, does the public have the right to elect a crook?" he said, laughing.

    In 1985, David Reville, an NDP member of the Ontario legislature, had a $10 000 business loan recalled by the Canadian Imperial Bank of Commerce because he supported striking credit card employees at the bank. The bank reinstated the loan when Reville made the incident public.

22. *Winnipeg Free Press*, 28 August 1988 ("Clark Aides Downplay Donation by Founder of Principal Group"). Susan Elliott, an assistant to Joe Clark, said that Cormie's $15 000 donation to Joe Clark didn't give him special access to Clark. However, she said, "There's likely to be a perception that people buy access to politicians. It is a perception problem rather than a reality problem."

23. *Vancouver Sun*, 26 August 1988 ("Principal Gave Clark $15 000 Donation"). Not only did the now-bankrupt Principal Group make a $15 000 donation to Joe Clark during the 1984 federal election campaign, but Don Cormie, the president of the Principal Group, donated $20 000 to the 1985 leadership campaign of Alberta Conservative Don Getty. The article implies that the large donations to the Conservative party may have been related to the slowness of the provincial government in taking action against the Principal Group.

24. Montreal *Gazette,* 26 August 1988 ("Gravel Won't Run Again: Aide"). Conservative MP Michel Gravel, who faces influence-peddling charges for allegedly accepting or seeking $230 000 in kickbacks from 11 contractors seeking work on the new Museum of Civilization in Ottawa, has decided not to run in the upcoming election because his constituency has disappeared through redistribution.

25. *Calgary Herald,* 28 April 1988 ("Donations Anger Saskatchewan NDP"). In a letter that Conservative party organizer Bruce Cameron wrote to party president Peter Matthews on 24 February 1988, Cameron stated that Dome Advertising Ltd. "should be expected to donate" services provided for the party's annual convention because the company has a "share of the provincial advertising budget." Premier Grant Devine, however, said that there is nothing wrong with asking for donations from companies with large government contracts as part of a province-wide fund-raising campaign.

26. Montreal *Gazette,* 11 February 1988 ("I Got Contracts without Tory Help: Businessman"). The engineering firm of Desmond Hallissey, Quebec director of the PC Canada Fund, was hired for $4 000 to evaluate land for two Old Port projects. Hallissey denied that his links with the Conservatives were the reason. However, he said that, when the Liberals were in power, his firm was systematically shut out of federal contracts. "The Liberals were kind of glad when the Conservatives got in," he said. "They said, 'Now, Desmond, you can get yours'."

27. *Globe and Mail,* 18 December 1987 ("Ontario Refuses to Order Probe of Developers' Campaign Gifts"). Municipal Affairs Minister John Eakins refused to order an inquiry into allegations that most municipal councillors in the Toronto area are beholden to the development industry because that industry pays for at least 75 percent of the campaign expenditures of most municipal politicians. Eakins has proposed legislation which would put caps on donations and spending, and require the disclosure of campaign finances.

28. *Globe and Mail,* 11 December 1987 ("Developers Give Generously to City Politicians"). Thirteen of 23 members of Toronto City Council received a total of $300 000 in largely undisclosed campaign contributions during the previous two years. During the same period, City Council has gone along with almost every major request from the development industry to build significantly larger buildings in the downtown core than are permitted under the city's official plan. In one area, on Bay Street between Bloor and Gerrard, rezonings requested or approved by City Council could produce $80 million in windfall profits for the developers, according to Toronto architect Alan Littlewood. An analysis by the *Globe* of the voting records of the 13 councillors most reliant on the development industry showed that they have supported most of the development proposals that sought increased density in the downtown core. Several developers said that they do not like making campaign donations to city politicians, but

feel under pressure to play the fund-raising game for fear of losing favour at city hall. "We get constant requests for money for Toronto politicians," one development company executive said. "It's not a nice game at the municipal level; it's ripe for abuse."

29. *Globe and Mail*, 25 November 1987 ("PQ Annoyed as Liberal Coffers Grow"). Saint-Hyacinthe Liberal MNA Charles Messier sent out a letter to local businessmen, inviting them to attend a benefit dinner for $125 per plate. However, if the businessmen paid a supplement of $375, they would be able to have a personal meeting with Paul Gobeil, president of the Treasury Board. Mr. Gobeil was described as "a man with great influence within the present government. Esteemed for his enterprising spirit, he will no doubt understand and listen to the desires and needs of the business people of the region." Embarrassed Liberal organizers cancelled the meeting after the letter was made public. At another fund-raising dinner, 85 businessmen paid $500 each for the privilege of meeting three Cabinet ministers. Liberal party director-general John Parisella said that there had been more than 300 such events during the previous year. According to legislation passed in 1978, all contributors of more than $100 to a political party must be publicly identified, and there is a limit of $3 000. Fund-raising dinners, however, are not covered by this legislation. The PQ claims that the Liberals are violating the spirit, though not the letter, of Quebec's election financing law by in a sense selling influence. Liberal party director-general John Parisella said that "it's not by ending the dinners with ministers that you're going to end the possibility of influence peddling. You don't think there are lobbyists around when a minister meets the people at a regional council meeting?"

30. *Globe and Mail*, 8 August 1987 ("Top Defence Firms Deny Donations to PCs Linked with Federal Contracts"). The contractors which got the largest defence contracts in Canada made sizeable contributions to the Conservative party in 1986. Bombardier contributed $21 187.75 to the Conservatives and $7 740.26 to the Liberals, and received a contract for the maintenance of CF-18 fighter planes. Pratt and Whitney contributed $5 000 to the Conservatives and $5 831.18 to the Liberals, and received $56.9 million in government aid. Litton Systems gave $3 553.78 to the Conservatives and $250 to the Liberals, and received contracts worth about $1 billion. Oerlikon contributed $3 000 to the Conservatives and received $678 million in federal contracts.

Deidra Clayton of Oerlikon, a Swiss-owned company, said that Oerlikon was led to believe that firms receiving government contracts in Canada were expected to make donations to the political party in office. She said that the company was approached by the Conservative party and that she said to the party spokesperson, "If others do it, then we will do it too."

Nicholas Locke, executive director of the PC Canada Fund, said that contributions come with no strings attached because the party is entirely separate from the operations of government. He also said that the party approaches the top 100 or 200 companies for support, without paying any attention to their relationship with the government.

Louise Boutin, public relations manager at Pratt and Whitney, indicated that the company gives to both the Conservative and Liberal parties as "an act of good corporate citizenship." If the company intended to buy favours, it would give substantially more than $5 000, she said. Charles Pittman, a Litton spokesperson, said that the company's contributions last year included mainly buying tickets for fund-raising dinners at which Defence Minister Perrin Beatty was the guest speaker.

31. *Calgary Herald,* 21 May 1987 ("Amoco Official Raising Money for Federal PCs"). Sherrold Moore, vice-president of Amoco Canada, is a fund-raiser for Calgary Centre MP Harvie Andre. Moore sent out a number of letters asking for money as part of the annual fund-raising campaign of the finance committee of the Calgary Centre Conservative riding association. Amoco Canada had made a $5.1 billion offer to buy Dome Petroleum, which must be approved by Investment Canada. Moore denied that there was a conflict of interest in raising money for Andre while Investment Canada was considering the issue.

32. *Winnipeg Free Press,* 4 April 1987 ("NDP Fundraising Pitch Called Abuse of Power"). Conservative MLA Gerry Mercier criticized the NDP for fundraising through selling tickets to dinners for $200 each where those attending would be able to meet 13 cabinet ministers. Mercier said that it appeared that to meet a cabinet minister, you would have to pay $200. (Tax receipts of $150 would be issued.) Mercier said that the provincial Conservatives once had such fund-raising dinners, but had cancelled them because they were unethical. Mercier implied that the fund-raising dinners represented a loophole in the province's election financing rules. The federal Conservatives, however, still have fund-raising dinners in Manitoba featuring federal cabinet ministers.

33. Montreal *Gazette,* 10 February 1987 ("Law Can't Force Party to Return Donations Illegally Gained: Hamel"). A federal Conservative party organizer, Pierre Blouin, pleaded guilty during the summer of 1986 to influence peddling in awarding a contract. Blouin arranged for a Drummondville businessman to give the Conservative party $50 000 in exchange for a $1-million contract. (In the end, the contract was given to another businessman with connections to the Conservative party.) Jean-Marc Hamel, chief electoral officer, compared the influence-peddling scheme to the system that Quebec's Union nationale had in place in the 1950s and 1960s, whereby businesses seeking provincial contracts had to pay a percentage of the contract into the party's "black coffer." Even though the $50 000 donation was obtained illegally, the law cannot force the Conservative party to give back the donation. As well, the law does not cover gifts of money to individuals who are not necessarily candidates. Although the federal law does not set a limit on the amount of money

which individuals or corporations can donate to a political party, Chief Electoral Officer Jean-Marc Hamel said that public disclosure effectively acts as a ceiling on contributions because "nobody wants to appear to be trying to buy his or her way to power." As well, setting limits on federal donations "would only address contributions to political parties and candidates at an election and not other types of activities. I think it [would deal with] a question of public perception."

34. Montreal *Gazette*, 31 January 1987 ("Tory MP Says Party Leans on Companies to Make Donations"). A Conservative MP, speaking to Southam News anonymously, said that it's an open secret that Quebec firms that want government business must contribute to the PC Canada Fund. As well, party fund-raisers "call companies [seeking government contracts], engineering companies for example, and say, 'Look, we're having a big dinner in Montreal – we'd like you to buy $5 000 worth of tickets.'" According to an article in *Le Devoir*, the Conservative party has a tollgating system in which companies in Montreal and Toronto are advised by Conservatives to engage the professional services of companies close to the Mulroney government, which then overbill their clients.

35. *Winnipeg Free Press*, 7 December 1986 ("Firms with Federal Contracts Filled Tory Political Coffers"). The chartered accounting firm Ernst and Whinney made a contribution of $41 906 to the federal Conservative party in 1985. The firm is Air Canada's auditor and was recently selected to audit the books of Canadair Ltd. Such contracts are awarded without tender and their value is kept secret. Previously, the Conservatives had commissioned Ernst and Whinney to audit the purchase of Petrofina by Petro-Canada and to review the performance of immigration officers at ports of entry. The partners of Ernst and Whinney may also have contributed, but such donations are difficult to pinpoint because of the reporting procedures of Elections Canada. Ernst and Whinney gave the Liberal party only $2 397.50. Donations by Arthur Andersen and Co. and Deloitte Haskins and Sells were also lopsided in favour of the Conservatives. Clarkson Gordon, however, gave $30 000 to the Conservatives and $28 000 to the Liberals. The country's major chartered banks contributed about the same amount of money to each party.

36. *Winnipeg Free Press*, 4 June 1986 ("Liquor Industry Tops NDP Donation Return"). Molson's, Labatt's and Seagram's each contributed about $2 000 to the provincial NDP in 1985. The companies are regulated by the provincial government. Sheritt Gordon Mines gave the NDP $1 000, and received a $2-million provincial loan, forgivable under certain conditions. In 1984 the company got a $10-million loan. Gravure Graphics gave the NDP $500 and received a $1.1 million loan.

37. Montreal *Gazette*, 3 May 1986 ("Magna Gave to Stevens's Campaign"). Not only did the Magna Corp. provide a $2.6 million loan to Sinclair Stevens's wife, but Magna also donated $2 000 to Stevens's 1984 election campaign.

Around the time of the loan and the donation, Magna was negotiating with Stevens for government grants and tax breaks. Magna eventually got $64.2 million in direct federal money, including $49.2 million in Industry Department funds personally approved by Stevens. Magna did not give any money to the Liberal candidate who opposed Stevens.

38. *Winnipeg Free Press*, 12 March 1986 ("Plohman Funding Appeal to Contractors Condemned"). Manitoba Highways Minister John Plohman sent letters to 39 firms with highway contracts from the provincial government requesting donations for his re-election campaign. Dan Jamieson, Plohman's official agent, said, "We need money to run a campaign and we don't get money from large businesses or corporations, so we have to get it where we think it is available." Only two groups received the letter: NDP supporters in Plohman's constituency, and highways contractors. Bill Jarand, executive director of the Manitoba Heavy Construction Association as well as a member of the provincial Conservative party, claimed that this fund-raising tactic was unethical because contractors would feel coerced to contribute to Plohman to keep their contracts. Nevertheless, one month after the letter was sent out, none of the contractors had made a contribution to Plohman's campaign fund.

39. Montreal *Gazette*, 10 October 1985 ("Ottawa Giving $363 000 to Firm Whose Owner Helped Dump Clark"). Walter Wolf, a "jet-set millionaire," said that he gave Frank Moores and Michel Cogger $25 000 "to work behind the scenes against [Joe] Clark before a 1983 party convention." Moores, however, denied receiving the money. "Other sources were quoted last year as saying Wolf's contribution to the dump Clark movement was as much as $250 000."

    Wolf's company, Wolf Sub-Ocean Ltd., subsequently received $363 000 from a joint development fund established by Newfoundland and Ottawa. Science Minister Tom Siddon confirmed that Ottawa had agreed, through the fund, to reimburse Wolf Sub-Ocean for 60 percent of its costs in a $1.1-million joint venture with another company. Siddon said that no bids were called from other companies.

    Members of the opposition said that Brian Mulroney is "paying off his friends" with the payment to Wolf Sub-Ocean. Siddon, however, denied that the deal had anything to do with Wolf's close association with Mulroney.

40. *Winnipeg Free Press*, 15 February 1985 ("Tory Ad Firm Gets $30 Million Plum"). Only three advertising firms were considered for the federal government's tourism advertising contract worth $30 million; all three are "tied closely to the Conservatives." The company which was awarded the contract was Camp Associates of Toronto, founded by Dalton Camp, a former president of the federal Conservative party. The president is Norm Atkins, a former Conservative campaign chairman. Tourism Minister Tom McMillan denied that politics was involved in the decision.

41. *Globe and Mail*, 7 January 1985 ("Federal Ad Deal to Generate PC Funds, Expert Says"). The federal Department of Supply and Services awarded a $60 million advertising contract to Media Canada. Peter Swain, who heads Media Buying Services, the largest advertising purchasing organization in Canada, was invited to join Media Canada, but refused because, according to the terms of the contract, part of the 3 percent commission would be turned over to the Conservative party for "educational purposes." Swain, a long-time Conservative, said that these terms were "unacceptable." Prior to the Conservative victory in 1984, the Liberal government also awarded government advertising to an "agency of record," but one associated with the Liberal party.

42. *Globe and Mail*, 21 November 1984 ("Alberta Opposition and Ministers Not Surprised that Firms Back PCs"). According to a *Globe and Mail* report, "companies doing business with the Alberta Government make the lion's share of contributions to the ruling Conservative party." The article also noted that the "vast majority of public contracts are tendered and awarded to the lowest bidder." Luscar Ltd., for example, contributed $15 000 to the provincial Conservative party during the 1982 election campaign, and later received "over $903 000 in contracts, [and a] Heritage Fund loan of $25-million." Thomas Chambers, the Minister of Public Works, said that in a province where 75 of the 79 seats in the legislature are held by the Conservatives, it is not surprising that most businesses support the Conservatives.

43. Vancouver *Sun*, 8 August 1984 ("Liberal Donations Probed"). *Le Devoir* conducted an investigation into the redevelopment of Quebec City's Old Port and discovered that 54 companies hired by a federal Crown corporation responsible for the Old Port donated more than $140 000 to the federal Liberals. Over five years, the federal funding for renovation on the harbourfront has cost more than $155 million, and $90 million was spent "without any control by Parliament."

    Jean Lambert, president of the Crown corporation, said that "it's not a disease to be ... Liberal. What's important is the competence of individuals and the companies [hired]." The 54 companies donated an average of just over $1 000 each during each of three years.

44. *Globe and Mail*, 8 June 1984 ("Peterson Alleges Coverup in Vote-Buying Charges"). Two days before a by-election in Stormont–Dundas–Glengarry, the Conservative government of Ontario gave $500 000 to Ault Foods, a company in the constituency. A "senior officer of the company then circulated a memorandum to all his employees urging them to vote for the Conservative candidate." The Conservative candidate won the by-election with ease.

    Liberal leader David Peterson accused the government of vote-buying, and demanded that the attorney general investigate. Roy McMurtry, the attorney general, said that "there was nothing to indicate any wrongdoing."

Agriculture Minister Dennis Timbrell and Premier William Davis "have conceded that the awarding of the grant two days before the by-election was not mere coincidence."

45. *Globe and Mail,* 7 June 1984 ("With Taxpayer Money"). This is an editorial which supports Liberal leader David Peterson's call for a police investigation into the $500 000 grant to Ault Foods, described above, to determine whether an indictable offence was committed. "In the politics of Ontario, there is a powerful link between grant and gratitude. It is part of that pulsating marketplace in which favours are exchanged, backs are scratched, obligations are planted, and services are rendered with a clear understanding that a debt has been incurred."

46. *Globe and Mail,* 13 May 1983 ("Two Liberal Fund-Raisers Fined $25 000"). Two former fund-raisers for the Liberal Party of Nova Scotia, Charles MacFadden and Senator Irvine Barrow, were convicted in the Nova Scotia Supreme Court of conspiracy to peddle influence and were fined $25 000 each. The two were found guilty of conspiring with J.G. Simpson, who had secured political contributions by pretending to have influence with the provincial government. Simpson pleaded guilty to the charges a year ago, and was fined $75 000.

    The amount of money collected for the Liberal party through the scheme was $593 000, of which Mr. Simpson collected $500 000.

47. *Globe and Mail,* 12 May 1983 ("Nova Scotia Liberals Found Guilty of Influence-Peddling"). Similar to the above article, but with more details. Liquor companies were asked to contribute a set portion of their annual sales at the provincial liquor commission, and in return they were told that they would get their brands listed at the liquor stores. Representatives of several companies testified at the jury trial that this tollgating practice had been going on in Nova Scotia for many years, under both the Liberals and the Conservatives. Officials of the four major distilleries testified that they paid 50 cents to the party in power for each case of their products sold by the liquor commission. A wine distributor said that he paid 25 cents a case.

    Contractors also were subjected to tollgating. A heavy-equipment contractor said that in 1971 he agreed to pay the Liberal party 3 percent of his sales to the government. The president of a Toronto contracting firm, Acres Consulting, said that he was asked to contribute 3–5 percent of his fees from government contracts, which amounted to half of his profits. He said that he had not encountered this practice in any other province. A Vancouver contractor withdrew a bid because of the demand for a party contribution.

    Crown Prosecutor Gary Hold stressed during the trial that he was not accusing the fund-raisers of making personal gains. "They did it on behalf of the cause they both believed in with great loyalty and passion – large "L" Liberalism, in effect the Liberal Party of Nova Scotia," he said.

Former Premier Regan and several former cabinet ministers testified that Barrow and MacFadden "did not influence their decisions, although Mr. Regan said the Senator did advise him on Government matters from time to time. Neither Mr. MacFadden nor Senator Barrow denied asking for contributions from companies doing business or hoping to do business with the province."

48. *Globe and Mail*, 31 March 1982 ("Slippery Stuff Can Stain," Orland French's Column). Ontario's provincial treasurer, Frank Miller, temporarily removed the sales tax from unsold 1981 model cars. The result was that $372 million worth of old inventory was quickly sold. On 10 May 1982 automobile dealers decided to have a fund-raising dinner for Mr. Miller's riding association to thank the minister.

   Bryan Rowntree, president of Golden Mile Motors, wrote to all members of the Toronto Automobile Dealers Association (TADA) to invite them to the dinner. His letter stated in part: "You will no doubt recall the problem of inventory that existed with some of us last fall. You will also recall how cooperative our provincial minister, Mr. Frank Miller, was in helping us by removing the provincial sales tax and stimulating auto sales at that time. The wholesale interest saving for dealers has been estimated in excess of $8 250 000 in December alone ... This successful event once again proves the benefit of dealers being united as in TADA and then of working closely with government. It is now our turn to say Thank You!"

   Liberal leader David Peterson asked the Speaker to investigate whether the fund-raising effort contravened the section of the *Legislative Assembly Act* relating to bribes.

   French was critical of the car dealers for being so blatant about the connection between the financial favour shown to them by Mr. Miller, and their fund-raising campaign for his riding association. "A little fund-raising dinner, with a certain unspecified guest list, would not have attracted the notice of the opposition Liberals."

49. *Winnipeg Free Press*, 10 October 1980 ("Ignorance is No Defence," Editorial). Winnipeg's Mayor Norrie refuses to disclose who his campaign donors are. His reasoning is that only his campaign fund-raisers know the donors, and that he insists on not knowing who they are so that his decisions cannot be influenced by them. If a list of donors were published, then this list could make him, in fact or in appearance, biased toward these donors.

   The *Free Press* was critical of this reasoning. "The more likely event would be a call to the mayor from one of his campaign fund-raisers suggesting that a given company, being an excellent corporate citizen, does not deserve the ill-treatment it is getting from the city. Not knowing who his contributors were, the mayor then does not know whether he is being subjected to donor's pressure or just a disinterested appeal to good sense. His ignorance of who financed his campaign, even if it can be sustained, is no defence against undue pressure."

50. Vancouver *Sun*, 20 February 1980 ("Liquor Industry Donations under Scrutiny in Alberta"). Attorney General Neil Crawford said that the RCMP is investigating the political donations by the liquor industry in Alberta to the provincial wing of a national party. Crawford said the party being investigated was not the Conservative party. The investigation involved the alleged use of political donations by distillers or brewers to gain influence in government decision making affecting them.

51. *Globe and Mail*, 14 February 1980 ("Distillers' Political Gifts Probed in Ontario, Maritimes"). Police in at least three provinces are investigating the possible link between sales of alcoholic beverages through the provincial liquor control agency, and donations to the Conservative and Liberal parties. Cheques made out by the distillers and wineries to the parties were for odd amounts, indicating that they may have been linked to sales. However, "police were never able to find evidence that there were any favours granted the companies in return for their donations." In British Columbia, "Insp. Douglas Linfield said the investigation foundered after about six months because no one would testify that money was being donated in return for favourable market treatment in liquor stores. 'You need somebody to say that's why the money was given ... we didn't have that evidence.'"

In Quebec, the provincial police made more than 200 raids during the past three years. "Twenty-six distilleries and wineries have been charged with giving money to liquor store employees in consideration for business dealings with the Government." Documents seized by the Quebec police which appeared to link political contributions to favours led to the investigations in the other provinces.

APPENDIX B
Category 2: Violations of Laws regarding Election Contributions or Spending Limits

The Starr Affair

1. *Globe and Mail*, 2 February 1989 ("Political Contributions Worry Charitable Group"). The president of the National Council of Jewish Women is worried that her organization may lose its charitable status because of the illegal political contributions made by the council's Toronto section.

2. *Globe and Mail*, 11 February 1989 ("Gifts to McDougall Drive Called Laundering"). When Patti Starr's charity originally applied for charitable status, the organization was turned down because only 60 percent of its housing project was devoted to charitable purposes rather than the required 100 percent. Nevertheless, Immigration Minister Barbara McDougall and her staff intervened with Revenue Canada, and Ms. Starr's organization eventually received charitable status.

ALLEGATIONS OF UNDUE INFLUENCE

Ms. McDougall was asked by the *Globe and Mail* whether the contribution to her campaign by Ms. Starr's organization was coincidental. "I don't see any connection," she replied. "The funds were for a fund-raiser, where 700 tickets were sold ... What we are looking at is if the money was given without the authorization of the group we'll give the money back." Revenue Minister Otto Jelinek said that Ms. McDougall's staff had simply made "routine contingency enquiries" about the status of the group's application for charitable status."

But New Democrat John Rodriguez saw the process very differently. "The Minister of Employment and Immigration intervenes, gets them a number, the minister gets a contribution, the housing project still does not conform to the regulations to get the charitable number. Mrs. Starr says that 60 percent of the units of the project are for charitable cases and 40 percent ... are obviously rented to people who can afford the going rate," he said. "And the profits are being funnelled back to politicians. This is a neat little laundering scheme." Otto Jelinek, however, told reporters that there was no problem concerning Ms. McDougall's involvement. "I can't understand exactly what the major concern is when it was dealt with in a very routine manner, and there was absolutely no influence whatsoever," he said.

3. *Globe and Mail*, 13 February 1989 ("OPP, Crown Attorney to Investigate Payments Made by Starr Charity"). Ontario's attorney general said that the allegations of illegal campaign contributions by organizations associated with Patti Starr would be investigated by the Ontario Provincial Police and a special Crown attorney. Opposition leader Bob Rae criticized Cabinet minister Lily Munro for recommending to Ms. Starr that Ms. Munro's mother should conduct a mail survey for the charitable organization. He also criticized David Peterson for not reprimanding Ms. Munro.

4. *Globe and Mail*, 13 February 1989 ("Contributors Linked to Starr Gave $2 500 to Back Keyes"). Five persons made campaign contributions of $500 each to former Ontario solicitor general Kenneth Keyes, and used the charitable organization controlled by Patti Starr as their mailing address. Three of the five work for Ms. Starr's charity (including Ms. Starr), and the other two are senior employees of Tridel Corp. It is possible that all five received the funds from Ms. Starr's charitable organization.

5. *Globe and Mail*, 15 February 1989 ("Charity Makes Political Donations Prohibited under Income Tax Act"). In addition to donations to politicians, Patti Starr said that she arranged for her charity to buy $400-a-plate tickets to a Conservative fund-raising dinner featuring Prime Minister Brian Mulroney in November 1988. She said that "she encouraged the council to make such contributions to raise its profile and support politicians whose positions it endorsed."

6. *Globe and Mail*, 16 February 1989 ("Law Firm Lists $82 000 in Payments from Starr"). The charitable organization controlled by Patti Starr paid out more than $82 000 in political contributions. The many recipients included

federal Immigration Minister Barbara McDougall, provincial Liberal ministers Elinor Caplan and Ed Fulton, Conservative MPP Susan Fish, Conservative MP William Attewell, and Toronto Mayor Arthur Eggleton. The PC Canada Fund also received a donation from Ms. Starr's charity.

7. *Globe and Mail*, 20 February 1989 ("Charity Got $14 400 from a Tridel Company"). A Toronto company associated with the Tridel corporation paid $14 400 into an account which was used by the Toronto section of the National Council of Jewish Women to make political donations to Ontario Conservative leadership contender Dennis Timbrell, Toronto Mayor Art Eggleton, and Liberal MPPs Joseph Cordiano, Ron Kanter and Claudio Poisinelli. It is illegal for a charitable organization to make political contributions.

8. *Sunday Star*, 11 June 1989 ("Liberals Got Funds Intended to Build Housing, Starr Says"). Patricia Starr has admitted that she diverted funds intended for non-profit housing to election contributions. However, she defended the donations. " 'It wasn't sinister. It wasn't sleazy. It wasn't political,' she said."

9. *Toronto Star*, 16 June 1989 ("Politicians Reeling at Reports of Donations"). Mayor Art Eggleton says that he will repay the $5 500 in campaign donations he received since 1985 from Patti Starr's charity. Since the donation cheques were signed by different persons for different companies, usually in amounts of $500, he had some difficulty in identifying the original source.

10. *Toronto Star*, 16 June 1989 ("Cabinet Ministers Confirm Findings"). Those politicians having received campaign contributions from the National Council of Jewish Women (Toronto section) include provincial Liberal Cabinet ministers Ed Fulton, Elinor Caplan, Hugh O'Neil, Bernard Grandmaître, Alvin Curling, Chaviva Hošek and Mavis Wilson. Other recipients were Dennis Timbrell, a former Conservative provincial cabinet minister, federal Immigration Minister Barbara McDougall, federal Conservative MP William Attewell, and federal Liberal MP Robert Kaplan.

11. *Toronto Star*, 16 June 1989 ("Funds Were Misused Public Trustee Says"). Ontario's public trustee has confirmed that more than $60 000 in charitable funds were misused as election contributions made by the National Council of Jewish Women (Toronto section).

12. *Toronto Star*, 16 June 1989 ("25 Politicians Shared $65 000 From Charity"). A confidential report leaked to the *Star* claims that 25 Liberal and Conservative politicians received over $65 000 in illegal campaign contributions from the charity controlled by Patti Starr. Besides those mentioned in the stories above, David Peterson, John Turner and Brian Mulroney are listed as recipients of the charity's funds through fund-raising dinners.

13. *Toronto Star*, 17 June 1989 ("No Sign of $9 800 in Starr Donations, Liberal Party Says"). The Toronto law firm of Goodman and Goodman prepared

ALLEGATIONS OF UNDUE INFLUENCE

a report showing that during 1987 and 1988 the Ontario Liberal party received $16 800 from Patti Starr's charitable organization. The party, however, can account only for $7 000 being received. Gordon Kushner, executive director of the Commission on Electoral Finances, pointed out that, although federal legislation makes it illegal for charitable organizations to make political contributions, under provincial legislation political parties are not prohibited from receiving donations from a charity. Most of the politicians who have received the donations from the charity, however, have now returned them.

14. *Toronto Star*, 17 June 1989 ("Starr's Slush Fund for Politicians: Where the Money Came from"). The Toronto section of the National Council of Jewish Women raised its money for political contributions from provincial sales tax rebates (which were supposed to be passed on to renters in their housing complex), and from "consulting fees" given to them by the Tridel corporation.

15. *The Globe and Mail*, 7 July 1989 ("Starr Handed Out More Than $150 000"). Ontario's public trustee has found that Patti Starr personally ordered the illegal disbursement of more than $150 000 from a charitable fund she controlled. A total of 126 separate prohibited payments were made to various beneficiaries, amounting to $160 053.84. The bulk of the money was paid out as contributions to political candidates and parties over four years, commencing in 1985. Two-thirds of that amount has now been paid back by those who received it.

Other Violations

16. Halifax *Chronicle-Herald*, 28 November 1988 ("Conservative MP under Investigation"). Conservative MP Richard Grisé resigned temporarily from the Quebec Conservative caucus after a Montreal television station reported that the RCMP had raided the business of Joseph Hamelin, former president of the MP's riding association. Published reports have suggested that the RCMP is investigating the alleged misuse of job-creation grants involving Hamelin's company, Mirabel Enterprises, and business links between Grisé and Hamelin. Grisé is chairman of the Regional Industrial Development Committee of Parliament and parliamentary secretary to Deputy Prime Minister Don Mazankowski.

17. *Winnipeg Free Press*, 17 August 1988 ("Indian Band 'Mistakenly' Donated $5 000 to Munro"). The Peter Ballantyne Indian band in Saskatchewan made an improper $5 000 contribution to John Munro's 1984 campaign for the leadership of the federal Liberal party. The $5 000 was described as a loan on a financial statement for a cabin renovation project by the band's outfitting company, Mista Nosayew Renovations. Later, it was marked "not an allowable expense" in an interim audit. Earlier this year, Sinco Developments Ltd., a now-bankrupt Indian-owned company based in Saskatoon, donated $50 000 to Munro's leadership campaign.

18. *Winnipeg Free Press*, 1 February 1988 ("Masse Requested Illegal Payment, Newspaper Alleges"). The *Globe and Mail*, quoting an affidavit sworn by an RCMP investigator, says that Lavalin Inc. paid $780.21 in election expenses for federal Energy Minister Marcel Masse because of a personal request by Masse. This amount was never included in Masse's campaign-spending declaration for the 1984 election, as required by the *Canada Elections Act*. Lavalin was Masse's employer before he was elected a Conservative MP. After an RCMP investigation, "three of Masse's campaign workers were charged with election campaign-spending irregularities. The company and two individuals pleaded guilty and were fined, the third has appealed the charges and the case is still before the courts. Masse was not charged and was welcomed back into the cabinet. Yet a confidential letter to Masse from elections commissioner Gorman dated Nov. 28, 1985, said that the minister had taken part in a campaign-spending infraction but it would not be in 'the interests of justice or the public interest' to charge him."

19. *Globe and Mail*, 18 February 1986 ("Firm Gave Illegally to Masse Campaign"). Lavalin Inc. pleaded guilty and was fined $2 400 on three charges of making illegal contributions to the campaign of federal Communications Minister Marcel Masse in the 1984 election. Lavalin gave Masse campaign worker Marthe Léfèbre $1 455 and $592 in two separate payments, and paid $1 456 to a Montreal travel agency for campaign-related expenses. Ms Léfèbre is charged with making illegal campaign-related payments after the election. Ms Léfèbre's lawyer says that she does not contest the facts but that she does challenge the jurisdiction of the judge. The judge is a special magistrate on a contract, and therefore may not satisfy the requirement in the *Charter of Rights and Freedoms* that all persons charged with an offence have a right to appear before an independent tribunal. Two other Masse campaign workers have also been charged under the *Canada Elections Act*. Gil Rémillard audited Mr. Masse's election return, and is charged with failing to report expenses of $9 000. John Vincent is charged with making four illegal campaign payments totalling $2 880, and with borrowing the $9 000 that Mr. Rémillard is charged with failing to report.

20. *Globe and Mail*, 8 October 1985 ("RCMP Probe Urged into Election Expenses of National Tory Party"). NDP leader Ed Broadbent charged that Marcel Masse was in trouble for exceeding his election spending limit partly because his campaign was forced to pay a bill that ought to have been paid by the national Conservative party. This is a $3 000 bill for transportation to a Brian Mulroney rally, which John Vincent, Mr. Masse's campaign chairman, said on the weekend ought to have been paid by the national party. Instead, Mr. Vincent himself paid the bill four months after the election. The national party was $2 500 short of its limit for spending, so if the national party had paid the bill, Mr. Broadbent said, then the party would have been liable to charges of breaking the law. Broadbent called for an RCMP investigation into the affair.

ALLEGATIONS OF UNDUE INFLUENCE

21. *Globe and Mail*, 16 February 1985 ("RCMP Examining Election Expenses of Two Candidates"). Lawrence Hanigan, the newly appointed chairman of Via Rail, is under investigation by the RCMP after a complaint of spending irregularities in his unsuccessful bid for a Montreal seat during the federal election of 1984. As well, independent Toronto MP Anthony Roman is under investigation. Elections Commissioner Joseph Gorman said that it is normal practice for the RCMP to investigate any allegations. Both candidates had spent within $500 of their spending limit.

22. *Calgary Herald*, 30 May 1984 ("Province May Outlaw Crown Firms' Donations"). In Alberta, the subsidiaries of provincial Crown corporations have donated money to a political party. Independent MLA Ray Speaker said that the current elections act allows provincial Crown corporations and their subsidiaries to make political donations. He claimed that such donations represent a conflict of interest. Premier Peter Lougheed said that the provincial government is considering banning such donations.

23. *Globe and Mail*, 19 March 1983 ("Wine Donations Probed by Electoral Watchdog"). A fund-raising dinner was held for Ontario Corrections Minister Nicholas Leluk in which 10 Ontario wineries provided free wine for 1 200 people. Mr. Leluk said that it was his understanding that wine does not have to be claimed as an expense. Any goods or services worth more than $100 must be listed as a political contribution, according to Ontario law; an individual or company cannot donate more than $500 to a riding association in a non-election year. The Ontario Wine Council's policy is to give wine to one major fund-raising event for each political party that asks once a year. The Liberals have also received such donations, but the NDP has never asked. The NDP House Leader Elie Martel called the wine donations "a blatant example of patronage." The Ontario Commission on Election Contributions and Expenses is investigating. The commission's executive director said he had never seen wines listed as a political contribution.

24. Montreal *Gazette*, 8 February 1983 ("Three-time Loser at Polls Guilty of Campaign Fraud"). Armand Léfèbvre, a three-time unsuccessful Conservative candidate in a Montreal South Shore riding, has been convicted of overspending and of filing a false return on his federal campaign expenses of May 1979. He spent at least $8 000 more than his limit of $31 917. Commissioner of Elections Joseph Gorman said it was the first conviction for this type of offence since the new *Election Expenses Act* was passed in 1974. Mr. Léfèbvre's campaign treasurer also faces two charges under the Act: not filing Léfèbvre's election return within the four month limit, and knowingly filing a false return.

25. *Winnipeg Free Press*, 24 August 1982 ("Election Charges Quashed"). Charges of overspending against four candidates in the last provincial election were quashed in court because the Crown attorney missed the six-month deadline for laying charges. The charges were the first to be brought under

the province's 1980 *Elections Finances Act*. The agents for two NDP cabinet ministers and two Conservative candidates had been charged.

26. *Winnipeg Free Press*, 1 June 1982 ("Financial Officers Charged Under Election Spending Act"). The financial officers of six provincial election candidates have been charged with spending too much on their campaigns in the first test of Manitoba's *Elections Finances Act*. There is nothing spelled out in the Act which would affect members of the legislature whose financial agents were charged.

27. *Winnipeg Free Press*, 23 February 1981 ("Alberta Investigates Political Fundraising"). Three political groups arguing for and against western separatism had been raising funds without permits. The West-Fed Association, Western Canada Concept and the Alberta Citizens' Coalition had not registered under the Alberta *Public Contributions Act*. "They'll have to cease until they get a permit," a government official said.

28. *Globe and Mail*, 30 April 1980 ("Diefenbaker Overspent by 40 Percent in Final Race"). An official report showed that, of the 1 424 candidates in the 1979 federal election, the first election to which the spending limits enacted in 1974 applied, only two candidates overspent. They were the late John Diefenbaker, who overspent by almost 40 percent, and George Kirby, the unsuccessful Conservative candidate in the Quebec riding of Argenteuil. The report of the chief electoral officer showed that the 282 winners spent an average of $22 900 or 83 percent of the spending limit, while the average spent by all candidates was $19 700, or 59 percent of the ceiling.

29. *Calgary Herald*, 15 December 1979 ("Politics: NDP's Unreported Cash"). Geoff White points out that it was the NDP that pushed for reform of the election financing laws to make disclosure of contributions mandatory in order to demonstrate that the old parties were "too closely linked to the business establishments to serve the interests of the average citizen properly. As it turns out, the campaign disclosures made to the chief electoral officer after the last election by the Conservative party read like a directory of big business in Alberta. Public enlightenment in this matter has served the public interest." But the NDP has also been embarrassed by the new law. The Alberta Union of Public Employees has admitted that it was wrong to make its donations in the way it did. "Union officials now claim they made money available to the NDP in the form of employee expense advances because many of the union's members would not agree with making contributions to the NDP. This is not the first time officials of a supposedly democratic union have ignored what they believe the will of their members to be."

30. *Calgary Herald*, 8 December 1979 ("Electoral Chief Investigating Donation to NDP Candidate"). Martin Van Kessel, a former negotiator for the Alberta Union of Public Employees (AUPE), has admitted that he secretly paid $500 to Alberta NDP candidate Bob Borreson under orders from top union officials. The union's constitution prohibits partisan political activity, and the

province's political contributions law, in effect for the first time during the last election, declares that any contribution to a party in excess of $250 must be disclosed. As well, Dennis Malayko, also an employee of AUPE, gave $800 to Borreson. Borreson said he believed at the time that the money from the two men was from their personal savings and not from union funds. The chief electoral officer said he has a list of five union employees who are willing to make allegations about improper union contributions to the NDP campaign. If he finds sufficient evidence, he can order a full public inquiry. The AUPE donations scandal is the second time since the election that the NDP has run afoul of the new contributions disclosure law.

APPENDIX C

Category 3: Donations to Candidates and Parties Made Public as Required by Law

Note: Only the references to these stories are presented here. Part of the content of the stories is summarized in the text under category 1, subheading "The Overall Picture regarding Political Donations." Readers interested in learning more about the nature of public disclosures of political donations should refer to the articles listed below.

1. Vancouver *Sun*, 31 March 1990 ("Big Business and the Tories").
2. Vancouver *Sun*, 31 March 1990 ("Some Donors Do Business with Feds").
3. *Toronto Star*, 15 July 1989 ("American Firms Gave Big Bucks to Tory Coffers").
4. *Calgary Herald*, 28 May 1989 ("Sunshine Owner Tops Election Donors List").
5. *Calgary Herald*, 6 April 1989 ("Oilers Helped Fuel Tory Machine").
6. *Winnipeg Free Press*, 14 July 1987 ("Wealthy Widow Leads List of Private Political Donors").
7. Montreal *Gazette*, 14 July 1987 ("Conglomerate and Receptionist Dig Deepest for Party Donations").
8. *Globe and Mail*, 3 May 1986 ("Donations Reveal Party Strengths").
9. *Toronto Star*, 12 July 1984 ("CP gave $102 000 to Liberals, Tories").
10. *Winnipeg Free Press*, 12 July 1984 ("Widow's $453 000 Gift to NDP Largest Political Contribution").
11. Montreal *Gazette*, 18 October 1983 ("Change in Election Act to Increase Spending").
12. Montreal *Gazette*, 26 April 1983 ("Party Figures Show Who Donated What").
13. Montreal *Gazette*, 18 February 1983 ("Pocklington Funded PC's Byelection Rival").

14. Montreal *Gazette*, 7 July 1982 ("Quebec Law Tightens Campaign").

15. *Globe and Mail*, 22 November 1981 ("Eggleton Says 43 Donors Get No Favors with $1 000").

16. *Globe and Mail*, 11 July 1980 ("Who's Who of Political Donors Unveiled").

17. *Winnipeg Free Press*, 8 July 1980 ("$18 813 147 Given to Political Parties").

APPENDIX D
Category 4: Weak Laws regarding Election Contributions or Spending

1. *Globe and Mail*, 25 November 1987 ("PQ Annoyed as Liberal Coffers Grow"). See appendix A, no. 29.

2. *Winnipeg Free Press*, 4 April 1987 ("NDP Fundraising Pitch Called Abuse of Power"). See appendix A, no. 32.

3. Montreal *Gazette*, 10 February 1987 ("Law Can't Force Party to Return Donations Illegally Gained: Hamel"). See appendix A, no. 33.

4. *Winnipeg Free Press*, 6 October 1986 ("Election Donors Remain Secret"). Manitoba's new *Elections Finances Act* came into effect in 1985. Under the Act, donors to candidates must be publicly identified. However, the NDP adopted a new centralized system for handling donations. All donations are sent to the provincial party, which issues tax receipts. The donations are then split; 30 percent goes to the federal NDP, the balance to the candidate. This system keeps the donor's name from appearing on a candidate's election-spending return. The NDP claims that the system was not adopted to promote secrecy, but for greater efficiency. In the future, the names of donors will be voluntarily disclosed by the NDP.

5. Halifax *Chronicle-Herald*, 16 April 1985 ("MacLean Wants Investigation of PC Election Fund"). Opposition leader Vince MacLean claims that the Department of Transportation makes $100 000 available to each government MLA in rural regions to spend on transportation projects as he or she wishes. MacLean claims that this makes a mockery of the legal spending limits in provincial elections.

6. *Globe and Mail*, 10 April 1985 ("Aldermen Get Cold Feet Over Funds Disclosure"). Toronto city councillors continued to resist introducing legislation which would require mandatory disclosure of campaign contributions. Only 11 of 22 council members have voluntarily disclosed their 1982 campaign expenses and contributions. Some councillors opposed draft legislation because they felt that although there would be a $500 ceiling on donations, this would not stop the NDP from pouring unlimited funds into its candidates' campaigns. An NDP councillor, however, said that each NDP candidate is responsible for his or her own fund-raising.

7. *Globe and Mail*, 21 November 1984 ("Alberta Opposition and Ministers Not

Surprised that Firms Back PCs"). Opposition members of the Alberta legislature have said that companies controlled by Alberta Energy Co. Ltd., which is 44 percent owned by the province, should not be allowed to give money to political parties. Such companies made four political donations in 1982.

8. Montreal *Gazette*, 28 June 1984 ("Publishers Happy Court Quashed Election Spending Amendments"). Mr. Justice Donald Medhurst of the Alberta Court of Queen's Bench ruled last Tuesday that amendments to the *Canada Elections Act* banning non-party interest groups or individuals from spending money to oppose candidates or political parties during an election violate free speech guarantees under the *Canadian Charter of Rights and Freedoms*. "We agree completely with the judge's decision," Jean-Robert Belanger, publisher of the daily *Le Droit* and chairman of the Canadian Daily Newspaper Publishers Association, said yesterday. "Newspapers have been fighting for freedom of speech, which the amendments partly denied. Freedom of expression during an election should be given to any group. This is the same government that gave us the Charter of Rights. For them to appeal the decision would be illogical and unreasonable."

9. Montreal *Gazette*, 27 June 1984 ("Law Limiting Election Spending to Parties Ruled Unconstitutional"). Justice Donald Medhurst of the Alberta Court of Queen's Bench has ruled that the amendments to the *Canada Elections Act* which ban campaign spending except by registered candidates or political parties violate free-speech guarantees under the *Charter of Rights and Freedoms*. The National Citizens Coalition (NCC), which has 30 000 members, spent more than $300 000 on legal fees and advertising in the fight. David Somerville, NCC vice-president, said that the organization has several issues it intends to promote and publicize during the next federal election. It wants the government to sell Petro-Canada and other Crown corporations, and dismantle the National Energy Program. It urges that the right to own private property be entrenched in the constitution, that the federal government balance the budget in three years or call an election on the issue, that indexed pensions for MPs and civil servants be abolished, that no Canadian be forced to contribute to union funds, and that all union strike votes be held in secret. Conservative House Leader Ray Hnatyshyn suggested that the government seek a reference from the Supreme Court to have the matter resolved before the next federal election.

10. *Calgary Herald*, 10 January 1984 ("Cabinet Plans $11 Million, Election-year Blitz") The Trudeau Cabinet is planning an $11 million advertising campaign prior to the expected federal election to provide information about what federal programs are available. Conservative MP Perrin Beatty, long a critic of Liberal government advertising policies, said that the campaign appears to be an attempt "to polish their own image in preparation for an election." But Employment Minister John Roberts said that the advertising will be purely informational, not advertising which merely promotes the image of the government. He added, however, "Obviously, as a

politician, if people know what our programs are and think they are effective, I hope eventually we will be worthy of their support."

11. Montreal *Gazette*, 3 July 1982 ("Quebec Law Tightens Campaign"). The director-general of political party financing, Pierre-Olivier Boucher, said that a new Quebec law will make political patronage more difficult. Bill 66, passed last week by the National Assembly, will require provincial and municipal parties to detail all revenues and expenses in a yearly financial statement. Boucher said that provision "will help opposition parties and the public identify whether a government, in its awarding of government contracts, is acting in conflict of interest." The bill tightens up a 1977 law which required parties to submit financial reports but did not demand precise details. The bill did not plug another loophole in the old legislation, however. "Corporations and unions which by law are not allowed to contribute funds to political parties in Quebec, can still donate all they want, in complete secrecy, at meetings when organizers pass around the hat. In the 1978 Montreal election, Jean Drapeau's Civic Party raised a full 44 percent of its $177 200 campaign fund from such anonymous sources, according to Boucher's records."

12. *Calgary Herald*, 18 March 1982 ("New Bid to Limit Vote Funds"). Calgary MLA Ed Oman has introduced a bill that would give cities and towns the right to set their own ceilings on the money which candidates can spend in a municipal election. He said that the bill, if passed, would free municipal politicians from allegations of back-room deals and big-money support. It would also allow candidates to run a campaign without the financial support of "just the rich or special interest groups." Oman had previously introduced a similar bill which would have set specific limits on municipal election spending, but some municipalities refused to support it on the grounds that it was too rigid. The flexibility of the new bill may gain it greater support.

13. *Globe and Mail*, 22 October 1981 ("NDP Says PCs Spent $8 Million"). Ontario NDP leader Michael Cassidy criticized Ontario's electoral laws for failing to set limits on election spending. He said that the Ontario Conservative party spent more than $8 million in the last provincial election campaign, more than twice as much as either of the other two parties. In contrast, the federal Conservatives and Liberals each spent about $10 million in the 1980 federal election for all of Canada. Cassidy said that the current law is inadequate because it places limits only on the size of individual contributions ($2 000 to a party and $500 to candidates with a maximum of $2 000 to candidates of one party) and the amount of media advertising. Cassidy urged the government to adopt the federal election spending limits, which have been found to be "quite comfortable" by the three parties.

14. *Winnipeg Free Press*, 8 July 1980 ("Tax Cut Proposed for Gifts to Parties"). Conservative Attorney General Gerry Mercier introduced legislation to tighten up Manitoba's election financing laws. Mercier said that the cur-

rent law has been flagrantly violated; 4 of 12 contenders in 1979 provincial by-elections ignored legal spending limits; in 1977, 39 candidates in the provincial election failed to file details of their expenses and donations within the 60-day limit. Under the new legislation there will be a tax credit on a sliding scale, with a maximum of $500 applying to a donation totalling $1 150 per year to a registered political party and/or candidate.

The law would be enforced by a commission made up of a Cabinet-appointed chair, the chief electoral officer and representatives of each party in the legislature. This composition would remove a possible conflict of interest. Greater disclosure provisions would act as a safeguard against undue influence by donors. Spending limits on advertising would be introduced, donations from outside Manitoba would be prohibited and federal party transfers to provincial party organizations would be limited to $100 per candidate. The names of contributors of more than $250 a year would have to be disclosed. Unincorporated associations and trust funds could make contributions, but would have to disclose the original sources of such money.

APPENDIX E
Category 5: Outside Interference in Election Campaigns

1. *Globe and Mail*, 29 November 1989 ("Tories Proposed Favours List, Papers Suggest"). The PC Canada Fund memo referred to in no. 2 below was prepared for a high-level, five-member committee chaired by Peter Clark, brother of Joe Clark. The memo suggested that the party's list of corporate donors (including U.S.-owned firms) should include information about "government contracts, grants or policy issues that profit the firm." Nicholas Locke, executive director of the PC Canada Fund, said that the recommendation that such records be kept was not implemented.

2. *Globe and Mail*, 21 November 1989 ("Tory Memo Advises Favours for Donors"). A PC Canada Fund official prepared a memo recommending that those who contribute more than $5 000 to the fund be given insider information. Major U.S. firms would be among the targets. The executive director of the fund said that this policy was never implemented.

3. *Toronto Star*, 15 July 1989 ("American Firms Gave Big Bucks to Tory Coffers"). American branch-plant companies in Canada – big beneficiaries of the free-trade agreement – were among the top contributors to the Conservative election campaign in 1988, Elections Canada documents show. Such major subsidiaries as Nabisco Brands Ltd. ($102 983.40), Merrill Lynch Canada Inc. ($105 469.11), and Budget Rent-A-Car ($100 000) helped the Tories raise a record $24.5 million for the 1988 campaign. Similarly, American-owned firms such as Imperial Oil Ltd. ($46 000) and Weyerhaeuser Canada Ltd. ($30 000) helped the Tories swell their war chest for the election battles. The Liberals raised $13.2 million and the

New Democrats $11.7 million. The contributions do not include the estimated millions spent by pro–free trade firms on an advertising campaign in support of the agreement. The figures, released yesterday, show a big-business tilt toward the Tories. The average financial contribution to the Liberals, for instance, was just $590. Federal election law does not limit size of contributions nor does it place any limit on the number of contributors. Any donation over $100 must be reported.

4. *Winnipeg Free Press,* 17 August 1987 ("Tories, Liberals Cash in on Out-of-Province Funding"). Manitoba's Conservatives and Liberals raked in sizable donations from non-Manitoba firms as they sought to unseat the NDP government last year. Of all the money collected from party contributions of $250 or more, 39 percent of the Liberal party money and 33 percent of the Conservatives' take came from individuals and firms listing addresses outside Manitoba. The documents deal only with contributions made directly to the parties, not to individual candidates. Toronto's Carling-O'Keefe gave $1 500 to the Tories. Banks, other financial institutions and Alberta-based oil companies gave thousands to the Conservatives. Meanwhile the NDP took in nearly $100 000 from unions, both in Manitoba and across Canada. The union donations accounted for more than 10 percent of the money collected through major contributions to the NDP.

5. *Toronto Star,* 19 November 1985 ("Hyundai Plant Has 'Nothing to Do with' Election, PM Insists"). Last week, Quebec Premier Pierre-Marc Johnson announced that a $300-million Hyundai auto plant will be built in the province. Ontario Industry Minister Hugh O'Neil said that the federal Tories gave Hyundai "an offer they couldn't refuse" to locate in Quebec. It was alleged that Mulroney favours a Parti Québécois re-election because he fears that a Liberal victory would help the federal Liberals. Mulroney has denied that the timing of the announcement had anything to do with the provincial election. He said it had "absolutely nothing to do with" the election campaign.

6. *Globe and Mail,* 14 April 1985 ("Strathroy Gets $305 000 Just as Miller Comes to Visit"). An hour before Conservative leader Frank Miller arrived in Strathroy during a campaign visit, the town received a letter by courier from Municipal Affairs Minister Dennis Timbrell announcing approval of grants and loans totalling $305 000. Miller claimed that he did not know about the money. But Mayor Thomas Wolder said, "Certainly, elections do seem to expedite public works." When Wolder, a Liberal, was asked if he would now vote Conservative, he said, "I don't deny it; everybody knows it. Well, I imagine it will sway a lot of people." Earlier in the day, Mr. Miller gave $500 000 to the Canadian Diabetes Association, then defended the gift as part of his job as premier. Because the money came from the Ministry of Health operating funds, it did not require cabinet approval. He said that the announcement was made in the centre of David Peterson's riding because it is simply the most convenient place to meet a lot of people.

7. Halifax *Chronicle-Herald*, 30 March 1985 ("Newfoundland Tory Campaign Receives $180 Million Boost"). Toward the end of the provincial election campaign, the provincial Conservative government received a boost when federal Justice Minister John Crosbie and Premier Brian Peckford announced a six-year highway construction program which will cost $180 million and create 1 000 jobs.

8. *Calgary Herald*, 24 July 1984 ("Free Ads May Tempt Federal Parties"). The National Citizens Coalition (NCC) has offered free ads to the three major national parties to make clear their stands on selected issues. The gambit is part of the massive $700 000 national advertising campaign the group plans to launch in this election. Since running full-page ads in the *Globe and Mail* and the *Toronto Star*, the NCC has netted $50 000 in donations.

9. *Calgary Herald*, 22 October 1982 ("Tory Vote-Buying has Backfired in Barrhead"). People in Barrhead, where Liberal leader Nick Taylor is running in a provincial by-election, are unimpressed by the collection of government give-aways announced in recent weeks. At election forums, voters did not understand why interest rates were being subsidized now, but not a year earlier when it would have done more good. One woman objected to the government's decision, announced during the election, to move the Alberta Correspondence School to Barrhead. She said that the government is attempting to graft on to the community an institution that does not belong there and whose employees will dislike living there, just to curry favour with voters and stave off a Taylor victory. As well, the announcement of the widows' pension fund, created by the government, was delayed until the election campaign began.

APPENDIX F

Category 6: Fund-raising for Leadership Candidates or Senior Party Officials Criticized

1. *Globe and Mail*, 7 September 1988 ("Turner Denies Funds Put in Trust for His Use"). *Maclean's* magazine published a story stating that some of the money raised for the 1984 Liberal leadership campaign of John Turner was for his personal use. Warren Chippindale, a senior executive with the accounting firm Coopers and Lybrand, who was chair of the fund-raising committee for Mr. Turner, said that the money collected exceeded expenditures on the campaign by "not more than $300 000." The excess, Mr. Chippindale said, was placed in an account to help cover Mr. Turner's living expenses in the months after the leadership convention. Turner denied that any of the funds raised were used for a personal benefit to him or his family, although he said that funds may have been used to cover transitional expenditures and on "the legitimate expenses for a party in the process of forming a government before it actually is the government."

2. Montreal *Gazette*, 8 October 1986 ("Grits Asked to Pay Off Campagnolo's Mortgage"). "Friends and admirers" of Iona Campagnolo, president of the Liberal party of Canada, hope to raise $75 000 for her as a retirement present to pay off her mortgage. A letter sent to typical large donors to the Liberal party explained that Ms. Campagnolo's lifetime of service to the public and the party has not permitted her to accumulate much in the way of savings for retirement. The names of the donors to the special fund will not be made public.

3. *Globe and Mail*, 29 July 1986 ("Riding Gave $147 000 in Tax-Exempt Funds to Timbrell Campaigns"). Dennis Timbrell's riding association contributed $147 000 in tax-exempt funds to his two unsuccessful attempts to gain the provincial Conservative leadership last year. Ontario's election financing law permitted riding associations to use funds for any purpose they wished, although they could not specifically collect tax-exempt funds for leadership campaigns. That loophole in the law has since been plugged.

4. *Globe and Mail*, 3 June 1986 ("Riding Gave $35 000 to Grossman in Party Races"). Conservative leader Larry Grossman's Toronto riding executive contributed $35 000 in tax-exempt donations to its candidate's two leadership campaigns last year, its annual report shows. This would appear to be in addition to $20 000 the association donated during the May election campaign.

5. *Globe and Mail*, 24 January 1986 ("The Contributors Nobody Knows"). This editorial claims that the lack of rules to force the disclosure of contributors to federal and provincial leadership campaigns constitutes a major weakness in electoral laws which require the disclosure of the names of contributors to parties. "By virtue of their selection by party members, these people assume important public trusts. When they subsequently run for office in a public election, names of major donors to their campaigns are publicized so that everyone knows to whom they are beholden. But that knowledge is something of a fiction if their real debt lies further back in the leadership campaigns."

6. *Winnipeg Free Press*, 16 November 1984 ("Tories Pressured to Reveal Funding," an Ontario Column by Eric Dowd). Traditionally, the Ontario Conservative party has chosen its leader without telling the public how much the candidates spent on their campaigns or who provided the funds, and it has also allowed candidates to spend as much as they could raise. There has been pressure to reform the process because of the trend to more openness in government. Because the new leader to replace William Davis will become premier, it is small wonder that people want to know who bankrolls the new leader. In contrast, the Ontario Liberal party, in choosing a leader in 1982, put a $75 000 ceiling on candidates' spending, but did not require donors to be identified; the NDP limited candidates to $30 000 each and required them to identify every contributor and the amount given. It is generally agreed in the Conservative party that each candidate

will need between $500 000 and $750 000 to have any chance of success. The Conservatives, this time around, have decided to require candidates to make public their total spending and the names of contributors, but not how much each individual contributor gave.

"Donors give to leadership and other political candidates for a variety of reasons. Not many people these days suggest a cash donation can persuade a premier to adopt a specific policy ... But some who give large donations hope their assistance will be remembered and at least assure them access to government to put their case, when the need arises. How else to explain the generosity of trucking firms toward the transportation minister, or nursing homes toward the health minister, as distinct from other ministers of the Crown, around elections?"

7. *Winnipeg Free Press*, 30 July 1980 ("Political Donation Disclosure Amendment Riles Opposition"). Opposition MLA Russ Doern has charged that the Conservatives have established a "slush fund" for Premier Sterling Lyon's retirement, and that the fund comes from contributions to the Conservative party. Last-minute amendments to the Manitoba *Elections Finances Act* will mean that the names of party donors who made their contributions before the Act is proclaimed need not be made public. Doern claims that this amendment is intended to prevent the NDP from knowing who contributed to the fund for Lyon's retirement.

(See also appendix A, no. 39, and appendix B, no. 17.)

APPENDIX G
Category 7: Campaign Contributions Used in Questionable Ways

1. Halifax *Chronicle-Herald*, 28 November 1988 ("Conservative MP under Investigation"). Published reports have suggested that the RCMP is investigating Tory fund-raising activities for MP Richard Grisé, and "whether all the money was used for political work." A former riding association president said that he resigned because he wasn't satisfied that the proceeds from fund-raising events were being used properly. He said he had to fight to get $20 000 raised at a dinner deposited into the riding's account.

2. Montreal *Gazette*, 26 August 1988 ("Montreal MPs Deny Fund-raising Charges as Liberals Hint PM Put Pressure on Them"). Montreal MPs Edouard Desrosiers and Claude Lanthier denied recent newspaper reports that suggested irregularities in handling of money from a 1987 fund-raising dinner. Lanthier told the Commons that he had been misquoted and badly translated by the Toronto *Globe and Mail*. The paper reported Monday that Lanthier had said he was concerned about possible diversions of money from political contributions. The quote referred to his concern about "the crumbs that drop off the table" after donations are made. Another Quebec MP, Vincent Della Noce, made a retraction after he was quoted as saying that the hardest thing about being an MP was staying clean and he could

put a dozen people in prison.

3. *Globe and Mail*, 26 August 1988 ("Tories Deny Wrongdoing on Donations"). Same as above.

4. *Globe and Mail*, 25 February 1983 ("Election Funds Buy Trip"). Toronto Mayor Arthur Eggleton plans to use a portion of the $49 293 left over from his 1982 election campaign fund to finance an eight-day trip to Britain for him and his wife. The mayor will participate in the opening phase of a European tour by the Toronto Symphony Orchestra. He will also make a speech to the Canada-United Kingdom Chamber of Commerce and meet tourist and travel executives to promote Toronto's 150th anniversary celebration next year. Eggleton said that there is no provision in the city budget to cover such an expense. He said that, if he decides not to seek a third term in 1985, the balance of the surplus, currently being held in trust, would become charitable donations.

APPENDIX H

Category 8: Friends of Government Party Get Favours (No Allegation Involving Money)

1. *Globe and Mail*, 13 February 1989 ("OPP, Crown Attorney to Investigate Payments Made by Starr Charity"). Ontario Opposition leader Bob Rae claimed that, despite the admission by Ms. Munro that she had intervened to get a contract for her mother, Premier Peterson had not publicly reprimanded her or asked for her resignation.

2. *Globe and Mail*, 2 February 1989 ("MPPs Want Probe of Ontario Place Contracts"). Opposition MPPs in Ontario called for the provincial auditor to investigate the awarding of an Ontario Place contract for $116 700 per year to Dino Chiesa by Housing Minister Chaviva Hosek. Mr. Chiesa worked in Ms. Hosek's campaign.

3. *Winnipeg Free Press*, 7 May 1987 (" 'Slush Fund' Benefited NDP Friends, Filmon Says"). Conservative leader Gary Filmon charged that the NDP government is using the Communities Economic Development Fund (CEDF) to reward former NDP members of the legislature. He said that the CEDF loaned Ken Dillen, a former NDP MLA, $100 000 although his eligibility was questionable. Northern Affairs Minister Elijah Harper denied the allegation, and reminded Filmon that the former Conservative government had used the fund to reward party workers, citing a CEDF loan to Centre Street Productions. After Centre Street Productions went broke, irregularities were discovered in the way the loan was granted.

4. Montreal *Gazette*, 19 November 1985 ("Ex-Crombie Aide Given $100 000 in Contracts to Study Native Funding"). Indian Affairs Minister David Crombie was criticized by members of the Opposition for awarding untendered contracts to his political friends. A Nova Scotia consultant who helped the minister set up his Ottawa office obtained federal contracts

worth about $100 000. And a company linked to a close friend will be awarded more than $100 000 to organize a native trade show. The friend is Bill Marshall, who ran Crombie's unsuccessful 1983 bid for the Conservative leadership.

APPENDIX I
Category 9: Ethics of Relying on a Few Large Donors or Accepting Money from Donors Who Violate Party Principles

1. *Winnipeg Free Press*, 17 June 1989 ("Media Donors Upset Uruski: MLA Suggests Gifts Show Bias"). Bill Uruski, an NDP MLA, said that it is hard to get the party's message out when those controlling the airwaves have blatant ties to the Tories and Liberals. For example, Izzy Asper, owner of CKND, individually and through his companies donated $5 850 to the Liberals in 1988 and $300 to the Tories. Moffat Communications Ltd. gave $4 500 to the Liberals and $12 000 to the Tories last year. Neither gave to the NDP. Employees of the stations, however, claim that knowing the political leanings of the owner makes them more vigilant than otherwise to ensure that reporting is unbiased.

2. Montreal *Gazette*, 4 May 1987 ("NDP's New Dilemma: Should It Accept Corporate Donations?"). Now that the federal NDP occupies second place in public-opinion polls, there is a real temptation to accept money from big business. Previously, the party's refusal on principle to accept such money was "rather like a person with no teeth boycotting steak on moral grounds." NDP national secretary Dennis Young says that he is returning unsolicited cheques from large businesses more often than before. The NDP refuses to accept funds from publicly traded corporations and many private companies.

3. *Winnipeg Free Press*, 4 April 1987 ("NDP Fundraising Pitch Called Abuse of Power"). Conservative MLA Gerry Mercier criticized the NDP for fund-raising through selling tickets to dinners for $200 each where those attending would be able to meet 13 Cabinet ministers. Representatives from banks or large corporations doing business with South Africa will be allowed to attend the NDP dinner but their donations will be returned to them. The NDP will not accept contributions from companies dealing with the apartheid-governed country.

APPENDIX J
Category 10: Pressure on an Electoral Boundary Commission by a Politician

1. Vancouver *Sun*, 6 August 1980 ("Inquiry Clears McCarthy"). The British Columbia attorney general said that his ministry has concluded that there was no wrongdoing in setting the electoral boundaries for the riding of Vancouver–Little Mountain. A former Electoral Commission employee

had sworn an affidavit stating that the Deputy Premier Grace McCarthy ordered the independent commissioner to make changes in her riding boundaries. The riding is shaped basically like a square, except there is a "finger" of land attached to it on one side. It was alleged that Ms. McCarthy demanded that the finger be attached to her riding.

APPENDIX K

Table 3.K1
All allegations of undue influence, 1979–90

	79	80	81	82	83	84	85	86	87	88	89	90*	Total
1. Relation between donation to party or candidate and favour, contract or grant to donor	2	1		1	1	2	2	8	10	7	15	6	55
2. Violations of laws regarding election contributions or spending limits	2	1	1	2	2	2	2	1	1	1	26		41
3. Donations to candidates and parties made public as required by law		2	1	2	4	2		1	2		3	2	19
4. Weak laws regarding election contributions or spending		2	1	3		3	2	1	1	3	1		17
5. Outside interference in election campaigns				1		3	6		1		2		13
6. Fund-raising for leadership candidates or senior party officials criticized		1				1		5		1			8
7. Campaign contributions used in questionable ways					1					3			4
8. Friends of government party get favours (no allegation involving money)							1		1		2		4
9. Ethics of relying on a few large donors or accepting money from donors who violate party principles										2	1		3
10. Pressure on an electoral boundary commission by a politician			1										1

*1990 includes only January–March.

Table 3.K2
All allegations of undue influence, 1979–90, by level of government

	79	80	81	82	83	84	85	86	87	88	89	90*	Total
1. Relation between donation to party or candidate and favour, contract or grant to donor													
M		1							3		4		8
P	2			1	1	1		3	2	3	5		18
F						1	2	5	5	4	6	6	29
Total													55
2. Violations of laws regarding election contributions or spending limits													
M											4		4
P	2		1	2	1	2			1	1	13		23
F		1			1		2			1	9		14
Total													41
3. Donations to candidates and parties made public as required by law													
M			1	1	1								3
P				1	1			1			1		4
F		2			2	2			2		2	2	12
Total													19
4. Weak laws regarding election contributions or spending													
M		1		2			1		1		1		6
P		1	1	1			1	1		2			7
F						3				1			4
Total													17
5. Outside interference in election campaigns													
M							1						1
P				1		2	3		1				7
F						1	2				2		5
Total													13
6. Fund-raising for leadership candidates or senior party officials criticized													
M													
P		1				1		3					5
F								2		1			3
Total													8

Table 3.K2 (cont'd)
All allegations of undue influence, 1979–90, by level of government

	79	80	81	82	83	84	85	86	87	88	89	90*	Total
7. Campaign contributions used in questionable ways													
M					1								1
P													
F											3		3
Total													4
8. Friends of government party get favours (no allegation involving money)													
M													
P										1	2		3
F							1						1
Total													4
9. Ethics of relying on a few large donors or accepting money from donors who violate party principles													
M													
P									1		1		2
F									1				1
Total													3
10. Pressure on an electoral boundary commission by a politician													
M													
P			1										1
F													
Total													1

Legend: M = municipal   P = provincial   F = federal.
*1990 includes only January – March.

Figure 3.K1
Allegations of undue influence by year

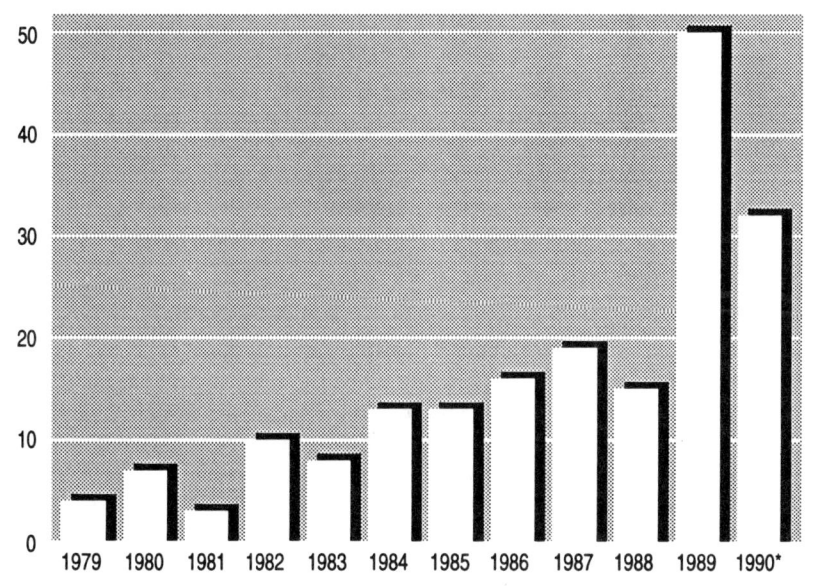

[Bar chart showing allegations from 1979 to 1990, with values rising from about 5 in 1979 to a peak of 50 in 1989, and 32 (extrapolated) in 1990.]

* The eight allegations for the first three months of 1990 are extrapolated to become 32 allegations for the entire year.

ABBREVIATIONS

C.A.	Court of Appeal
C.L.L.C.	Canadian Labour Law Cases
H.C.	High Court (Ontario)
O.P.S.E.U.	Ontario Public Service Employees Union
O.R. (2d)	Ontario Reports, Second Series
R.S.M.	Revised Statutes of Manitoba
S.C.C.	Supreme Court of Canada
S.Q.	Statutes of Quebec

NOTES

This study was completed 31 January 1991; references to the Patti Starr affair and to *Lavigne* were updated to 30 June 1991.

1. Nineteen seventy-nine was the first year that the *Canadian News Index* created a separate heading for "conflict of interest," an indication of a new awareness of political ethics issues.

2. All of these stories concern undue influence of one type or another except for category 3 (19 of 165 items), which simply includes reports on the public disclosure documents listing donors to political parties and candidates.

3. Ronald Dworkin, a contemporary legal theorist, summarized the application of the constitutional principle of equality as it applies to political institutions in Western liberal democracies this way: "We might say that individuals have a right to equal concern and respect in the design and administration of the political institutions that govern them... They possess [this right] not by virtue of birth or characteristic or merit or excellence but simply as human beings with the capacity to make plans and give justice" (Dworkin 1978, 180–82).

4. A review of stories on undue influence in the United States during the past two years indicates that the possible association between campaign contributions and public-office favours is the issue that has created the greatest concern south of the border. Most of the stories dealt with the Jim Wright affair, in which it was alleged that Democratic House Speaker Wright used his influence to help troubled savings-and-loans banks because of these corporations' financial support of Wright's campaigns. The relation between political contributions and interference by elected politicians in the activities of the federal regulators of the savings-and-loans banks is explored in Adams (1990).

5. The proportion of individual donors to the NDP is actually greater than one-third when original sources are considered. This is because the federal NDP received nearly 48 percent of its funds from the provincial party organizations in 1986 (Stanbury 1989, 362), and a substantial proportion of these provincial funds were most likely generated from individual donations.

6. Stanbury notes a single contribution of $93 943 to the NDP in 1986, and one of $453 365 in 1983. These large single contributions tend to present a distorted view of the NDP's reliance on the generosity of individual donors. The large contributions were both from Irene Dyck, a 76-year-old receptionist at the NDP's Calgary office. Ms. Dyck's husband had made a fortune when he sold some land near the outskirts of Calgary in 1979. The couple had been long-time supporters of the NDP, and the widowed Ms. Dyck decided to give part of the profit to the party. (Also see *Winnipeg Free Press*, 12 July 1984, and Montreal *Gazette*, 14 July 1987.)

    A list of newspaper stories reporting on the public disclosure of contributors to election campaigns is presented in appendix C.

7. This figure may not present a true picture of the donations received by the NDP from unions because the proportion of provincial party donations received from unions is not taken into account.

8. Stanbury (1989) arbitrarily defined "large" donors to be individuals who gave more than $2 000, or corporations which donated more than $10 000.

From the perspective of the newspaper reports on undue influence, however, a large donor would appear to be either an individual or corporation making a minimum donation in the $500–$1 000 range.

9. If the federal NDP were allowed to receive a maximum donation of $500 from each of the provincial parties, this would have the effect of promoting more independence between the federal and provincial wings of the party – something that party members themselves may be opposed to for policy reasons. However, there are non-financial methods of promoting integration between federal and provincial parties, and the benefit, from the perspective of NDP philosophy, of limiting the impact of large donors on the Conservative and Liberal parties may encourage members of the NDP to support such a proposal.

10. There seems to be no reason to treat corporations more leniently than individuals when setting limits because elected politicians are just as likely to do a favour for a corporation as they are for an individual in return for a donation.

11. Perhaps the strategy behind banning corporate donations is that this facilitates the enforcement of the spirit of donation limits by ensuring that a corporate owner cannot donate twice, once as an individual and once through the corporation. And if corporate donations are banned, union donations must also be banned for the sake of equal treatment of management and labour. Although the Quebec approach might well constitute a welcome long-run goal of election financing in Canada, it may be impractical in the short run because of the radical adjustment which all parties would have to make to their fund-raising strategies.

12. The Parker report (Canada, Commission of Inquiry 1987) contains a useful discussion of the disclosure and recusal method of discouraging conflicts of interest.

13. Most provinces now have conflict-of-interest legislation which prohibits Cabinet ministers and members of legislatures from participating in decision making in situations which could involve personal gain, even if such personal gain comes in the form of gifts funnelled through the decision-maker's party. The one exception is New Brunswick. The 1978 New Brunswick conflict-of-interest legislation required ministers to disclose benefits which they received from any sources to a judge, who would rule on whether these benefits placed the minister in a conflict of interest. Premier Richard Hatfield was found to be in a conflict of interest for receiving a series of salary supplements from the Conservative party. After the judge's decision, Hatfield repaid the salary supplements, but the government amended the legislation in 1980 so that Hatfield would not have to comply in the future. The judge who had found Hatfield in breach of the legislation resigned his position in relation to the conflict-of-interest code, claiming that the government had opened the door to pay-offs from party

supporters in return for public-office favours. The point is that salary supplements provided from a party to its leader are not unethical as such, but they should be regulated so that party members are aware of the use being made of their contributions and so that donors to the salary supplement fund do not receive special favours in return for their donation.

REFERENCES

Adams, James Ring. 1990. *The Big Fix*. New York: John Wiley.

Canada. Commission of Inquiry into the Facts of Allegations of Conflict of Interest Concerning the Honourable Sinclair M. Stevens. 1987. *Report*. Ottawa: Minister of Supply and Services Canada.

Dworkin, Ronald. 1978. *Taking Rights Seriously*. Cambridge: Harvard University Press.

———. 1985. *A Matter of Principle*. Cambridge: Harvard University Press.

Greene, Ian. 1990. "Conflict of Interest and the Canadian Constitution: An Analysis of Conflict of Interest Rules for Canadian Cabinet Ministers." *Canadian Journal of Political Science* 23:233–56.

Kernaghan, Kenneth. 1974. "Codes of Ethics and Administrative Responsibility." *Canadian Public Administration* 17:527–41.

Lavigne v. O.P.S.E.U. (1986), 55 O.R. (2d) 449 (H.C.), additional reasons at (1987), 87 C.L.L.C. 14, 044 (Ont. H.C.), reversed (1989), 89 C.L.L.C. 14, 011 (Ont. C.A.), affirmed (1991), 91 C.L.L.C. 14, 029 (S.C.C.).

Manitoba. *Elections Finances Act*, R.S.M. 1987, c. E32.

Ontario. Commission on Election Finances. 1988. *A Comparative Survey of Election Finance Legislation 1988*. Toronto: The Commission.

Quebec. *Election Act*, S.Q. 1984, c. 51.

Russell, Peter, Joseph Fletcher, Philip Tetlock and Paul Sniderman. 1987. "The Charter Project: Attitudes toward Civil Liberties in Canada." This project was funded by the Social Sciences and Humanities Research Council of Canada; data were collected by and are available from the Institute for Social Research at York University, Toronto.

Stanbury, W.T. 1989. "Financing Federal Political Parties in Canada, 1974–1986." In *Canadian Parties in Transition: Discourse, Organization, and Representation*, ed. A.G. Gagnon and A.B. Tanguay. Scarborough: Nelson Canada.

4

NEGATIVE POLITICAL ADVERTISING
An Analysis of Research Findings in Light of Canadian Practice

Walter I. Romanow
Walter C. Soderlund
Richard G. Price

POLITICS BY DEFINITION involves conflict. As the conflict management system of a society, politics unavoidably entails high levels of adversarial behaviour, which at times can become quite rancorous. Rules are therefore established, both formal and informal, regarding the ways in which individual citizens, groups and political parties will participate in the competitive process of determining "who gets what, when and how." By their very nature electoral campaigns, which decide who governs, are to a large extent acrimonious because the direct route to political office is through the process of attracting the vote of the electorate. This has always been true in Canada, even though in recent years new media have appeared on the scene that seem to enhance the element of conflict as political strategists have come to understand the suasive power of these media, especially television.

In assessing the phenomenon of negative advertising, it is important to appreciate that political campaigns in Canada's past were far from models of decorous behaviour. It is apparent that the tactic of attacking a political opponent has long been an attractive electoral ploy, particularly if the opponent happened to be an incumbent. Thus, it is important to stress that negative advertising is a technique that is built on a long historical tradition. What negative advertising does (and the reason why Canadians are concerned about it) is to utilize a very powerful medium (television) in an advertising context that is highly sophisticated and has proven effective in other fields.

Negative advertising can be said to have its genesis in competitive product advertising. This connection becomes all the more important as we recognize that from 1952, when political spot advertising was first begun (in the United States presidential campaign), those who conceived and produced political messages have been highly trained and creative executives in the advertising business. Thus, advertising as a factor in determining campaign outcomes has increased in importance, and it appears that negative or attack advertising is increasingly seen by those crafting messages as a particularly effective campaign tactic. It is possible as well to explain the popularity of the attack style of commercial campaign messages when one realizes that the "message" is in most cases likely to be 30 seconds or less in length. In such a brief period, it is virtually impossible to discuss complex issues on a cognitive level. Instead, appeals are made at the affective level to our "gut emotions."

There are further reasons why we believe broadcast campaign advertising is assuming greater importance as a decisive tool in determining electoral outcomes. First, studies show that approximately 25 percent of the Canadian population is functionally illiterate (Calamai 1987), and further that there is an additional 20 percent who choose not to read (Smith 1990). The conclusion follows that nearly half of the Canadian population is not very likely to read about campaigns or to be exposed to campaign advertisements in newspapers or magazines. In the same vein, Canadian newspaper editors have indicated concern that there appears to be no new generation of newspaper readers growing up. Thus, the young voter (18 to 21) is not likely to be a newspaper reader (Sutter 1990; Meyer 1985, 15).

Second, it has become apparent over the past two federal elections that the long-held view regarding the stability of voter choice with respect to political parties, subsumed under the concept "party identification," no longer holds true. Thus, short-term factors associated with the campaign period are going to have far greater weight than was assumed in the past.

Parties can no longer frame their electoral strategies primarily in terms of reinforcing and mobilizing their core vote. To an extent unprecedented in the past, all voters are in effect "up for grabs." Given the pattern of campaign expenditures, it is obvious that political parties see television advertisements as the preferred way of reaching the electorate with their messages. In short, the situation facing Canadian political parties as they enter the 1990s is one where the actual campaign period will be far more decisive than it has been traditionally; and within campaign strategy, advertising (particularly negative or attack advertising) is going to play a more central role.

In this study, we examine negative advertising in two ways: by reviewing pertinent research literature on the phenomenon, and by interviewing leading Canadian political strategists, advertisers and pollsters in order to ascertain their views on key aspects of negative advertising, including possible regulation.

DEFINITIONS

Negative Advertising

Negative advertising, according to Kern, is "generally defined as that which is directed to the failings of the opponent in relation either to character or issues" (1989, 93). Pfau and Burgoon restrict the definition of negative advertising to that which "stresses the negative attributes of an opponent" (1989, 53), although the research literature now strongly suggests that issues and candidate images are effectively intertwined in negative advertising. Taras describes negative advertising as an attempt "to tarnish an opponent through ridicule or by a straightforward savaging of their character or record in office. The competence, motives, intelligence and integrity of opponents are brought into question. The object is to draw blood, to inflict irreparable damage (at least for the duration of the campaign)" (1990, 219). Merritt's definition similarly focuses on the intended effect of the message, arguing that "negative advertising identifies the opponent and explicitly refers to either his general image or his specific policies with the goal of creating negative affect" (1984, 27). Further, according to Kern, negative advertising, operating in the affective domain, can be classified into three types: that based on "uncertainty appeals," raising serious questions regarding the integrity or competence of an opposition candidate; that based on "anger appeals," where it is suggested that the electorate will in some way be harmed by the policies of an opposition candidate; and that based on "harsh reality appeals," where the individual voter could become vulnerable "in the face of uncontrollable, powerful forces," for example, drugs and street crime (1989, 106–107).

Comparative Advertising

While we suggested earlier that negative political advertising could well have its basis in comparative advertising, it is important to point out that the two formats are identifiably different. Comparative advertising typically involves the comparison of two or more specifically named or recognizable brands (Coke/Pepsi/7-Up) of the same generic product class on the basis of a specified set of attributes (amount of caffeine) (Wright et al. 1984, 386–407). The distinguishing feature between comparative and negative advertising in a campaign context is drawn clearly: when a commercial focuses primarily on enhancing perceptions of a candidate at the expense of his or her competitor, such as in a comparison of voting records or policy positions, this would be considered comparative advertising. It is only when the commercial aims at "degrading perceptions of the rival to the advantage of the sponsor" that the commercial would be classified as attack or negative advertising (Merritt 1984, 27).

In sum, negative advertising contains these characteristics: the attack on a candidate is usually on more than his or her personal qualities; implicit or explicit in the commercial is advice to the electorate that some degree of damage will result to society or groups therein if the opponent is elected. Thus, in some instances, negative advertising may "draw blood" of the opponent, as Taras suggests. However, the extent of damage to society is left to the imagination of the voter.

Advocacy Advertising

It is inevitable in any discussion of competitive political advertising that a further category be considered: advocacy advertising. Advocacy advertising has been referred to by some as an "advertorial" or a paid editorial ("infomercial" is the broadcast equivalent) in that it presents a point of view on a public, usually controversial, issue. In a 1977 seminar sponsored by the Canadian Radio-television and Telecommunications Commission (CRTC), the Canadian Bar Association and the Faculty of Law of the University of Toronto, a clear distinction was drawn between advocacy advertising and other forms. Advocacy advertising "intervenes directly in the political arena on politically controversial issues. It attempts to influence the outcome of political debates that can be expected to affect the social, political and business climate of the advertiser. Broadly, it can also attempt directly to sell a political or economic philosophy to the public" (CRTC 1977, 15–16). Advocacy advertising in itself is neither good nor bad, and it can yield positive or negative social consequences, depending on the intent of the user.

Third-Party Advertising

Closely related to advocacy advertising, in that the operative strategy is to enter the arena of political debate, is what has been termed third-party advocacy. In the Canadian electoral context, third-party advocates are individuals or groups who, by registration criteria under the

Canada Elections Act, are not competing for office themselves; rather, they are outside the registration process and, rightly or wrongly, have not considered themselves subject to the requirements of the Act concerning such factors as budgets or prohibitions as to when commercials can be run, or to CRTC regulations dealing with equal treatment of parties and candidates. As advocates of a position, their tactics, as experienced in the Canadian campaign context, have been the free and open use of negative advertising, as defined above, targeted against particular parties or candidates. As these third parties enter the political debate uninvited (we assume), they serve two functions. First, they introduce issues into the debate that all political parties may wish to avoid (e.g., abortion or politicians' pensions). Second, they serve to deflect "flak" that is likely to result from a direct candidate-on-candidate attack. Thus, any assessment of negative advertising must of necessity examine the role of third parties in the campaign process.

HISTORICAL EXPERIENCE

Scholars have identified televised negative advertising in the United States as early as the 1952 campaign, the year in which television was first introduced in Canada as a popular medium. In that campaign, the Democrats rhetorically asked General Dwight Eisenhower, "How's that again, General?" – introducing the negative commercial as a form and "creating styles that would be repeated in years to come" (Diamond and Bates 1984, 84). Others have suggested that the first negative commercial was shown in the 1956 campaign, in which Democratic candidate Adlai Stevenson asked voters, "Are you nervous about Nixon?" (*Television/Radio Age* 1988).

While such examples appear tepid by today's standards, there is no doubt that the "Daisy" spot run by the Democrats against Republican presidential candidate Barry Goldwater in the 1964 campaign harnessed the full emotional impact of television. In the commercial, the picture of a young girl picking petals off a daisy, and counting them, segues into a man's voice taking over the count and ends with a mushroom cloud signifying a nuclear explosion. President Lyndon Johnson's voice-over told the audience, "These are the stakes ... We must either love each other or die" (Diamond and Bates 1984, 129). Although opponent Goldwater was never mentioned in the ad, it was clear that his militant stance on the possible use of nuclear weapons to deal with the growing Vietnam conflict was the target of the commercial. Supposedly by design, the ad was run only once. Yet even today, a quarter of a century later, the ad is recalled as a classic example of negative advertising in any discussion of the topic. Only the "Bear in the Woods" ad in the 1984 U.S. campaign and the infamous "Revolving Door" ad in the 1988 campaign appear as memorable in terms of perceived impact, and those were telecast on many occasions.

What has become evident is that negative advertising, through its emotional and dramatic impact, enhanced by the medium of television, tends to work. While specific research findings regarding the effectiveness of negative advertising are discussed in detail later in this study, the trend in the United States with respect to usage is clearly on the upswing. For example, in 1984, the ratio of negative to positive ads in U.S. Senate campaigns stood at 50 percent. In 1986, "in some cases, 80 and 90 percent" of ads were negative (Louden 1990, 1). In the 1988 presidential campaign, 39 percent of the Bush commercials produced and 49 percent of the Dukakis commercials produced were judged to be negative. Forty percent of the entire Bush campaign budget was spent airing what were perceived to be the half-dozen best negative ads, three of which were seen as having the greatest impact (Devlin 1989, 406). In an interview, Dr. Gina Garramone, a leading U.S. researcher on negative advertising, indicated that she believed the tactic would be widely used at the state level and even in local elections in the United States (1990).

The beginning of negative campaign advertising in Canada might be seen in the 1935 general election, with the "Mr. Sage" commercials. This advertising campaign was designed by a Toronto advertising agency on behalf of the Conservative party. The radio dramatizations attacked Mackenzie King personally in a manner that "made Liberals angry and most Conservatives ashamed" (Peers 1969, 166). Subsequent legislation prohibited such broadcast dramatizations.

With respect to television, Taras points out that political ads were used in the 1957 election, and quantities of specifically negative commercials were identified in the 1979 campaign with attacks on Pierre Trudeau on French television (1990, 220). In the context of negative advertising, Taras also describes the hard-hitting 1980 "House of Cards" commercial that mocked Joe Clark, as well as the 1988 "Erasing the Line" (the 49th parallel), which was aimed at undermining the Tories' Free Trade Agreement with the United States. This commercial was seen as so successful that the Progressive Conservatives found it necessary to produce their own commercial, "Replacing the Line." Taras also discusses the "Bomb the Bridge" ad campaign, in which the Progressive Conservatives attempted to undermine Turner's identification with Canadian patriotism, which was so effectively established during the leaders debate (ibid., 220–22).

Two further points about the Canadian historical experience need to be discussed. First, the Canadian advertising industry does not differ significantly from its counterpart in the United States. Indeed, most of the major players in the Canadian industry are owned by U.S. agencies. Since it is clear that Canadian parties have incorporated to a significant degree the assistance of advertising agencies and strategists in crafting campaigns, trends with respect to negative advertising in Canada are very likely to be similar to those that have become apparent in the United States. Although there are some subtle differences between the two political systems (which we shall examine later in this study), nevertheless, given the relative absence of Canadian literature on "measured effects" of negative advertising, we have no alternative but to turn to the research in U.S. studies.

Second, a brief overview of legislation on third-party advertising points to the significance of the Medhurst decision in the Alberta Court of Queen's Bench in 1984 *(National Citizens' Coalition Inc. v. Canada (Attorney General))*. In this judgement on a suit brought by the National Citizens' Coalition (which had challenged the prohibition of third-party advertising during campaigns on the basis of the guarantee of freedom of expression in the *Canadian Charter of Rights and Freedoms*), Mr. Justice Medhurst found no reason to limit freedom of expression in the political process, thus striking down the ban. The Liberal government at the time and the subsequent Progressive Conservative government both chose not to appeal this decision. Coming as it did just prior to the 1984 election, the consequences of the decision were not readily forthcoming in the 1984 campaign. By 1988, however, a number of groups taking positions on the issue of free trade, as well as on other issues, made it demonstrably clear that third-party advertising (if unchallenged) would play a major role in future electoral contests.[1]

At the moment, this means that registered political parties and candidates are significantly disadvantaged, since they are governed by a set of rules dealing with election expenses and major "blackout" periods for running ads during the campaign, while third parties are not. Clearly, the electoral "playing field" is not level, at least from the point of view of political parties.

Research Findings

Negative advertising as a political phenomenon in the United States has been studied by researchers over a number of years, employing a variety of research strategies, and the research continues. A reasonably coherent set of findings has emerged in the literature on short-term campaign effects of negative advertising. Commentary is abundant on long-term effects on societal attitudes toward politics and politicians, as well as other more subtle effects on the political process such as campaign negativism and recruitment of high-quality candidates; however, the research literature linking effects in these areas to negative advertising is much more speculative.

Short-Term Effects

The first effect of negative advertising is the finding that, when asked, people indicate that they do not like it. For example, in a September 1990 survey done in Michigan, where a number of national and state candidates were using negative ads, 58 percent of respondents said that they did not like the TV ads they had seen recently, and fully 85 percent expressed a "distaste for TV campaign ads featuring personal attacks on candidates" (Edmonds 1990, 1). This finding is widely substantiated in the research literature (Stewart 1975; Garramone 1984; Merritt 1984) and is seen in focus-group analyses of advertising messages as well (Colford 1986). On this particular finding, we have corroborating Canadian data. A November 1988 Canadian Gallup poll indicates that "60% of the Canadian public are opposed to political advertising which criticizes another party's policies and leaders" (Bozinoff and MacIntosh 1988, 1). During our interview with Gallup executives, further analysis was run on this question, and we found no statistically significant variations on this finding on such variables as region, mother tongue, occupation, income, education, and size of community in which the respondents lived. In other words, Canadians generally do not like it.

Nevertheless, in one recent U.S. study, while respondents indicated that they did not approve of negative political advertising, up to two-thirds of them indicated a high recall of negative ads (Johnson-Cartee and Copeland 1989, 893). Earlier studies support such a finding (Richey et al. 1975, 233). Further, it was found that these same respondents were likely to favour specific kinds of negative advertising. For example, advertisements that referred to a candidate's political or voting record, stands on issues, or criminal record were likely to be found favourable. However, advertisements that contained references to "medical histories, personal life, religion, sex life, family members and current or past marriages" were likely to be viewed unfavourably by respondents (Johnson-Cartee and Copeland 1989, 893).

This general societal dislike of negative advertising leads to the possibility of what has been called the "boomerang effect." As described by Garramone, "a strong attack on a candidate, if perceived by the audience as untruthful, undocumented, or in any way unjustified, may create more negative feelings toward the sponsor, rather than toward the target. Similarly, an attack perceived as unjustified may generate more positive feelings toward the target" (Garramone 1984, 251).

There is anecdotal evidence that negative advertising is coming under greater media scrutiny, thereby increasing the possibility of a boomerang effect or backlash. David Broder reports the views of an American ad maker: "The level of public tolerance [toward negative ads] is getting lower; the danger of a backlash is higher." Another political commentator noted that for the 1990 mid-term election campaigns:

> In every state I'm (working) in, at least one paper – and usually more – is taking each [negative] ad, as soon as it goes up, and saying what's true in it and what isn't ... And if a paper calls it sleazy, the next day the other side has an ad up saying, "*Herald* calls ad sleazy." (Broder 1990, 9A)

In our interview with Dr. Garramone, she indicated the obvious usefulness of having negative ad campaigns sponsored by third parties so that these sponsoring groups could absorb a possible boomerang effect (1990). Thus, there are clearly documented liabilities associated with the use of negative advertising. If the risks of doing harm to one's own campaign are considerable, why then, we ask, is there so much of it?

The answer is relatively straightforward and again is well documented in the literature – that is, negative advertising works (Sabato 1981; Will 1989). Moreover, we not only know that negative ads work, but we also have an excellent idea as to why they work. Two reasons appear crucial.

The first has to do with the dual impact of television as a medium of communication and an advertising strategy that increasingly attempts to generate emotional impact and perceptions through personalized appeals to fundamental values such as fear, patriotism and love of family (Lowery and DeFleur 1988; Blumler 1987; Kaid 1981; Hart 1982). As one of the Canadian political strategists whom we interviewed for this study indicated, the strategy of advertising during the 1980s underwent a change in focus: with too much information around, our senses are overloaded and advertisers have turned away from information-imparting ads to an approach that "goes for the gut," appealing to core values. Obviously, threats to these fundamental values result in a great deal of anxiety and uncertainty, which can be exploited fairly easily in negative ads (in the style of the Kern classifications cited previously). Issues such as abortion, street crime and nonavailability of health care offer seemingly limitless possibilities for emotionally laden, dramatic, negative messages.

As indicated, negative advertising is especially suited to the television medium, since television overtly seeks out the dramatic situation. Negative ads are crafted in the best dramatic tradition: they contain characterization (implicit or explicit), plot and conflict. In the 1988 Bush-Dukakis campaign, the producers of Bush's anti-Dukakis commercials specifically tested them for impact. As an example of the in-depth testing, two of the best-known commercials, "Boston Harbor" and the "Revolving Door," were tested in focus groups in colour and in black and white: the "Revolving Door" ad registered with more strength and impact in black and white, thus creating a memorable visual. The "Boston Harbor" pollution ad was run in colour (Devlin 1989, 394).

The second point underlying the success of negative advertising has to do with the characteristics of negative information. Simply put, negative (or disconfirming) information is more powerful in crystallizing decisions than positive (or confirming) information (Garramone 1984; Kaid and Boydson 1987; Roddy and Garramone 1988; Garramone et al. 1990). We tend to expect people to behave according to societal norms (e.g., a candidate comes home, pets and feeds the dog). When we hear that this is indeed the case, the information is accepted and quickly forgotten. However, should we hear that the candidate went home, kicked the dog and fed it rat poison, this we will remember. In politics, it is said, "mud sticks," and negative ads are the way in which seeds of doubt about an opponent are introduced and negative perceptions reinforced (Colford 1986).

Moreover, Garramone and colleagues point out that negative ads are more effective in allowing voters to distinguish between candidates (candidate discrimination):

> The superior informativeness of negative political advertising suggests that it may be especially useful to voters in developing their images (i.e., mental pictures) of candidates, and in differentiating or discriminating between those candidate images. By providing concrete substantive information, a negative political ad may allow voters to distinguish candidate qualities, positions, and performance more readily than would other types of political information that provide less explicit information. (Garramone et al. 1990, 4)

Although not a reason why negative advertising works, certainly a reason why it is used is that it is comparatively cheap and easy to produce: it is cost efficient (Nugent 1987, 49). The unique selling point of a commercial is quickly and readily identifiable, as a campaign strategist whom we interviewed quickly verified: "An incumbent has no chance [to escape negative ads] any more – no one's record is perfect." The hooks on which to hang negative ideas are all too easy to find.

Finally, with respect to the issue-versus-image dimension in negative advertising, the literature strongly supports the effectiveness of issue-based ads (Roddy and Garramone 1988, 425; Pfau and Burgoon 1989, 58). More recently Louden, in a study of the classic Hunt-Helms North Carolina Senate campaign of 1984, argues that the two types of negative ads have converged and that they should not be viewed as dichotomous:

> That is, when voters' perceptual processes are engaged, issue and image data are interpreted as interrelated ... The data from the Hunt/Helms race indicate that issues directly implicate voters' character evaluations. Rather than simply standing alone as justification for supporting a particular candidate, issues are transformed into character judgments ... The formation of a candidate's character information is best achieved through embedding image messages within issue-based commercials. (Louden 1990, 11)

Long-Term Effects

A 1984 commentary on campaign negativism stated:

> In a democratic society a healthy scepticism about power and those who wield it is a useful tool for maintaining a responsive government. However, when those who occupy decision-making positions are constantly portrayed as lacking in both morality and intelligence, the legitimacy of the decisions taken by the government may soon be called into question and the stability of the political system itself may be jeopardized. (Soderlund et al. 1984, 132)

These observations were based on poll data showing confidence levels in government ranging from 42 to 57 percent. A Gallup poll released in June 1990 indicated that only 27 percent evinced confidence in the House of Commons, while a mere 14 percent expressed confidence in political parties (*Windsor Star* 1990). In October 1990, a *Globe and Mail*/ CBC News poll conducted by Canadian Facts and based on interviews with 2 259 Canadians aged 18 and over, reported the following data regarding public trust and confidence in government and the political process in general:

- Level of respect for Parliament:
    55 percent reported respect went down; only 4 percent reported respect went up.

- Government "concerned" with views of the average Canadian:
    77 percent agreed or strongly agreed with statement that government "didn't care much"; 27 percent disagreed or strongly disagreed.
- Government "in touch" with people's problems:
    67 percent disagreed or strongly disagreed that such was the case; 30 percent agreed or strongly agreed.
- Politicians "telling the truth":
    77 percent indicated that the truth was being told only some of the time or hardly ever; 21 percent indicated just about always or most of the time.
- Degree of trust in government doing "what is right":
    76 percent indicated only some of the time or hardly ever; 23 percent just about always or most of the time.
- Can't get good people to run for office because of the way politicians are viewed by the public and the media:
    57 percent strongly agreed or agreed, 40 percent disagreed or strongly disagreed. (*Globe and Mail*, 29 October 1990)

What data such as these show collectively is that the Canadian political process stands on very shaky ground with respect to public confidence. Seemingly, only between one-third and one-quarter of Canadians have positive attitudes toward politics and the institutions that carry it out, while two-thirds to three-quarters are moderately to seriously disaffected with the political process on a number of related but distinct dimensions. Indeed, some may describe the situation reflected in these numbers as a crisis in public confidence, as there is no evidence that the trend has bottomed out and that the situation is improving: if anything, negativism and cynicism appear to be increasing.

Of course, it would be facile to attribute such social negativism either wholly or even in significant part to negative political advertising, which is present in the environment for relatively brief periods, usually about every four years. While negative advertising has an impact on the electorate in the context of the campaign, no one suggests that its impact approaches this magnitude.[2] Rather, it appears that negative advertising is but one of many factors that contribute to an unflattering view of politicians and the process with which they are involved.

Because of Canada's proximity to the United States, what happens in that country is extensively covered on Canadian television news (Surlin et al. 1988, 468). In the context of American politics, we witnessed day after day the abasement of the highest elected leader stemming from the events of Watergate, which followed on the heels of the vice-president being hounded from office over charges of corruption. In more recent years, the Speaker of the House of Representatives was forced to resign in the face of charges that he had violated congressional conflict of interest and income guidelines.

In Canada, as well, we have seen ministers of the Crown driven from office on a seemingly continual basis as a result of charges of conflict of interest, violation of oaths of office, and personal scandal. Clearly, the behaviour of politicians themselves (i.e., the violation of public trust) constitutes a major contributing cause for their abysmal evaluation by citizens. The TV dramatization of the murder trial of Colin Thatcher (Saskatchewan MLA and son of a former premier) was a highly popular mini-series that generated a good deal of critical commentary.

Among other events, Canadian senators in the very recent past achieved what critics have on occasion observed about the political process: that the behaviour of politicians had reached a new low. Canadians, political partisanship aside, observed the senatorial behaviour concerning discussions on the Goods and Services Tax which among many viewers must have created sentiments ranging from acute embarrassment to complete disgust with the political process.

Another factor contributing to low citizen evaluation of politics and politicians is media coverage in news and public affairs reporting. The penchant for the media to cover the dramatic and the novel rather than the routine event provides a beginning point for understanding the media's preoccupation with negative news. Especially for television, which is fundamentally an entertainment medium, it is likely that the dramatic event will be selected for inclusion in a news program over another event which, while by objective criteria might be more "newsworthy" nevertheless lacks audience appeal. If a story lacks visual support material (for example, action), it is even less likely to make it into a news program, and if it does, it is less likely to be featured in a prominent position. Evidence for this evaluation of television news began to accumulate in the late 1960s and early 1970s, particularly with news coverage of the Vietnam War by U.S. television (Singer 1975), and is now the standard interpretation of television news (Taras 1990).

As well, severe constraints on time (the average television news story is 90 seconds long) (Taras 1990, 102) lead to a tendency to simplify complex events, often by turning them into personal conflicts. Thus, the multifaceted problems of national unity and Quebec separatism which faced the country in the late 1970s and early 1980s were often conveniently portrayed in the framework of a battle between Pierre Trudeau and René Lévesque. This approach was doubly appealing as both protagonists understood the television medium and tailored their behaviour accordingly. In the context of personal conflict, the negative comment or attack is an extremely powerful way of gaining media attention. For example, in a study of the 1988 U.S. presidential campaign, it was reported that 68 percent and 71 percent of news stories on Bush and Dukakis, respectively, were negative (*Broadcasting* 1988).

In Canadian campaigns, it has become apparent that the party leaders have eclipsed both their parties and substantive issues as the dominant focus of media attention (Soderlund et al. 1984); the "follow the leader" strategy more and more is the operative media mode of covering a campaign (Taras 1990, 154–67). In the 1988 U.S. campaign, Garrick Utley estimated that there were two minutes of candidate coverage for every minute of issue coverage (*Broadcasting* 1988). The past two Canadian elections (despite the issue of free trade) boiled down to "Mulroney versus Turner." Candidates, to gain television exposure, understand that they must conform to television's criteria for newsworthiness, i.e., the material should be dramatic, confrontational, epigrammatic (sound bites in the U.S. 1988 campaign averaged 9 seconds), and should be backed by appealing visuals. The result is a leader-oriented campaign that features attacks on the opposition.

In a study of leader images in the Canadian 1984 campaign, it was found that 84 percent of the valenced descriptive words and phrases used in reference to Mr. Turner were negative. While overall Mr. Mulroney came out about equal, in fact he had a positive balance of descriptors in the French-language media and a negative balance in the English-language media (Wagenberg et al. 1988, 124–25). Indeed, going back to the 1979 and 1980 campaigns, of all the major candidates, only Mr. Broadbent had what might be described as positive media coverage (Soderlund et al. 1984, 67–68, 87–90).

Preliminary analysis of a study done on words and phrases used in the *Globe and Mail* to describe parties and candidates in the 1990 Ontario election underscores the phenomenon of campaign negativism. Election stories in the *Globe and Mail* were analysed for the duration of the campaign. Descriptive words and phrases used for all parties and candidates were recorded and coded as positive, neutral or ambiguous, and negative. The incumbent Liberal party and Premier David Peterson both came under heavy fire in the *Globe and Mail* in news and editorial items and in the reporting of opposition candidates' views on the premier and his party. Analysis reveals the following pattern: the Liberal party – 80 percent of descriptors were negative, 18 percent either neutral or ambiguous, and 3 percent positive; David Peterson – 49 percent were negative, 28 percent neutral or ambiguous, and only 12 percent positive.

Examples of some of the descriptors used for Mr. Peterson demonstrate our point that press coverage of campaigns can be every bit as vicious as negative advertisements: "hiding the facts" and "cover-up" (both about the Starr case), "lying," "cynical," "desperate," "neither believed nor trusted," "resorting to the rhetoric of fear in a last-ditch stand to win support," "responsible [as premier] for the loss of thousands of jobs," and "no friend of people who own, drive or require an automobile." This, remember, is not language contained in the tabloid press but that found in "Canada's national newspaper."

We have presented data from election campaigns when rhetoric tends to be at its sharpest. We are aware of the importance of the continuing coverage of politics in the time between elections and are prepared to concede that media rhetoric between elections may not be as dramatic as the examples we have cited. At the same time, there is little doubt that the media do in fact select from the political debate environment and that they use expressions akin to those we have identified. As one of our interviewees commented on campaign coverage, "There just isn't much positive going on out there."

CANADIAN PRACTICE

Negative Advertising in Campaigns

It is widely believed that negative advertising is less commonly used in Canada because of perceptions that it does not work as well as it does in the United States (Taras 1990, 219–22). While there remains some evidence supporting this conclusion, the experiences with negative advertising in the 1988 campaign led a majority of those whom we interviewed to the conclusion that the generalization no longer holds true.[3] As one respondent told us, "All of us assumed that negative advertising wouldn't work in Canada. We were wrong – it works and we'll all use it." Another was even more graphic: "No negative advertising in the 1988 campaign – no Tory victory."

Thus, the 1988 campaign appears to have altered in a fundamental way some of the long-established unwritten rules by which the country's major political parties have carried out "warfare" in past campaigns. Throughout our interviews we were struck by the number of respondents who remarked, unprompted by our questions, that the "old rules" about what was permissible in campaigns, particularly campaign advertising, had been shattered. While not dismissing obvious sins of past campaigns ("red baiting" of the CCF/NDP, for example), a number of those whom we interviewed felt that they had been dealt low blows in the last campaign, and at least some looked forward to settling the score. According to one respondent, "We never believed anybody could stoop that low. We were wrong. We'll shoot first next time."

All political strategists we interviewed (save one) readily acknowledged that negative or attack ads historically have played a significant part in the ad campaign tactics of the three major parties. Furthermore, while most admitted some uneasiness or discomfort (one indicated a "sense of dishonesty") with using negative ads, all saw them as effective in the right circumstances; and, given those circumstances, virtually all saw an increase in the use of a clearly demonstrated successful tactic. None would hesitate to use negative advertising to win.

Advocacy group spokespersons regarded negative advertising first and foremost as a constitutional right (one indicating that the term meant free expression), which also happened to be both legitimate and effective in raising issues and linking these issues to particular parties and candidates (the phenomenon of "targeting"). Also, on those issues where there is unanimity among the three major parties, "advocacy groups will challenge the consensus," and "if something very important is wrong" will alert society about it through advertising. Party strategists tend to fear the uncontrolled entry of advocacy groups into the campaign environment, which until the Medhurst decision had been their exclusive turf. One evaluated advocacy groups as follows: "They are single-issue fanatics with no sense of self-restraint – their ads are smart, tough and good."

Interviews with both party and advocacy group strategists confirmed their sense of the sophistication of their modern campaign advertising. A party's advertising "frames the leader and the issues" and is, to a large extent, research driven. While we do not wish to equate the practice of politics with, say, brain surgery, those making important and expensive campaign decisions are not "flying by the seat of their pants." Although there are some variations among the practices of the major parties (and it appears that some interest groups operate to a greater extent on "feel") the six steps outlined below represent a composite picture of the relationship among the three major sets of actors involved in the process of creating campaign advertising: political strategists, pollsters and advertisers. Those familiar with product advertising will immediately recognize some unmistakable similarities: there does appear to be some truth to the lament that candidates are packaged and sold much like underarm deodorant. The six steps are as follows:

1. *Political Strategists/Pollsters* Political strategists commission pre-election polls to determine the relative standings of the parties,

"firmness" of voter support, and the areas of weakness and strength for all parties, leaders and issues.
2. *Political Strategists* Political strategists analyse survey data to determine their own strengths and weaknesses, as well as those of the opposition parties. Their own strengths are outlined to advertisers to frame their own campaign and their weaknesses to anticipate the campaigns that will be used against them by the opposition parties. (In some instances, opposition negative ads are actually scripted, so as to simulate the real campaign and thus prepare counterattacks.) Opponents' strengths and weaknesses are pinpointed to provide ideas to advertisers for negative ads, targeted at specific groups in the electorate as well as at the mass media.
3. *Advertisers* Advertisers, taking the ideas given them by political strategists, produce a number of 20- to 30-second spots (both positive and negative) aimed at tapping a core emotional response in a target group (for example, party loyalists or weak identifiers with another party).
4. *Advertisers/Political Strategists* Advertisers or political strategists pre-test a battery of ads in focus groups representing the targeted population. Some use this step as a "disaster check" to make sure that the ads will not result in self-inflicted wounds; others check each component of the ad to see why it works. The "boomerang effect" in negative advertising is well known, and steps are taken to avoid it.
5. *Advertisers* Advertisers buy time or space in appropriate media and schedule ads in the most effective time slots to reach various targeted groups.
6. *Pollsters* Pollsters track voter response to the ads and monitor the changing campaign environment for new issues or weaknesses to exploit with respect to the opposition (if, for example, an opposition candidate is losing credibility with a key sector of the electorate) or new "problems" that demand a change in campaign strategy or tactics (such as Mr. Turner's debate performance occasioned for the PC campaign in 1988).

If all of the pieces fit together, the result is a campaign decision-making process that has at its core the following three elements: "good data" regarding the concerns and moods of the electorate; creative advertising people who are able to exploit emotional uncertainties in the electorate; and campaign strategists capable of orchestrating the process and responding decisively and correctly to unanticipated changes of direction. For this last dimension, one strategist indicated that his job during a campaign consisted of making literally thousands of minor decisions regarding day-to-day tactics and perhaps three or four key strategic decisions. It was the latter that he felt he had better "get right."

Canadian-American Differences in Negative Advertising

While on most issues dealing with the use of negative advertising a remarkable consensus was apparent among our respondents, there was no unanimity on the question of how differences between the systems in the two countries might affect the use of the tactic.

The strongest argument offered as to why negative advertising was not as useful in the Canadian context centred on the nature of campaigns in a multi-party as opposed to a two-party system. Of primary importance here is that in a two-party system, campaigning is a zero sum game, in that if through negative ads you can convince voters not to vote for the other party, you benefit: either the votes are not cast, or the votes may be cast for your party (both desirable outcomes). In a multi-party race, however, the process is more complex, as two or more opponents have to figure in the calculation. First, it is more expensive to target two or more opponents, which would have to be the case if one were unsure of who was the major opponent. Second, one has to consider what voters "driven" from an opposition party are going to do. Here there are three alternatives: non-voting, voting for another opposition party and voting for your party. Given the dynamics of a particular election, only the third option is a sure bet (witness the tag line on Progressive Conservative commercials in the 1990 Ontario election, "If you're thinking of voting Liberal, think again"). While the message may have been effective, as voters clearly did think again, they did not vote in a way that benefited the sponsoring party. While we realize that in many regions of the country the major parties are not equally strong, nevertheless, in a campaign where more than two parties are competing, purely negative ads are not enough. It is necessary to offer positive alternatives that will cause voters disaffected by negative advertising to be attracted to the sponsoring party, not to an opposition party. Thus, a mix of negative and positive ads are required in Canadian campaigns.

There is, however, one aspect of parliamentary government, as opposed to the U.S. presidential system, that makes negative advertising potentially more effective in Canada. As we pointed out in the literature review, negative advertising now employs the strategy of undermining leader credibility, not through direct attacks on character but through issue-based ads. A characteristic of a parliamentary system is that parties and leaders are clearly associated with an issue (the Progressive Conservative party, for example, with free trade, Meech Lake and the GST). Thus, there is no easy way in the Canadian political system for a party to avoid the consequences of holding what may be unpopular stands on issues. The U.S. system, however, is characterized by such features as separation of powers, checks and balances and weaker party discipline; as one respondent indicated, "No one knows who is responsible for laws." It is possible for candidates to disassociate themselves from a policy by blaming another branch of government or party for what is bothering the electorate or by adopting an ambiguous or dishonest rhetorical position. Which candidate, for example, represented the anti-Vietnam War position in 1964 (Goldwater or Johnson), 1968 (Nixon or Humphrey) and 1972 (Nixon or McGovern)? U.S. presidential elections are notoriously ineffective in deciding policy.

A final factor needs to be explored in this discussion. First, there are simply many more election opportunities in the United States. The entire House of Representatives comes up for election every two years, as does one-third of the Senate. Perhaps more important is that individual members of Congress and senators run expensive media campaigns, featuring heavy volumes of negative advertising. This is not the case with individual ridings in Canada. Again, there are 50 U.S. states, as opposed to 10 Canadian provinces, in which elections are held that can feature negative advertising.

In assessing these arguments, it is our conclusion that the multi-party system in Canada, combined with differences in the number of elections, over the long run will tend to mitigate the worst excesses of negative advertising as seen in the United States. However, this conclusion is tempered by the judgement of our respondents that third-party advertising, which is just beginning to be felt in Canada, will be heavily weighted in the negative direction. Moreover, with the clear attachment of parties to issues in the Canadian context, it will be extremely difficult for parties and candidates to disassociate themselves from unpopular policies.

Long-Term Effects
Will long-term societal and political harm result from negative political advertising? While most of our interview group admitted that there was at least a plausible link, few would go beyond that position, and no one believed that a link could be demonstrated in empirical research. The world of politics, our respondents felt, is concerned, after all, with winning the next election and thus gaining power: visions of "effects" tend to be constrained within these parameters.

VIEWS ON REGULATORY OPTIONS

Political-Party Advertising

All but two respondents expressed views that advertising (negative and positive) on the part of political parties should not be subject to any greater regulation than is currently called for in the *Canada Elections Act* and CRTC guidelines; that is, restrictions on expenditures, allocation of broadcasting time, and periods during the campaign in which advertising is not permitted. Most felt that the worst excesses of negative advertising by political parties would be adequately controlled through self-regulation. The comments we recorded on this issue include references to an élite political culture ("There is a reluctance in Canada to get down into the gutter") and a clear realization that a negative ad campaign involves playing with dynamite ("Using a negative spot badly is the most disastrous self-inflicted wound possible" and "Tasteless negative ads will kill you"). Two of those whom we interviewed suggested that regulations were needed for the content of negative ads in particular, but since these restrictions would apply to third-party advertisers as well, we shall consider them within that context.

Third-Party Advertising

Most of our respondents, when questioned on their views toward possible regulation of negative advertising, focused on the question of its use by third-party advocacy groups, which were seen to be "single-issue fanatics" who had no ties to the preservation of the political system. With respect to the regulation of third-party advertising, we can distinguish three positions.

The Libertarian or "Free-Fire Zone" Model

The first position, advanced primarily by third-party spokespersons, was that there should be no restrictions on participation in the electoral process by parties, interest groups or individuals. Before the introduction of third-party advertising, it was pointed out, political parties virtually controlled the electoral agenda. In such a situation, when there is unanimity among the three major parties on a question, the electorate is cheated as there is no "market-place competition." Third-party advocacy groups thus function within a classic "libertarian" interpretation of the political process. There is a strong sentiment among those associated with advocacy groups in favour of seeing this model continue in Canada, and there is no doubt that any attempts to regulate this would be challenged vigorously in the courts. The logical extension of this argument is that any existing regulations on advertising by political parties should also be abolished, although we must point out that no one explicitly brought up this point. In effect, this model would result in what one respondent described uncharitably as a "free-fire zone" of campaign advertising.

Regulatory Models
A significant number of party strategists argued for the regulation of third-party advertising by making the regulations currently in effect for political parties also apply to third parties. Two suggested strategies to regulate the content of advertising, regardless of whether it was produced by parties or by advocacy groups.

The regulation of advocacy groups through their registration under the *Canada Elections Act* and the enforcement of time and financial limits tended to have special appeal to Progressive Conservative strategists, who were concerned with the implications for freedom of expression stemming from a complete ban on third-party advertising. Arguments were offered that third parties should register under the *Canada Elections Act* and be subject to budgetary limits, disclosure of contributors and the obligation to file reports with the chief electoral officer or the broadcasting arbitrator. These regulations, it was argued, would "level the playing field" between parties and advocacy groups, while protecting the rights of citizens and groups to participate fully in the electoral process. Critics of this approach argued that such regulations could easily be circumvented through the multiplication of the number of groups registered (i.e., rather than registering one group concerned with an issue, five might be registered with different names and officers, thus increasing by a factor of five the amount of money that could be spent). As one respondent pointed out, "vocal special interest groups will always find a way to voice their concerns."

A second regulatory approach, related to the content of advertising, argues that the focus of regulation should not be on controlling the groups allowed to advertise, but rather on policing what is contained in advertising and how it is expressed.

Two specific proposals were advanced in this regard. The first proposed the creation of an Elections Communication Commission, envisioned as a blue-ribbon panel composed of experts in the field with impeccable credentials. All election ads (both party and advocacy group) would be submitted to this panel in advance of showing in order to be evaluated on the criterion of decency and cleared for use. The second content control proposal called for the creation of an "election advertising adjudicator" to whom parties aggrieved by negative ads could lodge complaints after the offending ad had been shown.

The adjudicator would have the power to withdraw the ad. In both instances the institutions proposed are new, and the question of whether they would function under the authority of the *Canada Elections Act* or the CRTC was not raised.

Arguments in favour of controls on content of advertising focused on the widespread existence of controls already in use in the advertising industry (food, pharmaceuticals, liquor and tobacco, for example), on the harm that negative advertising was perceived to have caused to public attitudes toward the political process and on the need to avoid further degradation. Good taste, it was pointed out, was unlikely to emerge on its own: one respondent indicated that no matter how mean-spirited an ad, "someone out there would make [use of] it."

Detractors of the content regulation proposals (and there were many) argued the virtual impossibility of defining in a precise way what negative advertising is. We were repeatedly asked for our definition of the term. When we replied, "Ads which focus on opposition parties and candidates in an unfavourable light," we would be asked, "What about critical advertising?"... "What about comparative advertising?"... "What about hard-hitting advertising?" Or we would be offered a sample script and asked whether we thought it fitted within the definition. Dr. Garramone reflected the same attitude when she said she felt that content regulation stood little chance of success because of the problems involved in defining negative advertising (1990). One respondent argued, in effect, that really good negative ads were made in such a way as not to appear negative.

What became apparent to us rather quickly was that negative advertising, as a generic term, is seen as a device which, if used properly in a political campaign, is tremendously powerful. Few were prepared to give it up. Negative ads, however, tended to be defined subjectively as those that were used against you, while the terms "hard-hitting ads" and "critical ads" tended to be applied to those that you yourself used in a legitimate way against the opposition. When pressed, most agreed that negativism was in the eye of the beholder. In addition, arguments were raised as to "who was going to be Solomon" in the process of determining what ads could or could not be run. Strategies of blitzing negative ads just before the election would serve largely to circumvent the power of the "election advertising adjudicator." In summary, most felt that proposals to regulate the content of ads "just wouldn't work."

Banning Third-Party Advertising

The final position on third-party advertising, that which tended to appeal to Liberal and NDP strategists, was, as one respondent put it, to "ban the buggers" during the campaign period. Another strategist we interviewed was only slightly less emphatic: "I hate it and I would want it banned." Arguments favouring the banning option focused on the Medhurst decision (*National Citizens' Coalition* 1984), which most felt should have been appealed – and that if it had been, it would have been overturned.

With respect to infringement of free speech, the argument was made that advocacy groups had total freedom to speak and advertise their points of view during noncampaign periods, that is, between elections, and that a ban on their advertising for about a four-week period about every four years simply could not be seen to be a major denial of freedom of expression. Moreover, it was argued that as third-party advertising was unrestricted while party advertising was restricted, real harm resulted from it. For example, a third-party advocacy group could advertise for the first 28 days of a campaign that "a candidate wasn't fit to sleep with pigs" and, as the law is now written, the candidate could not respond to such charges except through another advocacy group.

Also, it was pointed out that elections could be "bought" by those with the greatest resources (Canadian business), and that the single-issue interest groups could flood the campaign with emotional single-issue ads (on abortion, for example), thus distorting political reality, which tends to be multi-issued and complex. It was argued as well that banning really did not mean banning, since if advocacy groups wanted to advertise, it was not an unreasonable expectation that they would organize as political parties and register their intent with the chief electoral officer. In that status, they could participate on equal terms with their political opponents. In 1988 there were 14 registered political parties participating in the election, some being mainstream parties, while the majority were single-issue registrants.

In summary, the consensus among the group we interviewed about the regulation of negative advertising was as follows. There was little sentiment for greater regulation of advertising on the part of political parties. However, most wanted either restrictions on third-party advertising to level the playing field between political parties and advocacy groups (which was perceived to have been tilted unfairly to the disadvantage of political parties following the Medhurst decision) or the outright banning of third-party advertising during political campaigns.

CONCLUSION

There is a strong temptation on our part to link negative advertising to undesirable effects in society, in particular to the evident low level of regard in which Canadians hold politicians, political parties and the political process. However strong our feelings in this matter may be, we are obliged to echo the advice of one of the most experienced social science researchers in the area of negative advertising, that "it is hard to measure the more general effects of negative advertising on attitudes toward politicians and the political process" (Garramone 1990). A unilateral link has not been found in the research literature.

The great majority of those whom we interviewed, while acknowledging problems with negative advertising, clearly were not willing to give it up, nor were they even willing to entertain the thought of serious restrictions on its use. Political campaigns in Canada, our respondents felt, will feature more negative advertising than seen so far. However, for the reasons we have indicated, the proportional amount of negative advertising will not likely approach that seen in the United States. While self-regulation certainly can be oversold,[4] it does appear to us that all three major Canadian political parties are concerned with the boomerang effect. Canadian society is arguably more civil and polite ("kinder and gentler") than is the case in the United States, and given this situation, it will most likely be the goal of the political parties, as one respondent phrased it, to be "tastefully vicious" in their advertising. Unfortunately, the same set of restraints does not appear to apply equally to third-party advocacy advertising.

ABBREVIATIONS

Alta. L.R. (2d)	Alberta Law Reports, Second Series
c.	chapter
R.S.C.	Revised Statutes of Canada

NOTES

This study was completed in January 1991.

In compiling this review of the literature, we were assisted by Jean Pignal, an MA political science graduate of the University of Windsor. We gratefully acknowledge his contribution, as without his help we could not have completed the study on schedule.

1. At present, Quebec, Saskatchewan and Nova Scotia are the only Canadian provinces in which third-party advertising is restricted. Quebec is considered to be the most restrictive while Saskatchewan is regarded as the least restrictive (see Hiebert 1991). Under the Quebec legislation, third parties are prevented – directly or indirectly – from spending money to

promote a political party or cause during a campaign. Only a candidate or an official agent can authorize such expenses. Representatives of Quebec's federation of labour and largest employer group both claim to live happily with the law (*Gazette* 1988).

2. Interesting research on long-term effects of television more generally has been undertaken by George Gerbner and colleagues, particularly on the impact of televised violence. The central thesis emerging from this work is that those who tend to be heavy television watchers are also likely to develop beliefs that are consistent with those found in television content. It is in this sense that television content is said to "cultivate" attitudes (Gerbner et al. 1980).

3. In all, 19 interviews were conducted for the study with political strategists (both party and advocacy group), advertisers and pollsters. These were done from the middle of September to the end of October 1990. Seventeen of these interviews were conducted in person and two on the telephone. There were five others on our interview list. Three declined our request for an interview, while two were out of the country during the time we had allocated for doing the interviews. In-person interviews without exception were substantial, all lasting at least an hour, with many stretching to 90 minutes. Our thanks go to all those who shared their views with us: their names are listed following these notes. About half stipulated that the interview would be granted only on the condition of confidentiality. Since the total number of respondents is so limited, to fulfil that commitment we have deleted all identification of specific views. We felt that all respondents were remarkably forthcoming with their views on negative advertising and we owe them a huge debt of gratitude for their time and candour. Given the mandate of the study, the views of those we interviewed are in no way to be seen as representative of all Canadian society or of other élite sectors of society. Our purpose in seeking out particular people to interview was to ascertain and analyse views of those intimately and professionally involved in political campaigns.

4. David Broder points out the apparent failure of self-regulation in the United States, in that the American Association of Political Consultants has never seen fit to discipline a member for violating its code of ethics, which forbids members from intentionally disseminating "false or misleading information" and/or from "indulging in any activity which corrupts or degrades the practice of political campaigning" (cited in Hill 1989).

INTERVIEWS

Adams, Michael, Environics Inc., Toronto, 21 September 1990.

Atkins, Norman K., senator, Ottawa, 18 October 1990.

Bowles, Patricia, Martland Group, Toronto, 28 September 1990.

Bozinoff, Lorne, Gallup Canada, Toronto, 12 October 1990.

Corbin, Ruth, Angus Reid Group, Toronto, 28 September 1990.

Fingerhut, Vic, Fingerhut Madison Opinion Research, Washington, 22 October 1990, by telephone.

Garramone, Gina, East Lansing, Michigan, 17 September 1990.

Goldfarb, Martin, Goldfarb Consultants, Toronto, 11 October 1990.

Kaplansky, Ron, RK Studios Ltd., Toronto, 21 September 1990.

Kirby, Michael J., senator, Ottawa, 18 October 1990.

Knight, William, Ottawa, 20 October 1990.

Laschinger, John, PC Ontario, Toronto, 25 October 1990.

MacDonald, Donald, Ontario Election Finances Commission, Toronto, 11 October 1990.

MacIntosh, Peter, Gallup Canada, Toronto, 12 October 1990.

Mason, Julie, Toronto, 12 October 1990.

Near, Harry, Ottawa, 23 October 1990, by telephone.

O'Malley, Terrence, Vickers and Benson Advertising, Toronto, 21 October 1990.

Somerville, David, National Citizens' Coalition, Toronto, 20 September 1990.

Young, Dennis, Public Affairs International, Toronto, 27 September 1990.

REFERENCES

Blumler, Jay. 1987. "Election Communication and the Democratic Political System." In *Political Communication Research: Approaches, Studies, Assessments*, ed. D. Paletz. Norwood, NJ: Ablex.

Bozinoff, Lorne, and Peter MacIntosh. 1988. "Canadians Oppose Negative Advertising." *Gallup Canada*. Toronto: Gallup Canada Inc., 17 Nov.

Broadcasting. 1988. "Accentuate the Negative, Eliminate the Positive." 31 Oct., 27–29.

Broder, David. 1990. "Savvy Voters Are Rejecting Negatives, Demanding Honesty from Their Leaders." *Detroit Free Press*, 5 Sept., 9A.

Calamai, Peter. 1987. "5 Million of Us Can't Read." *Windsor Star*, 12 Sept., A12.

Canada. *Canada Elections Act*, R.S.C. 1985, c. E-2.

Canadian Radio-television and Telecommunications Commission. 1977. *Advocacy Advertising Seminar*. Ottawa: CRTC.

Colford, Steven. 1986. "POLLS Accentuate Negative." *Advertising Age* 57 (3): 104.

Devlin, L. Patrick. 1989. "Contrasts in Presidential Campaign Commercials of 1988." *American Behavioral Scientist* 32:389–414.

Diamond, Edwin, and Stephen Bates. 1984. *The Spot: The Rise of Political Advertising on Television*. Cambridge: MIT Press.

Edmonds, Patricia. 1990. "Political Ads Turn off Voters." *Detroit Free Press*, 28 Sept., 1A, 14A.

Garramone, Gina. 1984. "Voter Responses to Negative Political Ads." *Journalism Quarterly* 61:250–59.

Garramone, Gina, Charles Atkin, Bruce Pinkleton and Richard Cole. 1990. "Effects of Negative Political Advertising on the Political Process." Paper presented at the Association for Education in Journalism and Mass Communications (AEJMC) Conference, Minneapolis.

Gazette (Montreal). 1988. "Quebec's Third Party Spending Ban Unique." 29 Aug., A4.

Gerbner, George, Larry Gross, Michael Morgan and Nancy Signorielli. 1980. "The Mainstreaming of America: Violence Profile No.11." *Journal of Communication* 30 (3): 10–29.

Globe and Mail. 1990. "Political Discontent." 29 Oct., A7.

Hart, Roderick P. 1982. "A Commentary on Popular Assumptions About Political Communication." *Human Communication Research* 8:366–79.

Hiebert, Janet. 1991. "Interest Groups and Canadian Federal Elections." In *Interest Groups and Elections in Canada*, ed. F. Leslie Seidle. Vol. 2 of the research studies of the Royal Commission on Electoral Reform and Party Financing. Ottawa and Toronto: RCERPF/Dundurn.

Hill, Ronald P. 1989. "An Exploration of Voter Responses to Political Advertisements." *Journal of Advertising* 18 (4): 14–22.

Johnson-Cartee, Karen S., and Gary Copeland. 1989. "Southern Voters' Reaction to Negative Political Ads in 1986 Election." *Journalism Quarterly* 66:888–93, 986.

Kaid, Lynda. 1981. "Political Advertising." In *Handbook of Political Communication*, ed. D. Nimmo and K. Sanders. Beverly Hills: Sage Publications.

Kaid, Lynda, and John Boydson. 1987. "An Experimental Study of the Effectiveness of Negative Political Advertisements." *Communication Quarterly* 35:193–201.

Kern, Montague. 1989. *30-Second Politics: Political Advertising in the Eighties*. New York: Praeger.

Louden, Allan. 1990. "Transformation of Issue to Image and Presence: Eliciting Character Evaluations in Negative Spot Advertising." Paper presented at the International Communication Association (ICA) Conference, Dublin, Ireland.

Lowery, Shearon A., and Melvin L. DeFleur. 1988. *Milestones in Mass Communication Research*. 2d ed. New York: Longman.

Merritt, Sharyn. 1984. "Negative Political Advertising: Some Empirical Findings." *Journal of Advertising* 13:27–38.

Meyer, Philip. 1985. *The Newspaper Survival Book: An Editor's Guide to Marketing Research*. Bloomington: Indiana University Press.

National Citizens' Coalition Inc./Coalition nationale des citoyens inc. v. Canada (Attorney General), [1984], 32 Alta. L.R. (2d) 249 (Q.B.).

Nugent, J.F. 1987. "Positively Negative." *Campaigns and Elections* 7:47–49.

Peers, Frank. 1969. *The Politics of Canadian Broadcasting, 1920–1951*. Toronto: University of Toronto Press.

Pfau, Michael, and Michael Burgoon. 1989. "The Efficacy of Issue and Character Attack Message Strategies in Political Campaign Communication." *Communication Reports* 2:53–61.

Richey, Marjorie H., Robert J. Koenigs, Harold W. Richey and Richard Fortin. 1975. "Negative Salience in Impressions of Character: Effects of Unequal Proportions of Positive and Negative Information." *Journal of Social Psychology* 97:233–41.

Roddy, Brian, and Gina Garramone. 1988. "Appeals and Strategies of Negative Political Advertising." *Journal of Broadcasting and Electronic Media* 32:415–27.

Sabato, Larry. 1981. *The Rise of Political Consultants*. New York: Basic Books.

Singer, Benjamin. 1975. "Violence, Protest, and War in Television News: The U.S. and Canada Compared." In *Communications in Canadian Society*. 2d ed., ed. B. Singer. Toronto: Copp Clark.

Smith, Vivian. 1990. "4 Million Adults 'at Risk' of Illiteracy, Study Shows." *Globe and Mail*, 1 June, A4.

Soderlund, Walter, Walter Romanow, E. Donald Briggs and Ronald Wagenberg. 1984. *Media and Elections in Canada*. Toronto: Holt, Rinehart and Winston.

Stewart, C. J. 1975. "Voter Perceptions of Mudslinging in Political Communication." *Central States Speech Journal* 26:279–86.

Surlin, Stuart, Walter Romanow and Walter Soderlund. 1988. "TV Network News: A Canadian-American Comparison." *American Review of Canadian Studies* 18:465–75.

Sutter, Stan. 1990. "Nonreaders Uneducated Slobs? Nonsense." *Marketing* 95 (4 June): 14.

Taras, David. 1990. *The Newsmakers: The Media's Influence on Canadian Politics*. Scarborough: Nelson Canada.

Television/Radio Age. 1988. "Gauging TV's Influence on Voters: Debates, Negative Ads and Personality." 13 June, 34.

Wagenberg, Ronald, Walter Soderlund, Walter Romanow and E. Donald Briggs. 1988. "Campaigns, Images and Polls: Mass Media Coverage of the 1984 Canadian Election." *Canadian Journal of Political Science* 30:117–29.

Will, George. 1989. "The Pollution of Politics: Just When You Think You Thought It Was Safe to Turn the TV Back On – THEY'RE BACK! Negative Ads." *Newsweek* 6 Nov., 92.

Windsor Star. 1990. "Survey Impotent, Poll on Polls Shows." 5 June, A2.

Wright, John, Willis Winter, Sherilyn Zeigler and P. Noel O'Neal. 1984. *Advertising, First Canadian Edition*. Toronto: McGraw-Hill Ryerson.

5

CITIZENSHIP AND EQUITY
Variations across Time and in Space

Jane Jenson

CITIZENSHIP IS ONE of the most contested concepts in political thought. Because the concept organizes popular understandings of the relationship between the individual and the state, it has served as a principle for the mobilization of actions both for and against innumerable regimes. At the same time, claims in the name of citizenship have been made by all groups as they attempt to gain access to the political process. Moreover, contestation around such rights occurs precisely at those moments when the relationship between the citizen and the state is undergoing substantial alteration. Therefore, while all liberal democracies have followed a trajectory toward universal suffrage and the extension of citizens' rights, there have been significant variations in the ways and the extent to which such rights have actually been achieved in each country.

Citizenship does not have the same characteristics everywhere; while all states identify some individuals as members, the specificity of the definition of the nation and the representation of constitutive groups have differed in important ways throughout history and around the world. There have, however, been some common practices. Since the French Revolution, one philosophical basis for citizenship has been the notion of the reciprocal rights and obligations of citizens and the state. Citizenship has entailed a guarantee of protection against state interference for individuals and groups. Simultaneously, citizenship has also reposed upon the notion of equality of rights, with the state as guarantor.

It is this tension between *limits on the state* and *need for the state* in definitions of citizenship that first gave life to another fundamental concept of liberal democracy considered here, that of equity. From the beginning, it has been recognized that the principle of liberty, which imposes limits on state interference, may itself generate inequality. Moreover, equality rights formally guaranteed in law may not actually be fair in their effects. Thus, for both these reasons, definitions of citizenship have been modified by considerations of equity.

Equity principles involve a recourse to the principles of justice in order to correct or supplement some of the unequal effects of both liberty itself and the actual impact of legal guarantees of equality. The application of principles of fairness, involving rectification of weaknesses in law and justice due to their general nature, permits the application of the intent of those principles to meet the needs of specific cases. As a result of stressing rectification for specific citizens or categories of citizens, the concept of equity invokes the need for state regulation in order to achieve fairness.[1] Therefore, while basic concepts of citizenship necessitate both limits on state intervention and state guarantees, concerns about equity are more likely to lead to regulation because neither complete liberty nor formally defined equality rights alone can actually achieve the goals embedded in definitions of citizenship. It is, moreover, partly this concern with equity that gave rise to the concept of collective solidarity, a concept which also forms some societies' understanding of citizenship.

If equity is linked to definitions of citizenship in this way, it is obvious that the principles upon which the state acts in the name of equity will also vary across space and time. Such principles have meaning only in particular representational systems precisely because the notion of what is a "just outcome" can exist only in relation to societally designated desirable ends.

The rest of this study elaborates this approach to citizenship and its equity concerns. First, it sketches some of the general elements that have formed the definitions of citizenship. While Athenian democracy had a clear conception of citizens' rights and responsibilities, and these have helped to form subsequent understandings, modern citizenship dates from the 18th century. Therefore, the next section focuses on the legacy of the French Revolution's contribution of three basic elements of citizenship: liberty, equality and fraternity.

Next, as a result of the theoretical perspective described here of the variations across space and time in the very definition of citizenship, the bulk of the study analyses how these three elements of citizenship have been represented in Canada since 1867. This study identifies two basic notions of Canadian citizenship – one labelled place-sensitive and the other, nationwide – and describes the underpinnings of these representations in Canadian society and politics. Each of these definitions was accompanied by its own understanding of equity. Place-sensitive citizenship invoked equity claims for regions, while nationwide citizenship called for equity for individuals.

The last section of the study describes how the postwar understanding of nationwide citizenship has begun to crumble in the face of newly mobilized demands by collectivities for a less universalistic understanding of citizenship and for categorial equity.

DEFINITIONS OF CITIZENSHIP: SOME FUNDAMENTAL TENSIONS

The concept of citizenship has a long, often contested history, and has provided the backdrop to many political disputes because any definition of citizenship establishes the boundaries of social inclusion and exclusion. In other words, in its most fundamental sense, citizenship is about access. As such, it provides a clear statement of any society's definition of self, the way it represents itself both to itself and to others.

Since the time of ancient Greece there have been discussions of – and therefore struggle over – who is a member of the community and who is a citizen. The question is, who belongs? And even more importantly, how does such "belonging" translate into everyday political practice? Posing such questions raises the issue of power. Because the answers determine who will be powerful enough to deploy the resources of the state in the name of the population, definitions of who is on the inside and who is excluded have been central topics of political controversy in many situations.

In such struggles, there have always been proponents of the notion that belonging involves rights. Every citizen enjoys the rights of membership. Yet, from the beginning, many people have also promoted the notion that rights can exist only in relationship to reciprocal duties, because membership implies membership in a community that is greater than the sum of its individual parts. Therefore, a notion of collectivity is embedded at the heart of most understandings of citizenship.

Finally, conceptualizations of citizenship have included notions that formal rights are meaningless if they are not somehow translated into meaningful participation in the community (Hall and Jacques 1990, 175). This third criterion provides a justification for testing the appropriateness of the balance between rights and duties, as well as measuring the effects of that balance. Thereby, the space for considerations of equity comes into being.

Historical studies of citizenship find the concept present at least since the time of Athenian democracy. The criterion used in Athens to confer citizenship was the capacity to govern and be governed. That society's definition of who was capable of politics was, of course, extremely narrow, being based on full ownership of property.[2] Property ownership created political capacity because it freed time from manual labour for participation in decision making. Free time enabled citizens to undertake the responsibilities and privileges of governing.

Nevertheless, despite the very high threshold set for access to citizenship in Athenian democracy, entry to the charmed circle continued to involve a commitment to equal participation in the benefits and burdens of self-government. Thus, citizenship implied equality. The classic statement of principle is in Pericles' famous funeral speech extolling Athenian democracy. As he said: "No one, so long as he has it in him to be of service to the state, is kept in political obscurity because of poverty."[3] This statement reveals both a commitment to equality and a recognition of its fragility. From the beginning, then, there was philosophical attention paid to the limits to participation that might come from an unequal distribution of resources, or the differential status that might be attributed because of resources.

Such concerns provided the rationale for state action in the name of fairness. The first Athenian solution to the potentially negative effects of differential access and influence within the political process was to limit the definition of citizenship to those least likely to encounter such encumbrances – that is, those who already enjoyed equal status (free, Athenian-born males). These Greeks also clearly recognized that more positive steps were necessary. The rules of Athenian democracy guaranteed rotation in office, short terms in positions of authority, and payment for public services (Held 1987, 34 and chap. 1 passim). All of these measures were designed to ensure that the principles of self-government would be translated into fair practices by regulating the negative effects of wealth and social prestige.

We see, then, in the very first society to link citizenship and democracy, the centrality of the notion of equality. Yet, in order to be a citizen, one had already to be considered "equal"; thus citizens' social situations affected their political capacity. Moreover, it was the task of the state to guarantee the maintenance and realization of participation through the rules and regulations it established in the name of fairness.

Citizenship as a practical idea fell onto harder times with the rise of the Roman Empire and then the growing hegemony of Christian thought and practices.[4] Indeed, the concept as we now think of it is essentially a modern one. When resurrected in the 18th century, citizenship formed an essential concept in liberal thought. There were debates over the practices of citizenship, and different meanings were forged out of efforts to create a commonsensical understanding of the vast social changes that reshaped the face of Europe as capitalism transformed economies and as the drive for political rights remade state institutions. Therefore, while its philosophical roots might be traced to Athenian practices, it is most appropriate to discuss citizenship in terms of post-Enlightenment politics.

It is both impossible and irrelevant here to provide a historical account of the numerous philosophical and political controversies about how the principle of citizenship developed (Moore 1966; Macpherson 1977; Held 1987). I will, instead, simply assert the "modern" character of the discourse and use the famous phrase of the French Revolution – the event that gave us the Declaration of the Rights of Man and the Citizen and a commitment to liberty, equality and fraternity – to illustrate the inescapable tensions that have been at the centre of much of political thought about citizenship since the 18th century and that continue to bedevil our reform efforts today.

The concept of the citizen as we use it today depends upon the achievement of three large social changes that worked themselves out in western Europe after 1500. First, citizenship based on liberty and equality could exist only in a context in which hierarchical forms of social organization, such as feudalism, had lost most of their legitimacy. This change permitted the legitimization of horizontal and universalistic social relations, and at the same time, it created a political discourse within which the excluded could make claims for access. Those who were denied citizenship on the basis of lingering hierarchical criteria had a language with which to demand entry.[5] Thus, workers and those who did not own property in the 19th century could mount claims for civil, political and social rights as the fixed categories of feudalism's societal maps crumbled and were replaced by the more fluid ones of market relations and free-waged labour.

Secularization was the second important factor in the move toward modern citizenship. It carved out a public space that was not subject to the laws of the church and in which political identity was not reduced to religious identity. With a growing freedom of belief and choice, religion-based prohibitions on political rights crumbled: for example, Jews could make claims for access to citizenship. Only much later, however, did Catholic definitions of society – which kept women hidden in the family – weaken so that women in Catholic countries could join their Protestant sisters in demanding equality before the law (Jenson 1989b, 247–48). Indeed, the development of a nonparticularistic, nonascriptive, and formally rational legal system was the third change that made it possible for actors first to imagine the notion of citizenship and then to argue over who belonged within its boundaries.

The ringing rhetoric of Liberty, Equality and Fraternity announced France's move to abolish the remnants of feudalism, to establish free movement of goods and persons according to the practices of market exchange, to separate church and state, and indeed, to remake all social relations. The enunciation of this transition in the Declaration of the Rights of Man and the Citizen also reflected a movement toward a codification and legalization of principles, the third important social change. If the French Revolution invented the modern concept of *citoyen* and *citoyenne*, it also incorporated, in its very statement of principle, the tensions that now reside at the heart of modern citizenship. Such tensions, in turn, meant that concerns about equity would exist at the heart of this citizenship.

The first of the three – liberty – represented the consolidation in Western thought of the idea of the sovereign individual. Once 17th- and 18th-century liberalism had constituted the individual as the primary social unit, attention to protecting individual rights from excessive social, public and – above all – state intervention grew. Of primary concern was the establishment of a sphere of freedom from interference within which enlightened self-interest could be pursued. By placing liberty first in their trinity, the revolutionaries claimed their 18th-century inheritance and banished notions of feudal social relations, divine right of kings, and autocratic states.

Nevertheless, the extension of market relations – and thus the philosophical and spatial separation of the spheres of politics, economics and the social – also forced several issues onto the agenda. If the economic realm was one of self-interest, and if the social (sometimes termed the private) was the realm of higher virtue, it fell to politics to act as a check on the spill-over effects of each. Therefore, it became a question of how to sustain government and what form it ought to take. Evident, for example, in Madison's horror of factions is the fear of unlimited, unrestrained pursuit of self-interest, as well as of unrestricted democracy.[6] Jeremy Bentham and James Mill were able to overcome these fears, by developing a theory of democracy that tempered the effects of unrestrained liberty by institutional means, and set out a theory of "protective democracy," or limited democracy (Macpherson 1977, chap. 2; Held 1987, 60ff.).

For Bentham and Mill, the tyranny of the majority could only be controlled by careful constitutional design and a restricted franchise in a representative government. In this way, the accountability of the governors to the governed would be assured, and the dangers of arbitrariness would be reduced. The free market and the free vote went hand in hand to assure maximum well-being. Indeed, it was their simultaneity that provided the uniqueness of English 19th-century liberalism. Civil society required some freedom from state interference, but regulation was appropriate to provide security, to produce abundance, to favour equality, and to maintain security.[7]

English and American liberalism recognized, as did the Declaration of the Rights of Man and the Citizen, then, that complete liberty was neither a viable nor a desirable goal. Moreover, it recognized the effects of the unequal distribution of wealth and power in the realm of politics. Thus, such liberals were concerned to couple freedom with some attention to equality before the law, to equality of access, and to equality of rights, all elements of the definition of citizenship visible in the French Revolution's rallying cry. Commitment to liberty would be tempered by a commitment to equality of all citizens. With this pairing came the long dispute over who would be represented as a citizen and thereby gain access to equality rights. Individualism, and the concepts of the liberty of individuals, did not provide a unique set of answers to that question. A different set of philosophical principles was needed in order to address the complexities of the equality issue.

Without entering into all the convolutions, it is important to identify several competing notions of equality. A Kantian commitment to ontological equality generated few disputes because it was more a theological statement of principle than a practical social theory (Turner 1986, 113). Much more controversial in the discussions of equality was the distinction between equality of opportunity and equality of condition or outcome. If a liberal society, by its very nature, generated individuals with unequal endowments and resources, the immediate question was how to reinstate a meaningful form of political equality. Was it sufficient to open the gates and allow everyone the same chance to enter the field, or was it necessary to do more by taking positive action to ensure equality of results? Different philosophical traditions have answered this question by choosing one or another of the alternatives.

Despite the variety, however, in both these conceptions of equality we see the idea that society consists of more than sovereign individuals endowed with rights; it is also a collectivity that can express responsibilities for guaranteeing equality. The third term of the triptych – fraternity – expresses this goal of collective responsibility, not only in order to achieve equality of opportunity or condition but also in recognition of the organic qualities of society and the benefits of solidarity. By including this third term, it became possible to temper claims to liberal individualism in the name of both state action to guarantee equality and collective goals that might be other than simply the aggregation of individual interests.

In the rhetoric of the French Revolution, we see the complexity of the new notions of citizenship being invented at that time. From the beginning, citizenship involved an area free of the state (liberty) as well as an ill-defined terrain upon which state action was legitimate, and indeed necessary, in order to temper the effects of unrestrained liberty in the name of the equivalently valid goals of equality and solidarity. A consequence of the tripartite definition of citizenship was that it also created the possibility of state actions in the name of equity. Formal, even legal, guarantees of liberty and equality might be found insufficient when measured against alternative definitions of equality or against the goal of fraternity.[8]

Given the potential gap between formal rights and actual outcomes, the very definition of citizenship constituted in any society thus generated equity concerns and called forth discussions of the role of the state in regulating political practice with respect to both representation and rights.[9] Nineteenth-century attention to education-for-citizenship and to the right to collective action were followed in the 20th century by extended attention to the impact of wealth on representation and the inequitable distribution of resources. Then, by the end of the century, equity concerns also often implied state efforts to include groups – like women and minorities – systematically excluded by societal mechanisms of discrimination or by the actions of political actors.

All of this attention to equity was designed to increase equality and to realize solidarity in the name of a fully meaningful citizenship, even if such actions meant narrowing somewhat the sphere of unrestrained liberty.[10] Behind such equity concerns, we can see the fundamental question of citizenship – that is, the definition of who belongs and who has access to, and will benefit from, full citizenship rights. This question has been answered in different ways in every society because it involves finding, through real political practices, the exact social meanings of the three elements of the definition and employing the power of the state to regulate the mix in order to achieve each society's definition of fairness.

THE POWER OF DISCOURSE: DISPUTING CITIZENSHIP

The foregoing comments on citizenship and equity illustrate the general principles disputed in several countries since at least 1789. They remain, nevertheless, generalities until they can be concretized as reflections of political conflict and power in specific times and places.[11] To understand how the meanings of citizenship and concerns about fairness actually intersect, it is necessary to examine the weight given to each of the three elements in specific times and places. To do so, we need some concepts for understanding how the variations in the meanings and practices of citizenship came to exist. These can then be employed for an analysis of the Canadian experience.

Politics in any country is not simply a debate over who gets what, when and how; but, equally important, it is also a discussion about the boundaries of politics and about how politics should be conducted. As such, politics provides a definition of the kinds of conflicts that it can resolve as well as a designation of the actors involved. Such a perspective allows us to define politics as actors' efforts to carve out a constituency for themselves by mobilizing support for their preferred formulation of their own collective identity (and often that of their protagonists) and for the enumeration of their interests, which follow from that collective identity. This definition of politics depends upon an understanding of the dual aspects of representation.[12] One aspect of representation involves an actor's *representation of self* to others via a collective identity. The second, familiar from the language of liberal democracy, is the *representation of interests*. These two aspects of representation are closely linked by the fact that both involve power – the power to give meaning to social relations and thereby to represent and dispute interests. If political identities are social constructions, they are constructed by the successful exercise of power. The limits to the constitution of new identities come both from institutions, which solidify the relations of power expressed in earlier conflicts, and from the efforts by actors already in place to guard their hard-won successes.

The terrain on which actors struggle over representation of collective identities and the "naming" of actors is the universe of political discourse. Because actors with a variety of collective identities coexist in the universe of political discourse, their practices and meaning systems jostle each other for attention and legitimacy.

From this perspective, politics is conflict about collective identities – about who has a right to make claims – as much as it is conflict among groups and organizations over claims about who gets what, when and how. But politics is also struggle over where it occurs. Representation involves designating the spaces that actors understand to be "political." Whether they describe an issue as "public" or "private"; "national," "global," or "local"; or "of the family" or "of the state" is a crucial element of their representation of self and of their interests.

While politics always involves processes of representation and the social construction of collective identities, history shows us that not all times are equally likely to lead to innovation in identities, in their meaning systems, and in political practice. There are times when there is a relative societal consensus about the names of the actors, their interests and political spaces – about the "real world of politics," in other words. In times of relative consensus, conflict takes place within the terms of an ongoing system of representation, which is well regulated. At other times, there is turbulence in the universe of political discourse, with debates challenging not only distributional effects but also the very boundaries of politics and the right of some actors to make claims. Under such conditions of turmoil, alternative meaning systems and practices proliferate in the universe of political discourse.

A crisis cannot, then, be understood as being simply the result of reaching certain structural limits in the economy. Crisis is both manifested and resolved within the representational system. In a situation of crisis, actors newly visible and active in the expanding universe of political discourse will begin to present alternatives and to demand redress for their claims. Such new groups make demands not only for redress of specific complaints but also for the even more fundamental citizenship claims for recognition by the political process. New groups dispute the very terms under which representation occurs by asserting that existing categories exclude them and therefore make their needs invisible. Demands are often expressed in terms of citizenship claims because, in liberal democracies, that discourse provides a weapon to those seeking fairer access to politics.

This process can be explicated by comparing the two moments of turbulence through which Canada has most recently lived. In the 1940s, all actors in Canadian politics struggled to make sense of the economic, political and social restructuring associated with the Great Depression and the war years. At that time the Rowell-Sirois Royal Commission conducted a wide-ranging survey of the ills of Canadian society. The Commission was set up in response to popular mobilizations of discontent with federalism, social policy and economic relations, and was an opportunity for citizens to make their demands heard. A crucial element of the Commission's impact was to provide a new lens through which to view the representational needs of a modern, industrial society in which old-style federalism had failed; the power of the central government required extension. At the same time, the Commission contributed to a rewriting of Canadian philosophies of the relationship between the state and society. This work helped shape the whole of the postwar era, for the political parties and the state took up these ideas and reworked them for their own needs.

The contribution of the Rowell-Sirois Royal Commission to restructuring in the 1940s is invoked not as a historical curiosity but because Canadian society is now experiencing a similar period of rapid adjustment to social and economic turbulence. More than a decade of restructuring the economy and society has produced new pressures on the political system and new claims on the institutions of representative democracy. In the 1980s and 1990s, we too question the "fit" between the usual practices of existing institutions charged with organizing representation to guarantee citizenship rights and new claims mobilized by actors seeking access to the political process. In utilizing the discourse of citizenship rights, those who stand at the door demanding access raise issues of equity. They call on the state to act so as to make the fundamental categories of liberty, equality and collective solidarity work fairly for them.

CITIZENSHIP AND EQUITY IN CANADIAN POLITICS

Canadian political thought is a deeply divided and contested intellectual arena (Williams and Williams 1990, 107–108). Fortunately, this study does not need to resolve any of the long-standing disputes over the origins of our fundamental political principles.[13] There is general agreement among students of political thought that Canadian values reflect, at least in part, a collectivist tradition. While displaying a commitment to liberal principles, particularly the notion of limited government and individual rights, Canada has also been influenced by both the "Tory touch" and the social democratic traditions of social solidarity.

In his comparisons of Canada and the United States, S.M. Lipset (1965) isolated the absence of a "revolutionary moment" in the Canadian experience to account for this country's greater commitment to collectivism (Williams and Williams 1990, 111–14; Bell 1990, 147–48). Indeed, for Lipset the formative event for Canadian society – and its approach to citizenship values – was the counter-revolution, the immigration of Loyalists at the time of the American Revolution. These Loyalists, who were committed to Tory values, helped to ensure that Canada in the 19th century would be more elitist, particularistic and ascriptive.[14]

Lipset ignored, for the most part, the contribution of French-Canadian political thought to the substance of political culture in the last century. Other approaches have paid more attention to it, particularly the ways conservative Catholicism buttressed the Tory ideas of Loyalists. George Grant, for example, stressed the Catholic tendency to put virtue before freedom, a principle contributing to the legitimation of restraint of individual liberty in the name of the common good (Grant 1963, 75–76). To Grant, French-Canadian Catholicism fit well with the Calvinist Protestantism of English-speaking Canada. Neither religious tradition sought emancipation of the passions, and therefore, both inhibited the move toward the liberalism of self-realization, which

Grant described as characteristic of the hegemonic liberalism of the United States (ibid., 70–71).

A second description of Canadian political thought that stresses the contribution of French Canada to the collectivism of Canadian society is the "fragment thesis." Taking off from the argument of Louis Hartz (1964), Kenneth McRae and Gad Horowitz have shown how the pure liberalism of American political thought was tempered in Canada by the values of collectivism characteristic of both English Tories and French Catholics (Horowitz 1968, chap. 1).

Moreover, in the patterns of immigration and the relative tardiness with which Canadian political culture jelled, Horowitz found the reason for Canadian "exceptionalism": the presence of social democratic thought associated with left-wing parties and unions. For him, collectivist values were found in right- and left-wing thought, both of which combined a tempered enthusiasm for individual liberty and individual rights with a commitment to societal well-being. While left-wing thought took from liberalism a greater concern for equality than was found in the more hierarchical Tory map of society, both involved a reliance on the expression of the whole – usually through the state – against the individual, when necessary, in order to achieve the good.[15]

PLACE-SENSITIVE CITIZENSHIP: EQUITY FOR "ISLAND COMMUNITIES"

In early 20th-century Canada, we see the mix of these ideas about citizenship in a number of realms. Most often singled out is the willingness of Conservative politicians to utilize the state for the purposes of nation-building and economic accumulation.[16] The Canadian response to the "social question" associated with the dislocation created by massive immigration, urbanization and industrialization also expresses the collectivism of Canadian political thought. Both Tories and Socialists sought ways of ameliorating the destructive effects of these processes at the beginning of this century. Various combinations of state and private efforts to reassert "stability" emanated from Conservative politicians and their supporters, including reforming women of both English and French Canada (Jenson 1990b). But this discourse of reform was also important to the social gospellers who would later form the backbone of the movement that gave birth to the Co-operative Commonwealth Federation (CCF) in the 1930s.

The turbulent years from Confederation until the First World War were ones of fundamental economic, social and political restructuring. In time, however, the discovery of certain regulatory principles in each of these realms contributed the specific content of the meaning of citizenship, which held until the 1940s (Jenson 1990a). At this time, too, the tensions among liberty, equality and solidarity were visible. While the principles of liberalism provided the centre of gravity for the universe of political discourse, there was substantial space available for other views that mapped the world in more solidaristic ways, either from the left or the right (Christian and Campbell 1989).

Throughout this period, a fundamental concern was national development. Many considered the state's role was to unify the disparate social, linguistic and religious regions of the country while guaranteeing fairness to all. Profoundly important to Canadian political thought was the idea that the country's very existence depended upon the nation-building activities of a state that could act in the name of an as yet weak nation. Thus, the effects of market relations were supposed to be tempered by equity-generating actions for economic development (railway building and tariffs) that would create employment as well as generate trade and capital accumulation.

The parties of Macdonald and Laurier were supposed to be nation-building ones, even though they were anchored by strong ties to the emerging sectors of corporate Canada concentrated in Quebec and Ontario (Thorburn 1985, 4–5). Yet it took several decades to establish a national party system. Until that time, governments depended on their ability to cobble together support based on ministerialism, which involved promises for policy to certain areas in return for their electoral support. For example, the western constituencies remained ministerialist as long as they needed the railroad. "The westerners did not sell their support in return for the petty favours of the patronage machine and the pork barrel but only in return for the railway, the whole railway and nothing but the railway" (Reid 1985, 16). By 1896, however, a national party system was in place, but only for a short time. The election of 1911 marked a turning point in Canadian party politics for the two-party system so recently established fractured over issues of class, regional and cultural conflicts (Thorburn 1985, 6).

In this experience of fracturing, we see that despite – or perhaps because of – the emphasis on nation-building, the concept of citizenship constituted in these years was place-sensitive, and the universe of political discourse was dominated for the first four decades of this century by disputes over the factors contributing to regional inequalities. Other interests, reflecting the mobilization of linguistic, religious or class identities, were expressed in a regional discourse, and claims on the state for fair treatment of regions and their inhabitants were frequent. Such place-sensitive citizenship derived from a number of sources (Jenson 1990a, 670–74).

One source was that the lottery of resource distribution and the effects of industrialization via branch plants both mapped a regional cleavage into the heart of the Canadian working class and re-created, through time, a framework that interpreted class relations through the lens of region. In this way, class identities were more regional than national. The union movement in the West was dominated by workers in resource industries like logging, lumbering and mining. Their experience – often in one-industry isolated settlements – was very different from that of the craft workers in the factories of the East. As a result of differences in the forms of political organization, differences in the experiences of the workers themselves were veiled by a discourse of place. This then translated into a politics of regional conflict, which was sustained in part by support from farmers.[17] Regionally based farmers' protests took shape as western wheat farmers developed a dense network of institutions to protect themselves against the politics of the East and the notoriously fickle international market. Their goal was to use the state to achieve fairer treatment for their region from the railways, the banks and the international market.

Other actors also injected attention to place into political discourse. One important source followed from the crucial decision taken by French-Canadian élites at the end of the 19th century to concentrate their efforts to sustain their culture by reinforcing the power of the province of Quebec. Attention to the specificities of place, coming from links to the land, was reinforced by conservative nationalists and the Catholic Church's analyses of the dangers of geographical mobility – people moving to the cities or towns in search of jobs – to the continuation of the French "race" in North America. Thus, their contribution to definitions of citizenship was a representation of cultural politics and identities that emphasized place by designating the province as the space in which French-Canadians could realize their goals of religious and political survival.

The division of powers in federalism also contributed to a place-sensitive citizenship. Ottawa was not a major actor in social policy because the *Constitution Act, 1867* assigned such matters to the provinces. They, in turn, delegated their responsibilities to their dependants, the municipalities. The important role of municipal governments in building the infrastructural sinews of the city, as well as in providing relief services, meant that in rapidly growing cities, the "booster ethic" emerged, modelling municipal government on business practices (Weaver 1983). This discourse also linked economic prosperity to specific places, in this case, particular cities (Taylor 1987, 147).

All matters were shaped by this place-sensitive discourse of citizenship. The move toward female suffrage provides a good example, demonstrating the ways in which women's claims for fair access to the policy process and citizenship became demands that privileged representation of program over representation of social characteristics. Even before they got the vote, women helped constitute a definition of citizenship with a programmatic focus. This could occur because, in addition to utilizing the discourse of other groups to which they belonged, women contributed their own notion of place – based on the distinction between the private and the public – to place-sensitive citizenship. By the time they finally could vote, women were already living out the consequences of earlier actions that had created a notion of citizenship whose gendering effects were differentiated in ways that meant that they, too, ultimately became place-sensitive.[18]

The vision of gender relations embedded in this definition of citizenship put elements of place first for women, so that notions of their proper social roles were adjectival. Farm women, working women, French-Canadian women, Protestant women, western women and city women all had quite different collective identities depending on how class, religion and language entwined with place in Canadian politics. There was no single identity, nor was there a single women's politics. Therefore, as maternal feminism set out to "feminize" Parliament, advocating social reforms that would improve "public housekeeping," divisions within the movement due to place-sensitivity and the identities thereby mobilized meant that claims for representation of women gave way to demands for representation of women's interests, usually by men who were similar to them in terms of language, class or region.

In the terms of this definition of active citizenship, the construction of women's identity as reformers was more integrative than gender-specific, more collective than egalitarian and liberal. If women were "natural mothers" and if the world needed mothering and housekeeping, then men could, if properly nurtured, actually organize the change. Therefore, while maternal feminists were absolutely central to the movements for social reform described above, these women came late to the realization that their reformism required that they be voting citizens. Indeed, throughout the crucial years at the end of the 19th century when the notions of citizenship were crystallizing, groups like the National Council of Women never utilized an electoralist discourse.[19] They elevated the collective principles of social reform far above demands for emancipation or individual rights (Bashevkin 1986, 250).

The discursive weight in considerations of citizenship was also on the collectivity for Catholic feminists in Quebec at the end of the 19th century (Lavigne et al. 1979, 21ff.). The metaphor was, however, different. For Protestant, English-speaking women the image was of "housekeeping," while for French-speaking women, the language was one of "protection." Women, organized as women, joined male nationalists and priests in trying to protect Quebec society from urban ills (Trofimenkoff 1977, 108ff.). One result was that, while empowering women, such feminism could not make claims for equality because the church, as well as much of the male power structure, was adamantly opposed to female suffrage for nationalist and religious reasons. By aligning with such groups, women found that talk of the vote for women became impossible.

There were identifiable consequences for Canadian society, then, in the ways claims for fairness were generated in these years. Women did not make strong gender-based claims for equality. Instead, to each group gender was important, but its meaning was linked discursively to other social relations in a variety of ways, and these links were not simply discursive. Women were divided by class and religion into groups that sought political expression through the political parties and movements that had taken shape in the economic and political restructuring at the turn of the century. They were willing to focus their demands more on the representation of policy positions – their reform concerns – than on the representation of women qua women. Their equity claims focused more on the possibilities of access of new policy positions, and the political formations advocating them, than on access of specific kinds of persons.

A second consequence was visible in the way demands for equity were made by other groups. While Canadian politics in the turbulent years at the beginning of the 20th century was anchored, to be sure, by a liberalism that drew clear distinctions between state and civil society, there were also grounds for claims for solidarity of regions and provinces. From all these strands, then, a place-specific response to fundamental political questions emerged as the meaning of being "Canadian" took shape. The nation was coming into being, but it was a nation of "island communities."[20] The result was a citizenship cleaved by language, religion and class. Moreover, it was a citizenship with a new consensus on the basic terms, which were to maintain the diversity of the island communities defined in spatial terms. This agreement, then, served to bound conflict. Although competition continued over the actual operation within that definition of citizenship, a framework had been set down.

Among the basic principles of this definition was the idea that the collectivity required careful tending if the liberalism of the market was to be prevented from reorganizing space so as to remove the border, so painfully constituted by Confederation, between Canada and the

United States. Moreover, distributional justice depended on representation of the regions at the centre, thereby reflecting their diverse needs. Because regions were different, they could not be reduced to a single interest, nor could they be represented in ways that blurred their distinctiveness. Therefore, virtually all efforts to generate equity focused on efforts through the party system and cabinet government, to recognize the specificity of spatially based needs. Place-sensitive citizenship also generated social movements organized according to such logic (trade unions, for example), just as it allowed for the continued separation of the two cultural solitudes.

The party system provided an institutional expression of these representational forms. The intensely local party system created by the post-Confederation patronage system gave way to the politics of regional accommodation in the first decades of the century (Smith 1989, 131). The brokerage system, constituted most successfully by Mackenzie King, "places a premium on the regional representativeness of the executive and encourages the emergence of regional power brokers as key cabinet ministers, who thus play a double role as administrators and as political leaders of regions" (Whitaker 1985, 146). This system provided for the vertical integration of subcultures concentrated in particular places and for mechanisms of horizontal accommodation by élites acting as brokers. In this process, the party system itself took on a "federal" form (Reid 1985, 17; Smith 1989, 134).[21]

Thus, this party system was uniquely designed to represent the demands for equitable treatment of regions and for fair representation. Each place could see its representatives in the Cabinet, if not "in action." Each place could hope that its sectional needs – whether those of class, language or religion – would be well represented by the ministers from that place. Furthermore, this party system contributed to a representation of Canadian society to itself as being first and foremost a country where region mattered and where politics was about fair treatment of such diverse spaces. This representation reinforced a citizenship that stressed collectivities over individuals, that emphasized difference more than equality, and that defined fairness in spatial terms.

NATIONWIDE CITIZENSHIP: EQUITY FOR INDIVIDUALS

This representational complex of meanings and practices did not last, however. After the crisis of the Depression and the political and economic restructuring that occurred during the war, this version of a place-sensitive citizenship gave way to other understandings. By 1945, the universe of political discourse was dominated by a new language of nation-building in which attention to region was attenuated.

Individuals – as citizens, as consumers and as producers – began to have greater discursive visibility. Identities and interests shifted as a new designation of space came into being.

Economic and political regulation during and after the Second World War came to involve, among other things, a rebalancing of federal-provincial powers because of the mounting influence of the federal government. At the same time, the question of Canada's relationship to the United States began to occupy more attention. Even if by the mid-1950s the Royal Commission headed by Walter Gordon had begun to inquire into, and criticize, the structuring effects of a strategy of trying to build a national economy by encouraging continental ties, economic regulation using Keynesian principles provided a unifying schema. It justified an active central government, as well as an active government *tout court*, to regulate a single unit, that of the nationwide economy (Jenson 1989a).

In such an economy and politics, concepts of space changed; political discourse represented Canada less as a conglomeration of regions and more as a single space north of the 49th Parallel with one labour market, universal standards for social programs and a central government responsible for assuring the well-being of the whole. After the wartime "seizure of power" by the federal government, Canada entered the postwar decades with its federal institutions partially reconstructed. For the first time there was a centralized system for income security. The rationale for such programs was that they were a means of eliminating the interregional disparities related to the differential income sources of provincial governments by paying benefits to individual citizens. A national level of income security that could accommodate the mobility of workers in the postwar national labour market was achieved (Jenson 1990a, 681–82). One concurrent result of this understanding of economic restructuring was that in the 1950s and 1960s attention focused on the workings of capitalism and technology to an extraordinary extent (Cairns and Williams 1988, 234).

A recomposition of citizenship around a basic policy and discursive consensus had taken place, sponsored by the Liberals, supported by the Tories, and claimed as a victory by the CCF. To the mainstream parties, reforms were meant to meet national needs for social justice. Social spending was represented as part of the state's proposals for reconstructing the nation after the travails of wartime mobilization. Keynesian and social policies stressing redistribution via transfer payments – like unemployment insurance, social assistance and family allowances – tended to address Canadians more as individuals than as members of collectivities.

The shift, however, was not only in the meanings and practices attached to citizens as economic actors. By the 1950s, the notion that the federal government's responsibility legitimately extended to monitoring a single national economy went hand in hand with the notion that it was responsible for nationwide cultural, scientific and educational institutions. Thus, these years saw a flurry of policies to strengthen national culture and to distinguish the autonomous Canadian state from its colonial past. Canada's very visible independent role in founding postwar international institutions like the United Nations and the General Agreement on Tariffs and Trade was accompanied by a partial elimination of Westminster's oversight of Canadian constitutional arrangements and by an attenuation of the colonial symbols of "Dominion" and "royal." The *Citizenship Act* of 1946 went in this direction, as did the establishment of the Massey Commission, a Royal Commission on the Arts, Letters, and Sciences, and the national extension of CBC television. Thus, as the turbulence of the 1930s and war years gave way to the postwar boom, a new universe of political discourse, with quite different actors predominating, stabilized.

When the federal government addressed Canadians after the war – in election campaigns (as the Liberal party), in federal-provincial conferences, and in policy documents – it claimed to speak for the country, which had weathered the threat of war thanks to the massive regulation of economic life by the central government. Now it faced a future in which only that government had the know-how, experience and good sense to avoid a repetition of the 1930s' crisis. Only the central government, giving guidance to the provinces, could speak for the whole. All this meant that the discourse of politics was a national one, albeit one tempered by the recognition that federalism prevented the central government from seizing too much initiative, and "free enterprise" meant that the role of the state would be limited.

The contribution of the party system to the representational complex also changed in these years. The brokerage politics of Mackenzie King, based on regional barons and backroom negotiations, began to founder under the new conditions of the postwar period. The influence of the bureaucracy rose as ministers turned to their departments for "expert" advice; "political savvy" served less well than previously (Whitaker 1985). In the new times of technocracy, supposedly ushered in by the 1950s' "end of ideology," expertise and adjustments at the margin were more important (Brodie and Jenson 1988, chap. 7). But the pressure for nationwide politics also generated other kinds of political responses, ranging from the discourse of an "unhyphenated Canadian" citizenship deployed by John Diefenbaker in his successful bid to unseat the "government party" in 1957, to the "pan-Canadianism" of Lester Pearson and Pierre Trudeau when they returned the Liberals to hegemony in the 1960s.

With these shifts, national symbols redefined Canadian citizenship, making it one founded upon a particular reading of not only cultural relations but also the economy and the technology of modernity. Thus, citizenship was a national identity based on the spatial commonality of all residents of a large and dispersed country. Citizenship identified the country's natural resources, rather than its workers, as the source of its greatness.[22]

In this way, one sort of place-sensitive definition of citizenship replaced another. Macroeconomic policies and a national "responsibility" for some social spending were grafted onto traditional ideas about defensive expansionism. The recomposition of the space of citizenship made the Canada-U.S. couplet particularly important, along with the French-English one. By the mid-1960s, these two couplets, within a national vision of citizenship, were being profoundly debated. Once again, the mix of liberty, equality and collectivity was on the agenda as Canadians tried, in the context of the postwar world, to define their national identity. This self-definition involved not only a process of differentiation from the United States (which is how it is often read) but also a debate about fundamental values, especially collective ones. In this debate, the state's ability to contribute to society's representation of itself by tempering individualism in the name of the other values of citizenship and of fairness was a central theme.

It is important to note that in this debate the national level predominated discursively; citizenship was based on allegiance to Canada. Thus, the two problematic couplets (Canada-U.S.; English-French) were interpreted through a lens that could view the whole and that privileged that whole, a lens that fitted with the regulatory patterns established after 1945 for both the economy and politics. Thus, as the mechanisms sustaining such patterns entered a more turbulent period in the late 1960s and 1970s, there was a shift in the optic, a refitting of the lens in ways that were more fragmented, less national, more local and much more disputed. In the mid-1960s, however, controversies were confined within discussion of the terms of a national citizenship. I will explicate this debate by referring to three key texts of the time: Pierre Trudeau's *Federalism and the French Canadians* (1968); George Grant's *Lament for a Nation* (1963); and Charles Taylor's *The Pattern of Politics* (1970). Taken together these texts reflect the major terms of political discourse utilized in those years.

Trudeau's writings through the late 1950s and 1960s were part of the hugely creative postwar movement in which many forces in Quebec society struggled to extricate themselves and their society from the influence of a conservative church and politics (Trudeau 1968, viii ff.). Looking back to Quebec history and engaged with his contemporaries who were already constructing an argument for a distinct role for the Quebec state in representing that community's aspirations for the future, Pierre Trudeau opposed the move to neonationalism (ibid., xx–xxi). In doing so, he contributed to Canadian political thought a political manifesto founded on liberal principles.[23] His primary concern was to push his francophone compatriots into modernity by tying them to a project of democratic renewal that involved a commitment to individual over collective rights. Trudeau's opposition to discourses of nationalism was based on his interpretation of the nationalist past of Quebec, which he read as both inward-looking and profoundly conservative. For him, the future must involve an opening to the larger society, both in Canada and internationally.[24]

Trudeau dealt with the English-French couplet by calling for a "federal society" in which language and cultural differences would gain recognition within national institutions.[25] In this way, the central government could provide protection for francophones; a strong provincial state would not be necessary. As for the second couplet, there was an uneasy tension between Trudeau's commitment to the values of a liberal internationalism and Canada's relationship with the United States. In 1965 his argument against Quebec's independence was that both Canada and Quebec were "largely dominated by the economy of the United States" (Trudeau 1968, 9) and would necessarily be so if the benefits of economic development and technology were to be realized (ibid., 12–13). The role of the state was to direct and develop as much as possible without using "legal or moral violence against its citizens ... On these matters as well, a constitution of free men must be free from bias" (ibid., 12).

It was the Canadian–American relation that most occupied George Grant and Charles Taylor. Their definitions of Canadian citizenship included at their heart a notion of the differentiation between Canada and the United States, as well as the need to sustain such differences if fundamental Canadian values were to survive. Both Grant and Taylor, starting from an analysis of the postwar economic order, laid the problem at the door of powerful large corporations who deployed their technological paradigms for generating mass production for mass consumption.

Grant's lament was for a past of order and stability, a tradition that had been undermined by rampant liberalism, carried by the postwar influence of the United States. To Grant, the "Canadian nation" was an impossible dream in a technologically advanced society dedicated to the constant expansion of variety in order to satisfy unrestrained passion. If liberalism meant choice and pluralism to Grant, the enthusiasm for affluence and consumption at the core of the postwar boom was the epitome of liberalism. Gone from this citizenship heavily weighted toward individual freedom, or liberty, was any commitment to the search for the good society. Only with this principle was it possible to derive a distinctive vision of Canadian citizenship, a vision that would define "the national" in contradistinction to the sceptical liberalism of the United States, where the values of organic solidarity no longer existed (Grant 1963, chap. 5). In this way, Grant linked an attack on continentalism to a diatribe against technology, unrestrained passion and brokerage-style politics.

Taylor explored many of the same issues, but he composed his story in a different way to produce less of a lament and more of a call to battle. His shibboleth was the "politics of polarization," which he advocated as a substitute for the "politics of consensus" organized by the "New Young Leader," embodied in Pierre Trudeau. Taylor's goal was to create a specifically Canadian space in which it would be possible to experiment with a politics of "resacralization." He identified democratic participation as the only antidote to the starvation of the public realm, which had occurred because of an excessive liberalism and which had allowed large corporations to have their way with Canadian society. The goal of resacralization was to promote a sense of community, of identity, by reinfecting Canadian society with its traditional commitment to collectivity. This sense of identity, however, would arise neither from Tory visions of hierarchical society nor from church-based ones. Rather, it would be secular but sacred and based on the reinvention of man's relationship to nature. Thus, again, postwar technology and production relations loomed large in the argument not only because of analyses of their effects on the distribution of social power but also because of notions about how they shaped the very way in which Canadians constituted their own political identity in de-sacralized (that is, noncommunitarian) ways.

Therefore, for Taylor as for Grant, Canadian citizenship depended upon the boundary drawn at the 49th Parallel because it created a space for a protective mix of values. Moreover, like Grant, Taylor ascribed to the state and to politics a fundamental role in guaranteeing this space.

In these postwar debates bridging the two kinds of collectivism as well as in the predominant liberal position, there was a specification of "modernity." The modern was industrially and technologically defined and organized around certain fundamental values. This meant that the market, production and indeed economic activities in general occupied a privileged discursive position. The Canadian nation was, to be sure, a space north of the 49th Parallel. But that space was an economic one; Canadian identity depended not only on political separation from the United States but also on the identification of a separate economic space. This notion of a single market for goods, services and manpower was one defining feature of Canada's postwar representation of citizenship. Thus, while Grant lamented the activities of American corporations in Canada because they brought liberal values with them, he stressed the shaping effects of economic activities. In lambasting the state's failure to guarantee the economic sovereignty upon which cultural and political distinctiveness depended, Taylor confirmed the unity of the condition of the private economy and the public good.

In these formulations, then, considerations of the state's role in guaranteeing equity tended to focus on the economic, on the power of money and on the distribution of resources. Fair dealings across regions were replaced by concerns about equitable treatment of individuals. This distribution-based conceptualization of equity arose out of the discursive interlinking of the terms and concerns described above. The individualism of liberalism found its expression in the Keynesianism of income transfer; Canadians became citizens who might be recipients of social benefits. Notions of economic redistribution expressed the concern for equality, just as the principles of universality and some notions of social citizenship rights translated into commitment to solidarity. In all of this, the state's role was to ensure that the basic mix worked and to intervene as necessary to ameliorate the distribution of wealth and foster economic growth.

The political parties also reorganized themselves. The system of regional brokering in Cabinet gave way to an institutionalized and relatively unmediated relationship between the centre, especially the leader, and the voters. The brokerage politics of these years was based less on the regional organization of power-handlers than on a system of interest representation that stressed the leader and his ability to represent, through creative cross-cleavage brokering, the immediate concerns of the people (Clarke et al. 1984, chap. 1; Smith 1989, 142). Thus, the national parties created out of such postwar politics were leader-focused and had little staying power in the ways they dealt with the great issues of the day.

The concerns about equity upon which such institutions of representation could focus were primarily those of funding and access for those who were less endowed with the material resources with which to participate. Public funding of election campaigns, limits on election expenditures and access to the communication media were implemented to improve equity at the price of some limitations on liberty of action in election campaigns (Paltiel 1970, chap. 1).

Of lesser importance in this representational complex, however, was the attention to collective solidarities. An assumption informed the thinking at the time; while the state might have to intervene in the economy to guarantee fairness, the institutions of liberal democracy – once purged of the risk of undue influence associated with corrupt practices or excessive wealth – would produce a viable, even desirable outcome. Thus, little attention was paid, in the context of the assumptions about postwar citizenship, to the special needs of particular groups, whose access to democratic institutions might be hindered in a process weighted more toward liberalism and formal equality rights.

This assumption made sense in the context of the definition of citizenship then in place; only individuals could be endowed with rights. Thus, to the extent that there was a move from the 1960s until the 1982 *Canadian Charter of Rights and Freedoms* to strengthen the legal guarantees of individuals, the notion that society was also composed of collectivities became harder and harder to recognize. Yet, the last 20 years of Canada's history is testimony to contestation around exactly that notion. Even as the finishing touches were being put on a representational system organized around definitions of a single national citizenship, a national space and fairness for individuals, new politics were emerging to contest all three of these definitions in the name of specificity, difference and alternative collectivities.

A FRAGMENTED CITIZENSHIP: CATEGORIAL EQUITY

The first site in which the postwar definitions of "belonging" began to come apart was in the contestation over Québécois nationalism. The insistence by that nationalist movement on the difference – or distinctiveness – of its cultural identity challenged the fundamental principles of Canadian bicultural citizenship being institutionalized by the federal government in the *Official Languages Act* of 1969 and the procedures of fiscal federalism. Accommodation of the Québécois identity could only result in a challenge to the representational capacity of the party system. Substitution of executive federalism as a route to representation was a result of that challenge and accommodation just as constitutional politics became conflicts over competing definitions of Canada (Cairns and Williams 1988, 240; Jenson 1989a).

Yet, it was not only the Québécois nationalist movement that contributed to this decomposition of the party system. Dissatisfaction with the new forms of brokerage politics as well as province-building provincial governments generated criticisms of the parties and greater enthusiasm for federal-provincial negotiations as the arena for resolving such competition. Thus, new conceptions of space began to emerge as the provinces and regions again became crucial places for conducting both economic and cultural politics.

It was not only contestation within federalism that encouraged this decomposition of the national space and its economic language. A "politics of identity," which severely challenged earlier notions that collective identities and politics followed in a straightforward, even unmediated, way from economic activities and technological innovations, began to develop.[26] The new social movements of the 1970s and 1980s rejected the long-standing notion that the primary political spaces were Parliament, workplace and nation. As these movements now struggle to make sense of their own identities and to legitimate them in the social and political world, the spaces for and of politics proliferate. Such movements incorporate, in their practice, the idea that there has been a shift in the locale of politics from the national to both the global and the local. Feminists, anti-racists, ecologists and gays insist on creating new space for new politics in the family, the city, the environment and the community. Geographical space contracts, as such movements develop ties around the globe, linking the new politics of Canada with those of Third World women, anti-apartheid struggles, Amazonian Indians, and peace and Green activists, East and West. In the process, Canada's border becomes even more permeable, for such movements around the world provide support to Canada's indigenous people trying to settle land claims, to ecologists attempting to block large-scale development projects or to save the seals, and to women seeking abortion and equality rights.

This shrinking of the political globe, and its attendant permeability of borders, is a characteristic of the third major period of turbulence in Canada's history as a country. The economic and political strategies of the postwar years have reached the limits of their technological paradigms, labour processes, monetary systems and state programs. Moreover, just as in the other two periods of crisis and restructuring, alternatives for the future are being contested in this turbulent moment.

The response from some of the business community has been to become more mobile, to seek less expensive and less truculent sources of labour not only in the Third World but also in the peripheries of already industrialized countries. New labour processes have been put into place, including new management strategies to increase "flexibility." Neo-liberal political movements have mobilized around the idea that there must be limits to social spending. Collective bargaining rights, the hallmark of the postwar labour regimes, have come under fire.

Business is not alone, however, in mounting severe attacks on postwar arrangements (Breton and Jenson 1991). As described above, provincial governments have struck out on their own in search of their particular restructuring strategies. Moreover, social movements, including the labour movement, have mobilized around their own criticisms of labour processes that granted little control over execution to the workers themselves; of state programs that were excessively rigid and insufficiently client-friendly; and of the general lack of democracy in the postwar arrangements. Indeed, a demand for democratization unites the new social movements of these years with the labour movement, forging alliances among new and more traditional actors.

Coming from a large variety of sources, then, is the demand for recognition of new political spaces, for less statist politics and for much more democracy. Involved in all of this is a renegotiation of citizenship and, in particular, the assertion that more actors "belong" in the political process than can be recognized by a single nationwide undifferentiated definition of the citizen.

As a result, a search for the proper balance among the three elements of liberty, equality and solidarity is again underway. The previous consensus about space, about identities and about interests has been undone, and the ordering principles of politics are being renegotiated. Fairness needs respecification and several alternatives are on the table. The selection of one or the other of these will set Canada in motion down the road to the future. Not surprisingly, then, concerns are grave and conflict is intense, as revealed by the last two great debates of Canadian politics, during the 1988 Free Trade election and the struggle over the Meech Lake Accord.

Experience with the constraining effects of global competition has led to expectations that restructuring of labour-management relations, state spending and citizen entitlements will occur. Neo-liberals *pur et dur* have pressed for more space for market relations to shape not only the economy but also politics and, therefore, for a minimization of state intervention in the affairs of citizens. Neo-liberals' analysis of the postwar past stresses the deforming effects of too much state regulation, and they seek a "leaner and trimmer" political process.

Other groups, in contrast, are seeking a more balanced mix of the space for individualism and a recognition of the need to generate meaningful equality and to sustain solidarity. Some actors seek, in a reconsecration of democratic politics and national institutions, a better balance between liberty and equality. These involve a search for ways of strengthening national institutions in the face of the decentralizing effects of recent constitutional politics and the realignment of the Canadian economy on a north-south axis.

For yet others, the future means revived attention to collectivities as groups make claims in the name of collective rights and solidarities. Feminists, for example, have sought not only the right to strive for equality with men but also the acknowledgement that achievement of that goal could involve, at times, recognition that women are a collectivity distinct in many ways from men. As a result, affirmative action has been pressed. Similarly, Québécois seek constitutional entrenchment of their collective distinctiveness through language rights as well as in the Meech Lake process and beyond. Indigenous peoples make claims for recognition of their historic rights as First Nations and recognition of their collective distinctiveness. Such formulations explicitly reject the 1960s' vision of assimilation of individuals – an equality-based strategy – and seek instead a recognition of collective rights.

While these notions of collectivity are reminiscent of traditions of collectivism, they have been somewhat modified from previous versions. In the past, collectivities tended to be more traditional groups, rooted in particular spaces, whereas now there is greater fluidity to collective identifications and a great deal of movement through space in the ways already described. Traditional notions of fairness to regions cannot satisfy these demands.

In this context, then, definitions of equity have also begun to change. It is no longer satisfactory to these groups – whether they stress equality or solidarity – to reason simply in terms of the financial barriers to access or in terms of access for certain policy positions. More and more groups are now making demands for access for those "like them," representatives who can symbolize their integration into citizenship by their presence in the highest political offices. Concerns about exclusion of whole categories of citizens – women, Aboriginal peoples and visible minorities – have exploded in conjunction with these processes of renegotiation of political spaces and representations of citizenship.

Armed with arguments about what is fair, groups call on the state to guarantee effective justice in the face of a situation where formal equality of rights – supposedly guaranteed by a national citizenship blind to gender, race or history – has failed to generate institutions that are representative of the categories of Canadian society.

Moreover, other institutions, including the political parties, are being pressed to represent these new pictures of Canada. National institutions can no longer organize representation only around a regional definition of the country or on the basis of undifferentiated individuals.

More and more collectivities seek expression – both inside and outside national institutions – of their differences. They demand fairer representation for all categories of the population.

We are living through disputes about – and the creation of – the Canada of the 21st century. Not surprisingly, then, the terms "Canada" and "Canadians," as well as "citizen" and "fairness," are again hotly contested. The ways they will combine commitments to individualism, to social and economic equality and to collective solidarities will emerge out of the politics of this moment. Only if this conflict is again resolved and some consensus is reached about fairly assigned citizenship rights, will the next "Canadian identity" acquire meaning and practical content. This is the task at hand as we move into the future, constrained by past choices, to be sure, but also at liberty to shape the future within those constraints.

NOTES

1. The *Concise Oxford* defines equity as fairness. Thus, these two notions can be treated as synonyms.

2. In this way, manual workers, slaves and freed slaves, and women and children were usually excluded from citizenship. According to Aristotle, such wide exclusions were justifiable (Turner 1986, 13–14).

3. As quoted in Held (1987, 16).

4. This, however, was never a completely black time for these ideals. The Romans tended to fear a potential conflict between the autonomous individual and the claims of public life, while Christian teachings promoted the religious over the secular (political) life. Nevertheless, both societies did keep alive a certain notion of universality, albeit on different grounds than the capacity to participate in self-government. Thus, the Abrahamic religions stressed a universality of faith, which established the boundaries of community, and provided a concept of "equality in the eyes of God" (Turner 1986, 16–17; Held 1987, 36–37). For Protestant women, in particular, this religious notion of equality provided a stepping-stone toward their claim for equality before the law and in politics in the 18th and 19th centuries.

5. Macpherson (1977, 19ff.) explains how women were excluded from full citizenship rights until the 20th century because they were considered to be "in" but not "of" civil society. Thus, like children, they did not fully merit the benefits, nor were they able to assume, the burdens of citizenship.

6. According to Macpherson (1977, 15–16), Madison's fear of democracy, and his insistence that the right to property took precedence over even liberty, excluded him from the ranks of pre-19th-century liberal democrats. Held (1987, chap. 2), in contrast, labels him a founder of the theory of "protective democracy."

7. These four definitions of legitimate state action were provided by Bentham in his *Principles of the Civil Code* (Held 1987, 68).

8. In the French Revolution, public assistance was defined as a sacred duty. With this emphasis on solidarity in order to achieve liberty and equality, the French definition of citizenship distinguished itself from that of the American Revolution, which declared only liberty and equality as its goals (European Documentation 1990, 10).

9. There is a large literature on citizenship and rights derived from T.H. Marshall's famous distinction among types of citizenship rights and their historical development. For Marshall, the 18th century was the century of the development of civil rights, while the 19th century brought political rights, and the 20th, social rights. Clearly this dating of access to rights is both Euro-centric and biased in that it reflects only the experience of men. Women did not gain access to civil rights and/or political rights in several countries until much later.

10. For the rest of this study, I will substitute the term "solidarity" or "collective solidarity" for the classic "fraternity." There are two reasons for this. The first is quite simply that "fraternity" suffers from not being gender-neutral. The second is more analytically important, however: In 18th-century France, the notion of fraternity provided a particular definition of solidarity. Since definitions of solidarity are also societally specific, it is more appropriate to use the general rather than the particular term. For the more extended – and contested – use of solidarity, see the European Community's discussion of citizenship in post-1992 Europe (European Documentation 1990).

11. For example, according to the European Economic Community, fraternity in post-1992 "social Europe" implies the existence and extension of "economic and social rights" (European Documentation 1990, 39). In Canada, the tradition of social rights was never really established after the Second World War. Therefore, the definition of solidarity is quite different in Canada, giving rise in turn to quite different equity concerns.

12. This theoretical apparatus is elaborated in Jenson (1990a, 662ff.).

13. For an overview of these approaches and disputes see Bell (1990) and Williams and Williams (1990).

14. This selection of labels for values in Canada comes, of course, from the political sociology of Talcott Parsons. This structural-functional approach to explaining societal integration and values has had a profound influence on thinking about Canada, not only with regard to political culture but also for our understandings of party politics and the role of the state (Brodie and Jenson 1989, 31–33; Jenson 1991).

15. George Grant, whose distinctions between American liberalism and left-wing thought are very close to those of Horowitz and Hartz, points to the centrality of the idea of the perfectibility of man in left-wing thought. This

notion provides a justification for the role of the state that is absent in liberal thought, especially that of the sceptical variety (1963, 59–63).

16. The difference between the views of the state in the United States and Canada in the early 20th century is striking here. Where the Canadian state was considered a legitimate tool for fostering economic development and organizing social well-being, in the U.S. these years were marked by a Supreme Court that insisted on "freedom of contract" to block any move toward legislated regulation of social relations. This situation has been described as a "state of courts and parties," in which the presence of national legislative institutions was weak (Skowronek 1982; Jenson 1989b).

17. Grounding for regional identities lay in the shared interests of eastern workers – mostly organized in the Trades and Labour Council – and those parts of the business community that promoted the National Policy. The particularities of the Canadian economy made eastern unionists, concentrated in the manufacturing enterprises of central Canada, dependent upon the maintenance of tariffs. Divisions within the movement over partisan strategy, forms of organization, and styles of militancy limited the impact of labour, especially in electoral politics. For example, whereas the Gomperist Trades and Labour Council sought partisan representation in the mainstream parties and feared industrial unionism, the One Big Union and Socialist Party of Canada organized widely in the West around a quite different union and electoral strategy (Jenson 1990a, 670–71).

18. There is an unspoken comparison in this statement. These observations about Canada are developed as a contrast to the gender-differentiated citizenship of the United States and France. I have labelled citizenship in the United States elsewhere a "bifurcated citizenship." For France, where gender differentiation passed through the family and was based on roles in production and reproduction, I have labelled citizenship as "citizen producer" (Jenson 1989b). All three of these notions of citizenship had important gendering effects, helping to delineate the possibilities for women's social roles and setting out the terms under which they would participate in politics. Thus, for example, the bifurcated citizenship of the United States helped sustain a series of social programs that were gender specific. The "women's state" was organized by standards of assistance and the "men's state" according to universal principles.

19. Only in the first decade of the 20th century did the National Council of Women put suffrage forward as the last plank of its long platform "to secure better housing conditions, to have the feeble-minded cared for and segregated, so that the imbecile population would not eternally be multiplying," and overall, to assure public cleanliness (Roberts 1979, 22–23).

20. Veronica Strong-Boag uses this term in her description of the goal of the nationwide organizations taking shape at this time. These groupings were "attempts to find collective solutions to the similar problems of the Dominion's 'island communities'" (1977, 87).

21. As Reid wrote in 1932 (1985, 17), "In caucus the party is sectional. In public it is homogeneous. In reality it is federal ... Out of the alliances of sectional parties are created the federations of sectional groups – the national Conservative and the national Liberal parties."

22. A discourse of productivism, which would have granted social and political power to workers because of their place in the postwar boom, never took hold in Canada.

23. John Saywell wrote, in the introduction to *Federalism and the French Canadians*, "Trudeau's state is one that exists for the individual; one must find the precarious balance between order and liberty; one that, as he says, 'must take great care not to infringe on the conscience of the individual'" (Trudeau 1968, xiii).

24. As Trudeau wrote in 1961, "Ouvrons les frontières, ce peuple meurt d'asphyzie!" (1968, xi).

25. "Canada must become a truly bilingual country in which the linguistic minority stops behaving as if it held special and exclusive rights, and accepts the country's federal nature with all its implications" (Trudeau 1968, 5).

26. Such politics challenge not only long-standing leftist notions, then, but also those of observers who saw the end of ideology in the economic boom of the 1950s and 1960s, and of the political business cycle as the mechanism for regulating electoral conflict. They do not, however, support a straightforward "post-materialist" interpretation of current political conflicts. Groups currently very visible – like indigenous peoples or clients of the welfare state, for example – have hardly had their "material" needs met before engaging in a politics of democratization and empowerment.

REFERENCES

Bashevkin, Sylvia. 1986. "Independence versus Partisanship: Dilemmas in the Political History of Women in English Canada." In *Rethinking Canada: The Promise of Women's History*, ed. Veronica Strong-Boag and Anita Fellman. Toronto: Copp Clark Pitman.

Bell, David. 1990. "Political Culture in Canada." In *Canadian Politics in the 1990s*. 3d ed., ed. M.W. Whittington and Glen Williams. Scarborough: Nelson Canada.

Breton, Gilles, and Jane Jenson. 1991. "After Free Trade and Meech Lake: Quoi de neuf?" *Studies in Political Economy* 34 (Spring): 199–218.

Brodie, Janine, and Jane Jenson. 1988. *Crisis, Challenge and Change: Party and Class in Canada Revisited*. Ottawa: Carleton University Press.

———. 1989. "Piercing the Smokescreen." In *Canadian Parties in Transition: Discourse, Organization, and Representation*, ed. Alain G. Gagnon and Brian Tanguay. Scarborough: Nelson Canada.

Cairns, Alan, with Doug Williams, ed. 1988. *Constitutional Government and Society in Canada: Selected Essays by Alan Cairns.* Toronto: McClelland and Stewart.

Christian, William, and Colin Campbell. 1989. "The Political Culture of Canadian Parties." In *Canadian Parties in Transition: Discourse, Organization, and Representation,* ed. Alain G. Gagnon and Brian Tanguay. Scarborough: Nelson Canada.

Clarke, Harold, Jane Jenson, Lawrence LeDuc and Jon Pammett. 1984. *Absent Mandate: The Politics of Discontent in Canada.* Toronto: Gage.

European Documentation. 1990. *A Human Face for Europe.* Brussels: European Community.

Grant, George. 1963. *Lament for a Nation: The Defeat of Canadian Nationalism.* Toronto: McClelland and Stewart.

Hall, Stuart, and Martin Jacques, eds. 1990. *New Times: The Changing Face of Politics in the 1990s.* London: Lawrence and Wishart.

Hartz, Louis et al. 1964. *The Founding of New Societies.* New York: Harcourt, Brace, and World.

Held, David. 1987. *Models of Democracy.* Stanford: Stanford University Press.

Horowitz, Gad. 1968. *Canadian Labour in Politics.* Toronto: University of Toronto Press.

Jenson, Jane. 1986. "Gender and Reproduction: Or, Babies and the State." *Studies in Political Economy* 20 (Summer): 9–46.

———. 1989a. " 'Different' but not 'Exceptional': Canada's Permeable Fordism." *Canadian Review of Sociology and Anthropology* 26 (1): 69–94.

———. 1989b. "Paradigms and Political Discourse: Protective Legislation in France and the United States before 1914." *Canadian Journal of Political Science* 22:235–58.

———. 1990a. "Representations in Crisis: The Roots of Canada's Permeable Fordism." *Canadian Journal of Political Science* 23:653–83.

———. 1990b. "Wearing Your Adjectives Proudly: Feminism in Early 20th-Century Canada." Paper presented to the Annual Meeting of the Canadian Political Science Association, Victoria.

———. 1991. "*Ce n'est pas un hasard:* The Dangers of Political Elitism." Paper presented to a Conference on Canada's Century: Governance in a Maturing Society, Queen's University, Kingston.

Lavigne, Marie, Yolande Pinard and Jennifer Stoddart. 1979. "The Fédération Nationale Saint-Jean-Baptiste and the Women's Movement in Quebec." In *A Not Unreasonable Claim: Women and Reform in Canada, 1880s–1920s,* ed. Linda Kealey. Toronto: Women's Press.

Lipset, S.M. 1965. "Revolution and Counter-Revolution: Canada and the United States." In *The Revolutionary Theme in Contemporary America*, ed. T. Ford. Lexington: University Press of Kentucky.

Macpherson, C.B. 1977. *The Life and Times of Liberal Democracy*. Oxford: Oxford University Press.

Moore, Barrington. 1966. *Social Origins of Democracy and Dictatorship: Lord and Peasant in the Making of the Modern World*. Boston: Beacon Press.

Paltiel, K.Z. 1970. *Party Finance in Canada*. Toronto: McGraw-Hill.

Reid, Escott. 1985. "The Rise of National Parties in Canada." In *Party Politics in Canada*. 5th ed., ed. Hugh G. Thorburn. Toronto: Prentice-Hall.

Roberts, Wayne. 1979. " 'Rocking the Cradle for the World': The New Woman and Maternal Feminism, Toronto, 1877–1914." In *A Not Unreasonable Claim: Women and Reform in Canada, 1880s–1920s*, ed. Linda Kealey. Toronto: Women's Press.

Skowronek, Stephen. 1982. *Building a New American State: The Expansion of National Administrative Capacities, 1977–1920*. Cambridge: Cambridge University Press.

Smith, David E. 1989. "Canadian Political Parties and National Integration." In *Canadian Parties in Transition: Discourse, Organization, and Representation*, ed. Alain G. Gagnon and Brian Tanguay. Scarborough: Nelson Canada.

Strong-Boag, Veronica. 1977. " 'Setting the Stage': National Organization and the Women's Movement in the Late 19th Century." In *The Neglected Majority: Essays in Canadian Women's History*, ed. Susan M. Trofimenkoff and Alison Prentice. Toronto: McClelland and Stewart.

Taylor, Charles. 1970. *The Pattern of Politics*. Toronto: McClelland and Stewart.

Taylor, John. 1987. "Sources of Political Conflict in the Thirties: Welfare Policy and the Geography of Need." In *The 'Benevolent' State: The Growth of Welfare in Canada*, ed. Allan Moscovitch and Jim Albert. Toronto: Garamond.

Thorburn, Hugh G. 1985. "The Development of Political Parties in Canada." In *Party Politics in Canada*. 5th ed., ed. Hugh G. Thorburn. Toronto: Prentice-Hall.

Trofimenkoff, Susan M. 1977. "Henri Bourassa and 'the Woman Question'." In *The Neglected Majority: Essays in Canadian Women's History*, ed. Susan M. Trofimenkoff and Alison Prentice. Toronto: McClelland and Stewart.

Trudeau, Pierre E. 1968. *Federalism and the French Canadians*. New York: St. Martin's.

Turner, Bryan S. 1986. *Citizenship and Capitalism: The Debate over Reformism.* London: Allen and Unwin.

Weaver, John C. 1983. "Elitism and the Corporate Ideal: Businessmen and Boosters in Canadian Civic Reform, 1890–1920." In *The Consolidation of Capitalism, 1896-1929,* ed. Michael Cross and Greg Kealey. Toronto: McClelland and Stewart.

Whitaker, Reg. 1985. "Party and State in the Liberal Era." In *Party Politics in Canada.* 5th. ed., ed. Hugh G. Thorburn. Toronto: Prentice-Hall.

Williams, Cynthia, and Doug Williams. 1990. "Political Entanglements: Ideas and Identities in Canadian Political Life." In *Canadian Politics: An Introduction to the Discipline,* ed. Alain G. Gagnon and James Bickerton. Peterborough: Broadview.

6

Fairness, Equity and Rights

Kathy L. Brock

THE *CANADIAN CHARTER OF RIGHTS AND FREEDOMS* has altered the way Canadians perceive and behave toward their political institutions. By codifying rights and providing a means for enforcing those rights, the Charter has encouraged the political mobilization of certain individuals and societal groups and has legitimized their demands on government. As a result, political institutions are being subjected to intense scrutiny and new standards of evaluation. The "new" rights discourse is influencing perceptions of fairness and equity. The electoral system is one area that has come under review and re-evaluation.

What impact is the Charter having on the way Canadians regard the electoral system? This study proposes to answer that question by examining which groups are responding to the Charter, what their expectations are, how they are using the Charter to make the electoral system more responsive to their demands, and how the political and judicial systems are responding to these demands. The study argues that the Charter has introduced a tension between rights and perceptions of fairness and equity in Canada. This tension must be resolved if the legitimacy of the electoral system and our system of political representation is to be maintained.

The study is divided into three main sections. The first section offers a description of the Charter provisions relevant to the Canadian system of political representation. The second section outlines the impact of the Charter on society and the "new" rights consciousness that has developed. The third section examines the conflict between rights and broader concepts of fairness and equity as they pertain to the electoral system. Some of the leading Charter cases that affect the electoral system will be reviewed in this section. The study concludes with a short evaluation of what the new perceptions of fairness and equity hold for the Canadian system of political representation. It cautions against any "quick fixes."

KEY POINTS OF CONTACT

There are three main points of impact between the *Canadian Charter of Rights and Freedoms* and the electoral system. The three areas of the Charter are the democratic rights (sections 3 to 5), the equality rights (section 15), and the fundamental freedoms (section 2). Each of these will be discussed briefly.

Democratic rights provide the clearest example of where the Charter impinges on the elective system of representation. Two of these sections on democratic rights concern the legislative bodies. Section 4 provides for a maximum duration of five years for Canadian legislative bodies, except in times of "real or apprehended war, invasion or insurrection," when more than two-thirds of the members of the body concur. Section 5 requires annual sittings of Parliament and the legislatures. These two sections replace section 91¶1 of the *Constitution Act, 1867* and extend the five-year term to federal and provincial legislative bodies equally. If Parliament or a provincial body chose to extend its term beyond the five-year maximum, it could be challenged to justify that action in the courts under the grounds specified in section 4(2).[1] These limits on the legislative bodies allow the citizens' rights specified in section 3 to be realized.

Section 3 of the Charter comprises two rights that are integral to our democratic system of government. Section 3 provides that "[e]very citizen of Canada has the right to vote in an election of members of the House of Commons or of a legislative assembly and to be qualified for membership therein." Thus, this section constitutionally recognizes the right of Canadian citizens to vote for the first time in Canadian history (Hogg 1985, 723). It also entrenches the right of Canadian citizens to stand in federal and provincial elections. Implicit in this section is the recognition of Canada's tradition of representative democracy.

The rights to vote and to hold office are fundamental in a liberal democracy. They symbolize political equality. This fact is recognized in the Charter. By making the rights applicable to all citizens, the Charter places the onus on the governments to justify departures from the rights before the courts. Although these rights were recognized in Canadian statute law prior to the Charter, there were significant limits on the franchise throughout Canadian history (Boyer 1981, 121–37). The Charter does not create these rights, but it does strengthen them. Of the democratic rights, section 3 has been subject to the most litigation and is having the most significant impact on the electoral system.

The democratic rights are among the least controversial sections of the Charter. As Gerald Beaudoin writes, "the democratic rights are probably those upon which the consensus between the various governments in Canada has been the easiest to achieve" (Beaudoin 1989, 299–300). They were exempted from the override clause in the Charter, which permits Parliament or the provincial legislatures to declare that a piece of legislation will operate notwithstanding a conflict with a Charter right. Just as the importance of mobility and language rights are underlined by the fact that section 33 does not apply to them (Russell 1983, 38), the centrality of the democratic rights to our system of government is underscored by the same fact. However, these rights are not absolute but "subject only to such reasonable limits prescribed by law as can be demonstrably justified in a free and democratic society" (*Canadian Charter of Rights and Freedoms*, s. 1). As will be seen later, these limits are important.

Section 15 of the Charter enumerates the equality rights. Subsection 15.1 provides that: "Every individual is equal before and under the law and has the right to the equal protection and equal benefit of the law without discrimination and, in particular, without discrimination based on race, national or ethnic origin, colour, religion, sex, age or mental or physical disability." The guarantee of these rights is followed by a subsection that allows for affirmative action programs for any of the groups specified in subsection 15.1. Section 15 came into force on 17 April 1985, three years after the Charter. The delay was premised on the assumption that the equality rights have "the potential to be the most intrusive provision of the Charter" (Hogg 1985, 787). It allows substantial room for the courts to remedy the shortcomings of the Canadian political system. The delay allowed the federal and provincial governments time to review their legislation and to bring it into line with the Charter.[2]

Section 15 is complex. It must be read with other provisions in the Charter. First, like the democratic rights, it is subject to the reasonable limits clause contained in section 1. Second, section 28 complements section 15 by providing that all rights are guaranteed equally to female and male persons. Thus, while section 15 provides for equal treatment under the law, section 28 guarantees rights to men and women equally. Third, although section 15 has been important to visible minorities in protecting their rights,[3] ethnically defined Canadians have placed more hopes in the multicultural statement contained in section 27 (Cairns 1989b, 128). The latter section stipulates that the "Charter shall be interpreted in a manner consistent with the preservation and enhancement of the multicultural heritage of Canadians." Fourth, section 15 must be read with section 35(1) of the *Constitution Act, 1982*, which affirms and recognizes "existing aboriginal and treaty rights."[4] Section 35(1) recognizes the special rights of Aboriginal peoples. These sections are mutually reinforcing.

Section 15 is one of the most important sections of the Charter, and yet its wording is curious. The rights are guaranteed to "individuals." Although this word was used so as to exclude corporations, the courts have used it to include corporations as well as natural persons under other sections. However, it is doubtful whether the courts would extend section 15 protection to corporations (Gibson 1990, 53–54; cf. Hogg 1985, 667, 798). The wording also moves away from the use of "person." Given that the word "person" has been defined to exclude women, Indians, Mongolians and Chinese in Canada's past (Boyer 1981, 130; Brodsky and Day 1989, 13; Baines 1988, 159–70), "individual" is a preferable alternative, although not legally significant in this sense.

The wording in section 15 is both awkward and ambiguous. According to Peter Hogg, the right to equality is formulated in a number of different ways in the section to avoid the restrictive interpretations that had been given to equality rights in the past (Hogg 1985, 798; cf. Baker 1987). He explains:

> Section 15 of the Charter speaks of being equal "before and under the law". The words "and under" were intended to abrogate the "administrative" definition of equality ... applied ... in the *Lavell* case, and to make clear that judicial review under s. 15 extended to the substance of the law and not just to the way in which it was administered. Section 15 also speaks of "equal benefit of the law", a phrase which was intended to abrogate a suggestion by Ritchie J. in the *Bliss* case that the legislative provision of "benefits" was not subject to equality standards. Finally, s. 15 uses the phrase "equal protection ... of the law" ... The use of this phrase implies that the American jurisprudence on equal protection, which the Supreme Court of Canada has hitherto ignored, is relevant to the interpretation of s. 15. (Hogg 1985, 798)[5]

Women's groups in particular fought for this drafting, which they hoped would depart from previous interpretations and strengthen equality rights.

This section is important in two ways. First, the equality rights are beginning to be the source of much litigation. Despite the fact that equality rights were delayed in coming into effect, they were the fourth most frequently cited rights in the first 100 Charter decisions of the Supreme Court. In the first 100 decisions, legal rights were argued 125 times, exclusion of evidence 37 times, fundamental freedoms 20 times, and equality rights 11 times. In contrast, democratic rights were not argued.[6] This indicates that equality rights cases will most likely become more numerous in relation to the other sections since equality rights are now in effect. More significantly, "Now that the Court has begun in *Andrews* [its first case on equality rights], to lay the foundation of equality rights jurisprudence, a larger portion of the cases coming before the Court will likely deal with equality rights" (Morton et al. 1990, 11). Second, the equality section, especially together with sections 27 and 28, has encouraged the political and legal mobilization of individuals and groups within society. These sections validate the fight for equality, as will be discussed below. Section 15 of the Charter is having a significant impact on the legal system and on how Canadians view social relationships and political institutions.

The equality rights touch upon the electoral system indirectly. Political boundaries and related matters are affected by perceptions of equality. Similarly, the proportionate representation of the provinces may be affected by equality rights (Gibson 1990, 15). Finally, restrictions on voting rights may be challenged under this section. Links are being established between sections 3 and 15 in cases involving voting rights and the system of representation. Section 15 is often used as a supplementary or supporting argument to section 3 arguments, and may be used subsequently when section 3 cases are defeated (Greene 1989, 110–25). At the very least, the Supreme Court will have to clarify the legal link between equality rights and section 3 as the British Columbia Court of Appeal began to do in *Dixon* (1989). Cases involving these rights will be discussed later.

Section 2 of the *Canadian Charter of Rights and Freedoms* also has an impact on elections and parties in Canada. Especially important are the guarantees of "freedom of thought, belief, opinion and expression, including freedom of the press and other media of communication," 2(*b*), and "freedom of peaceful assembly" 2(*c*), and "freedom of association" 2(*d*). Freedom of expression is held fundamental to the operation of the Canadian political system (Hogg 1985, 713–14; Beckton 1989, 196–97). This freedom affects the ability of the government to regulate the political activities of citizens and public servants, the funding of election advertising by third parties, and the distribution of political literature on public property. Freedom of peaceful assembly and of association may provide protection for groups who wish to demonstrate for or against parties, to attend political meetings, and to be members of political parties (Norman 1989, 230–31, 259, 260–64). As in the case of equality rights, these freedoms are subject to both the override clause and the reasonable limits clause contained in the Charter. As will be seen below, these rights are important in determining what is fair and equitable for elections and the electoral and party systems.

To understand the effect of these sections on the electoral system and how it is perceived, it is first necessary to understand the impact of the Charter on the Canadian civic consciousness. The next section begins that task.

A NEW CANADIAN CONSCIOUSNESS

The Charter has ushered in a new era of openness in Canadian politics. More groups are arguing for inclusion in the mainstream of Canadian political life. They are demanding that the political institutions be more representative of the diversity in Canadian society and that the norm of equality be respected and applied more rigorously than in the past. The electoral and party systems are guilty of excluding certain groups and interests in favour of others, albeit unintentionally. This section of the study briefly reviews changing perceptions of representation, provides examples of exclusion, and then examines the new political consciousness in Canada.

On the surface, the Canadian political system seems among the most open and accessible in the world. As Mishler and Clarke point out, "In an open society such as Canada there are many ways in which citizens can attempt to influence government, directly or indirectly, individually or in groups, legitimately or illegitimately" (Mishler and Clarke 1990, 158). Forms of political activity include voting, working for parties, contacting political representatives and participating in demonstrations. There are few formal barriers to participating in political parties or running for office in Canada. However, certain groups and interests tend to be underrepresented among the politically influential.

The concept of political representation is becoming more central to discussions and studies of Canadian political life. Questions concerning the legitimacy of political parties and institutions are increasingly based on the representative character of these institutions. The nature of the discourse has changed from being founded on the tradition of responsible government, to one rooted in the principles of pluralist democracy (Dupré 1989, 245–46; cf. Smith 1990, 13–14). Citizens demand that political institutions reflect the diversity in society.

This demand for "mirror representation" has been challenged. Jennifer Smith has observed that the concept of mirror representation is "repugnant to any independent-minded citizen" because it implies that leaders of organizations speak for that societal group only on the grounds that they are "one of them." Their right to speak for people of a specific group is questionable unless they possess some form of political and government organization and wish to be included within those structures, as in the case of Native people (Smith 1990, 18). Further, she maintains that representatives of interest groups argue from the perspective of one set of issues and thus have a partial concept of justice. Other citizens "rely on governments to save them from interest groups, not expose them even further to their claims" (ibid., 19). Elected politicians and political parties provide a broader understanding of justice and the public good, and of how to balance competing demands.

This view is persuasive and offers an admirable defence of the Canadian parliamentary tradition and practices. However, it is fundamentally unsatisfactory for two primary reasons. First, numerous studies in the 1970s and 1980s, beginning with the Royal Commission on the Status of Women, contradict the assumption that men can and should represent the interests of women in political life (Baines 1990, 8–9, 15–16, 19).[7] This logic can be extended to include other groups. Second, regardless of whether policy or constitutional output is more reflective of certain interests, the symbolic and perceptual dimensions of representation are important. Paul Thomas uses the approach developed by Eulau and Karps to broaden the question of representation to include the issue of responsiveness – to whom should legislators be responsible? In his discussion, he suggests that symbolic responsiveness is important, especially since the Charter conferred recognition on certain social groups: individuals from such groups may have less confidence in the institution of Parliament if they are underrepresented in its membership (Thomas 1990). Usually, there must be a material reward for the symbolic representation to be effective, but the electorate perceives that there are finite limits to the efforts of legislators to be responsive to particular interests. The rationale underlying the call for more inclusive institutions of governance is not that individuals cannot speak outside their own experience, but rather that an unrepresentative system appears to exclude or disregard certain interests. These concerns cannot be allayed by simple assurances to the contrary. These points are illustrated in the following discussion of exclusion in the Canadian political system.

Much criticism has been directed against the Canadian political élite for being exclusionary. John Porter's classic study of the political élite from 1940–60 illustrated that the Canadian élite tends to be homogeneous. These findings were reinforced by Dennis Olsen's 1980 study *The State Elite*. Olsen found that the political élite had not changed much from Porter's study, which noted that it tended to underrepresent women and Canadians of other than French and English backgrounds.

The political élite tended to be overrepresented in terms of white, Anglo-Saxon, Anglican, middle and upper-middle class, English-speaking males (Porter 1972, 386–90; cf. Olsen 1980).

This characteristic of the political élite still holds. Sylvia Bashevkin's study of the representation of women at all levels of political organization (from local constituency organizations to cabinet) corroborates these findings. She concludes that "combined with our review of patterns of political candidacy, legislative office-holding, and cabinet appointment, these figures offer strong evidence that higher, more powerful, and more competitive political positions in English Canada remain overwhelmingly in the hands of men" (Bashevkin 1985, 79). Despite significant increases in the last six years, if the current rate of increase of female members into Parliament holds, then it will take 45 years before men and women are represented equally in Parliament (Maillé 1990, 10). Although French-speaking males have made significant advances in terms of representation, other groups have not.

The limited inclusion of ethnic Canadians in the political élite also continues to hold. Daiva Stasiulis and Yasmeen Abu-Laban have examined the role of ethnic minorities in party and electoral politics overall, as well as in the 1988 federal election. They conclude that "the November 1988 federal election failed to transform the face of the House of Commons in a direction more representative of Canada's multicultural and multiracial diversity; in fact, the number of MPs of non-British or non-French origin actually dipped slightly to 49 from 51 in 1984. Although approximately 150 ran in the 1988 federal election, according to the Ethnocultural Council of Canada only 16.6 percent of MPs elected have minority ethnic backgrounds, in comparison with the approximately 30 percent of all Canadians of non-Native, non-British, non-French ancestry" (Stasiulis and Abu-Laban 1990, 594–95). Minority candidates have some success in Montreal and Winnipeg, but the Toronto ridings with small populations of non-British and non-French immigrants and their descendants offer the greatest opportunities for election. However, minority Canadians of different ethnic and racial backgrounds remain underrepresented in both the parties and the elected élite. A cursory scan of the elected representatives in the House of Commons reveals that the same remains true for Aboriginal Canadians.[8]

These findings are not new or shocking. Their significance lies in what they tell us about the Canadian electoral and party systems. First, they reveal little about representation. It does not necessarily follow that the exclusion or limited inclusion of certain interests results in unrepresentative policies. Conversely, "there is no *necessary* link between someone who comes from a particular ethnic or class background and the behaviour he or she will exhibit as a member of the elite" (Panitch 1990, 188). Inclusion of all groups in society would not necessarily result in better government. Indeed, given the voting power of the unrepresented groups, elected and bureaucratic actors cannot afford to overlook the interests of minority and female Canadians. Instead, the significance of this information lies in what it reveals about perceptions of the electoral system.

The second point concerns these perceptions. The electoral and party systems are perceived as offering informal and often intangible barriers to the participation of minority Canadians and women. Williams argues that the most powerful barriers to nontraditional candidates seeking party nominations are psychological rather than legal or financial (Williams 1981, 87–88). However, Stasiulis and Abu-Laban explain that women and ethnic Canadians are impeded by informal barriers:

> The efforts of ethnic minorities to attain direct representation in the House of Commons raises another issue pertaining to party accessibility. Bashevkin argues, with respect to women's political representation, that the more competitive the constituency is, the less likely it is that women will be found as candidates ... Similarly, the perception of many ethnocultural minorities (especially visible minorities) continues to be that the established parties do not want minority candidates to run in winnable ridings. Exclusion of ethnocultural and visible minority candidates may be attributable to several factors – prejudice in the party establishment, sensitivity to the Canadian electorate's racial and ethnic discrimination, or the fact that minority candidates, part of the more recent wave of immigration, may be perceived as not yet having gained sufficient exposure or commitment to the party in which they seek representation. (1990, 591–92)[9]

These candidates face more obstacles within the party in getting elected than the traditional party members. Although the Liberal party has made limited overtures to minority groups, the Conservatives and the New Democratic Party have been even less encouraging (Stasiulis and Abu-Laban 1990, 592–93). The electoral system does not compensate for this process of exclusion.

Third, the barriers to representation may lie within perceptions of "appropriate" forms of representation. The highest offices in Canada often alternate between individuals from Quebec and from the rest of Canada. This system tends to result in traditional French-speaking and English-speaking Canadians holding these offices. When there is a departure from this convention, it is obvious and not dismissed lightly. For example, the fact that Jeanne Sauvé was the first female governor general was often noted when she was mentioned in public. Similarly, the Ukrainian background of Governor General Ramon Hnatyshyn was widely remarked on when he succeeded Jeanne Sauvé. His appointment to this position revealed another dimension of Canadian attitudes to elected and appointed offices. Key political spokespersons criticized his appointment because he was "not bilingual" at a time of national crisis over the rejection of the Meech Lake Accord. Recently, this criticism was repeated in Quebec during the Spicer Commission hearings. A presenter noted that he is not bilingual and that "if you had such a thing in Belgium, there would be riots in the streets" (Poirier 1991, A4). Although Hnatyshyn is not bilingual in the two official languages, he is bilingual in English and Ukrainian. This attitude sends a direct message to ethnic Canadians of diverse linguistic backgrounds that they may be excluded from higher office unless they learn not one, but both, official languages. This puts them at a disadvantage to English-speaking and French-speaking Canadians who need to learn only one other language. Given the tendency of the parties to choose leaders and key officials bilingual in the two official languages, the power of this message to minority Canadians should not be underestimated.

There is one final but significant way in which the party and electoral systems are seen as unrepresentative. Provinces and regions are often either underrepresented or not represented in the governing party. Alan Cairns's seminal study of the Canadian electoral system clearly illustrated the tendency of the electoral system to make "sectional cleavages between the parties much more pronounced in Parliament than they were at the level of the electorate," and to deny parties representation in certain regions (Cairns 1989a, 118, 116–17, 119). This can result in the perception and the reality that parties are insensitive to regional needs (ibid., 124–28). This view of the electoral system is reinforced by the fact that Ontario and Quebec hold the largest number of seats in the House of Commons and traditionally have influenced the development of policies. While the regional views can be accommodated within party caucuses, the private nature of caucus debates leaves the public with the impression that their views are not represented (Thomas 1991). In the past, these facts have led to the perception in western Canada that the electoral system unfairly rewards central Canada at its expense (Elton and Gibbins 1982, 90; Gibbins 1990, 292–93; cf. Elton and Gibbins 1980).

Therefore, the party and electoral systems foster the impression that minority groups are not welcome as full and equal participants. The electoral system also reinforces regional differences, which are not reconciled by the parties. Although gains have been made in making the electoral and party systems more representative in recent years, the systems still have substantial room for improvement.

The exclusionary nature of the electoral and party systems flies in the face of the new civic consciousness of Canadians being ushered in with the *Canadian Charter of Rights and Freedoms*. The change in the public attitude toward political institutions is evident both in the rise of rights consciousness and in the rise in litigation. Canadians are arguing for more open and inclusive institutions.

The impact of the Charter is evident in the increased mobilization of individuals and in certain groups within society. Alan Cairns observes: "The Charter brought new groups into the constitutional order or, as in the case of aboriginals, enhanced a pre-existing constitutional status. It bypassed governments and spoke directly to Canadians by defining them as bearers of rights, as well as by according specific constitutional recognition to women, aboriginals, official language minority populations, ethnic groups through the vehicle of multiculturalism, and to those social categories explicitly listed in the equality rights section of the Charter" (1988, 122; see also Cairns 1986, 66–67; 1989c, 18–19). By explicitly recognizing or enhancing rights in the Charter and Aboriginal people's rights provisions of the *Constitution Act, 1982*, the governments encouraged citizens to identify themselves and to formulate their demands in terms of these constitutional categories. Moreover, it is constitutionally recognized that these identities and demands have a legitimate place within Canadian political discourse. While the effects of mobilization of these groups were most visible in the opposition that arose to the Meech Lake Accord, they are also evident in other areas.

The Charter significantly altered the nature of constitutional discourse and broader political debates in Canada. Cairns identifies a number of salient features of the constitutionally inspired ethnic and Aboriginal minority discourse. Five of his ten points are especially relevant here (1989b, 126–30). First, the discourse is nonofficial and challenges élite domination of the course of constitutional change. Aboriginal and ethnic communities are suspicious of the ability of elected government leaders to deal fairly with them. This quality is also characteristic of the attitude of these groups to political issues and policy making. As illustrated above, women share this distrust. Second, these groups are not complete outsiders any longer. Constitutional recognition of their rights gives them a place in constitutional debates that impinge on those rights. In contrast, other groups, such as the gay community, have not received constitutional recognition and thus remain outsiders in constitutional debates. Also, the Constitution provides the recognized groups with a greater sphere of influence over policy making. The groups jealously watch to see if policies reflect their interests and agree with the rights entrenched in the Constitution (cf. Cairns 1986, 66–67, 72–77). If policies depart from those rights, then they protest and often challenge them in the courts. The Constitution is a lever in this battle. Third, "Their language is often highly emotional. It is the language of shame, pride, dignity, insult, inclusion or exclusion, humiliation or recognition" (Cairns 1989b, 127). This is equally true in the political arena. Debates over affirmative action programs, pay equity and Aboriginal self-government attest to this. Fourth, there are important differences among the "new" Charter groups (whether female, Aboriginal, ethnic or racial); and fifth, these Charter groups are proliferating. The resulting discourse sometimes seems cacophonous and divisive. In the political realm, this means that more demands are being made on government (cf. ibid., 77).

Hence, like the constitutional discourse, the debates over political issues have been affected by the new rights consciousness. These "new" Charter groups with clearer perceptions of their rights, their status and their stakes in the political system are altering the nature of political and constitutional discourse. They are calling for the process of decision making to be more open, so they can guard their rights, and to be more more inclusive, to acknowledge their "new" status.

The change in attitude of Canadians is evident in the rise in litigation and in the changing perception of the courts of their role in the political system. Individuals as well as groups are resorting to the courts more frequently. In only eight years, Charter cases have come to represent 25 percent of the Supreme Court of Canada's output. This is roughly equal to the percentage of the load of the American Supreme Court dealing with rights cases. By contrast with the 1960 *Canadian Bill of Rights*, the Supreme Court heard only 34 cases between 1960 and 1982 (Morton et al. 1990, 2–3). The moderate activism of the Court has stimulated public use of the courts to challenge and to strike down unfair or discriminatory legislation (ibid., 3, 5, 8).[10] The attitude of Supreme Court justices has also contributed to the tendency to turn to the courts. Former Chief Justice Brian Dickson said in 1985, lawyers, legislators and judges must balance "the tension between change and tradition" but "recognize the importance of equality in a multicultural confederation" (Dickson 1987, 6, 7). New Charter Canadians, whether individuals or socially defined groups, cannot help but be encouraged to challenge accepted policies that adversely affect them. The Charter provides them with the leverage and the means to make policies and services more responsive to the changing nature of Canadian society.

It is not surprising then that these Charter Canadians are using their new weapons to challenge structures like political parties and elected institutions of government.[11] As illustrated above, these bodies have been exclusionary and have operated along the traditional lines of parliamentary democracy. This is inconsistent with the new concepts of representation and responsiveness. In the first instance, challenges come from within these bodies. Individuals advocate reforms that are consistent with Charter rights. In the second instance, challenges come from without, through the courts. As Andrew Heard notes, "Because political parties are an essential element of Canadian legislature, it might seem reasonable to suggest that their activities within their legislatures are indeed subject to the Charter" (Heard 1991, 85). However, he continues on with the observation that parties have been held exempt from the Charter on the grounds they are private associations, and the internal workings of Parliament that make up party operations have also been exempted. He concludes by suggesting that Charter scrutiny would be neither desirable nor feasible (ibid., 85–87).

This view toward parties may change. If they were to become exclusive actors in elections, or if their roles as integrative forces and research bodies were to be strengthened, or if they were to assume a greater part in policy formulation, then it would become less tenable to exempt them from Charter scrutiny on the grounds that they are private associations. They will be perceived increasingly as public bodies and as part of the governing apparatus. Similarly, as Charter norms become increasingly pervasive, legislative bodies and associated actors will be expected to conform to those standards. This will likely alter basic components of the system such as party discipline and legislative procedures.

The electoral system also has been affected by the tendency of these groups to turn to the courts for remedies. In his report on the 1988 federal election, then Chief Electoral Officer of Canada, Jean-Marc Hamel, commented: "The 34th General Election will surely be remembered by my staff as the 'litigation' election. Court actions were numerous and followed our every step. Much time and energy were spent in responding to them ... it is evident from the experience of the last election that the *Charter of Rights and Freedoms* has had and will continue to have a very significant impact on Canada's democratic process" (Canada, Elections Canada 1989, 27). The increase in litigiousness among the general population was evident in the challenges mounted to the electoral process. As Hamel commented to the press, "People were far more conscious of their rights this time" (Delacourt 1988, A5).

Court actions were undertaken in a number of areas (Canada, Elections Canada 1989, 27–29). Restrictions on voting were challenged by the Canadian Disability Rights Council and several individuals on behalf of persons with mental disabilities. The Federal Court struck down paragraph 14(4)(*f*) of the *Canada Elections Act,* which denied the vote to persons whose liberty of movement and property management is restrained because of mental disease. Two federally appointed judges were successful in the Federal Court in challenging the denial of voting rights to federally appointed judges. Prison inmates launched various actions to restore their right to vote with mixed results at the provincial high court levels. As many as 12 actions were begun by unregistered electors who contested the provisions in the *Canada Elections Act* that permit rural but not urban electors to be vouched for and thus to vote on election day (cf. Delacourt 1988). "All cases except one were dismissed summarily on the principal ground that constitutional matters should not be decided in interlocutory proceedings without the benefit of an adequate trial" (Canada, Elections Canada 1989, 27). Other cases involved candidacy requirements, printed advertisements (s. 72) and broadcasting regulations.

The Charter figured prominently in most of these actions. New criteria were being applied to the democratic system to make it more representative of the changes in Canadian society. Societal groups wielded the Charter as a new weapon to challenge outmoded, discriminatory or offensive provisions in the Act. As a consequence, the chief electoral officer recommended a thorough review of the conflict between the Charter and the *Canada Elections Act* and lamented the failure of Bill C-79, which would have corrected many of the inconsistencies (Canada, Elections Canada 1989, 29, 10–11). These actions reveal the need for legislative action to avoid court-imposed solutions or vacuums in the legislation.

THE CONFLICT BETWEEN RIGHTS AND FAIRNESS

In the Charter battle involving the electoral system, the ideas of fairness, equity and rights interact on three planes. On the first level, the new rights protection afforded by the Charter conflicts with traditional understandings of fairness and equity. On the second level, the new concepts of rights cause differing perceptions of fairness to collide. On the third level, the three concepts of fairness, equity and rights operate to moderate each other. Each of these should be explained as an introduction to the discussion of the four specific areas of interaction discussed below.

The new rights consciousness is prompting a re-evaluation of traditional understandings of fairness and equity with respect to the system of political representation. Traditional forms of accommodation are found lacking by the standards introduced by the rights contained in sections 2, 3 and 15 of the Charter. It is no longer sufficient that the barriers to running for office are low. The Charter groups (whether women, Aboriginal peoples, ethnic and racial minorities, or persons with disabilities), are demanding that positive action be taken that will enable them to participate equally in the system. For example, the recently elected deaf member of the Ontario legislature, Gary Malkowski, justified the government expense of sign-language interpreters for him with the argument: "I'm a taxpayer as well ... And so, don't I have a right to participate in society just like everybody else?" (Allen 1991, A4). The right to vote and equality rights are being wielded in such a way as to make the system more open and equal.

On the second level, perceptions of fairness collide. The Charter has given rise to differing perceptions of fairness. By recognizing rights, the Charter provides for new definitions of what is fair and equitable. The equality rights suggest that fairness must be consistent with equality. Individuals now express a right to their "fair share," that is, an equal share of political goods. In the context of voting, this means that individuals assert that their vote must be equally persuasive. Minority citizens, whether defined according to place of residence or personal characteristics, demand that their vote be weighted more heavily so that their voice will be as equally persuasive to legislators as the majority voice. These different perceptions of fairness result in calls for electoral redistribution and guaranteed representation. What is important is that different perceptions of fairness are promoted by the Charter. These perceptions compete, and they must be balanced if the legitimacy of the system is to be maintained.

On the third plane, fairness, equity and rights collide and compete but also influence each other. When considering rights under sections 2, 3 and 15, the courts will also consider limitations under section 1. Considerations of fairness and equity based on past practices will be used to define and shape the rights. Similarly, decisions involving these rights will alter these practices. As a result, the definitions of what is right, fair and equitable will be evolving constantly. As the dialogue based on rights becomes increasingly familiar to the public, the notions of fairness and equity will evolve further. Through this interaction, a new concept of justice will emerge.

There are a number of areas in which the new rights protection of the Charter is coming into conflict with the perceptions of fairness and equity in the battle over the electoral system. This section of the study will review four of these areas and evaluate possible solutions to the conflict. The areas include the principle of "one person, one vote," representation, interest group spending and voting restrictions.

One Person, One Vote

The Charter has initiated a new dimension in the debate over representation in Canada. Does the section 3 right to vote imply equality of voting power and representation? Does the section 15 right to equal protection and equal benefit of the law require greater equity in the redistribution of electoral boundaries? These questions raise important concerns regarding federal electoral boundaries. Different conceptions of fairness and equity clash in these debates.

Historically, the electoral boundaries in Canada have not strictly corresponded to the norms of representation by population. In the past, departures from the principle of one person, one vote were tolerated when other overriding objectives were at stake. As Kent Roach comments, historically, the distribution of seats in the House of Commons among the provinces and territories has been a matter governed by federalist concerns about equity between provinces (Roach 1991). Similarly, the ideal of equal representation has been compromised by concerns with quality of representation in the interests of fairness (Boyer 1987a, 105). For example, a strict application of population quotas would impair the quality of representation in northern ridings because they would be quite expansive. Members of Parliament from large ridings face increased travel, less contact with constituents, higher office maintenance costs because they will have to keep more than one constituency office, and a wider spectrum of constituency demands involving a wider array of government services than members from smaller, more concentrated ridings. Although special compensation assists these MPs with costs, and technology has improved travel time and distance problems in comparison with the past, citizen demands have increased. These representatives face a heavier burden than other MPs. If the representation in these constituencies is to be equitable to that provided in others, then size must still be controlled. In Canada, departures from the norm of one person, one vote have been tolerated in response to the population imbalance, the size of the country and the country's peculiar history. Population is an important but not the sole criterion in determining electoral boundaries (Sancton 1990, 450 quoting Dickson C.J.C.).[12]

A look at Canada's history of representation in the House of Commons illustrates that the "overall record of electoral districting in Canada since confederation might be characterized as a typical Canadian compromise" (Cameron and Norcliff 1985; cf. Boyer 1987a, 101–12).

In the *Constitution Act, 1867,* section 37 stipulates the size of the House of Commons, and section 51 provides for representation to be based on the population of the provinces. However, the principle of representation by population is qualified by the requirement that no province will have fewer seats in the House of Commons than the Senate and that no province will have fewer seats than it received in 1976. The principle is further compromised by the provision in the *Representation Act, 1985,* that electoral boundaries commissions should "respect the community of interest or community of identity in or the historical pattern of an electoral district in the province," or "maintain a manageable geographic size for districts in sparsely populated, rural or northern regions of the province." The standard principle of variation between electoral districts is 25 percent of the electoral quota for the province.

Three results follow from this method of determining representation in the House of Commons. First, the principle of one person, one vote is diluted. After a review of Canadian electoral representation, Donald Blake concluded that "Judged by this standard, and by comparison with countries like Australia and the United States, Canada presents glaring inequalities at the federal level" (Blake 1990, 18). The 25 percent rule is much greater than the 2–3 percent and the 10 percent variations tolerated in the United States and in Australia, respectively. Another problem is that the provincial boundary commissions can use the allowed latitude differently when responding to historical, community or geographical considerations (Courtney 1988, 679–81; Sancton 1990, 445–47, 453–54). This increases discrepancies between constituencies.

Second, while some provinces are overrepresented in the House of Commons, others are underrepresented in relation to each other. This results in the overrepresentation of provinces such as Prince Edward Island, Nova Scotia and, as of the last redistribution, Quebec in relation to Ontario (Sancton 1990, 452). Some ridings in Metro Toronto are larger than Prince Edward Island, which has four seats. After the 1991 census and redistribution, only Ontario, British Columbia and Alberta will have their representation in the House of Commons based on population alone. The variation in ridings can be substantial. In the 1984 election, the average number of voters per riding varied from 14 657 in the territories and 21 804 in Prince Edward Island to 61 919 in Ontario and 66 183 in British Columbia (Cameron and Norcliff 1985, 33).

Third, intraprovincial representation also departs from the principle of equal voting power. There is a substantial discrepancy between rural and urban ridings and between northern and southern ridings. Donald Blake observed that the "distribution record varies between provinces, however, with Saskatchewan constituencies relatively equal (the range is +15 percent to -7 percent). By contrast, the ranges in Ontario and Quebec are -41 to +38 percent and -37 to +57 percent respectively" (Blake 1990, 18; cf. Courtney 1988, 683–84; Sancton 1990, 445–47). The discrepancies may be substantial to account for geographical, historical and social differences. The urban-rural split is especially noticeable in the west, while the northern-southern split is especially evident in Ontario.

These results are giving rise to Charter challenges under sections 2, 3 and 15. Cases have arisen on these grounds in British Columbia, Alberta and Saskatchewan. In Alberta, two cases have been launched on the grounds that discrepancies between provincial ridings are too large. In total, 43 of the 83 constituencies exceed a +/- 25 percent margin. Under the scheme proposed by the 1990 Electoral Boundaries Committee, variances could be as high as 75 percent between certain ridings. Urban voters in densely populated ridings are arguing that the system is not fair because their votes are worth less than votes in less populated rural ridings. Rural voters respond that the imbalance is necessary if their special needs and concerns are to be recognized by politicians, and if urban ridings are to be prevented from exercising the same control over provincial policies that Ontario and Quebec do over federal policies (Geddes 1990; Dafoe 1991).

In Saskatchewan, the debate has proceeded further with the recent unanimous Alberta Appeal Court decision on the new provincial electoral boundaries. The Court of Appeal has held that the boundaries are unconstitutional because the required division between rural and urban areas "creates a stranglehold in the hands of non-urban voters and assumes that an arbitrary apportionment of rural and urban interests is required in representative democracy in Saskatchewan" (Burton 1991). The Court also found that the +/- 25 percent variation was not acceptable. Previously, the difference was held at +/- 15 percent (Bergman with Eisler 1991, 19). The timing of the decision was poor since the Saskatchewan government must call an election by October. To have the boundaries in operation for the election, it will likely appeal the decision to the Supreme Court of Canada. The case should have ramifications across Canada.

The most telling case is *Dixon v. British Columbia (Attorney General)*.[13] In April 1989, the provincial Supreme Court handed down its decision on the provincial boundaries. Under the scheme adopted by the provincial legislature, rural ridings were assigned a greater weight than urban ridings, and population deviations between ridings reached as much as 86.8 percent below and 63.2 percent above the norm. Beverly

McLachlin C.J.S.C. held that these discrepancies infringed on section 3 of the Charter and could not be justified under section 1. She recommended that a scheme similar to the one recommended by the Fisher Commission on boundaries, which allowed for a +/- 25 percent variance, be adopted (*Dixon* 1989, 283). Given that McLachlin has since been appointed to the Supreme Court of Canada, this case may provide insight into how the issue will be resolved at that level.

The basic argument used to challenge the provincial schemes of representation has been that diluting the vote violates the norm of equality established by the Charter. This equality principle is important as Justice McLachlin acknowledged in *Dixon* (1989, 259): "The concept of representation by population is one of the most fundamental guarantees. And the notion of equality of voting power is fundamental to representation by population. The essence of democracy is that the people rule. Anything less than direct, representative democracy risks attenuating the expression of the popular will and hence risks thwarting the purpose of democracy." However, as McLachlin proceeds to observe, the idea of absolute or radical equality of voting power is a departure from the Canadian tradition. The principle of equality is tempered by the principle of good government or quality of representation. Thus, she struck down the British Columbia system as having too many unjustifiable discrepancies, although she indicated a willingness to consider reasonable departures from the norm of equality (ibid., 271, 272, 263–64).

McLachlin's decision captured the fundamental tension in Canadian thinking about the electoral system. The Charter encourages Canadians to push toward a more equal system of representation. From this perspective, equality of voting power equals fairness. However, as shown in the discussion above, there is a rival perception of fairness that maintains that representation concerns more than numbers. If differences between provincial seats, or between urban and rural ridings, or between northern (low-population) and southern (high-population) ridings are reduced to +/- 10 or 15 percent, then the influence of the less-populated areas declines accordingly.

Who is affected? Those affected will tend to be: the have-less and have-not provinces who believe that their interests are not effectively represented in the House of Commons; if its birth rate continues to decline, Quebec, which is at a critical juncture in its relations with the rest of Canada; Aboriginal peoples who reside in the north of many provinces and the territories; and rural voters who are seeing a decline in their way of life and in their influence on policy. These groups increasingly will be forced to question the legitimacy of a political system that denies them effective political expression and representation. This perception of fairness conflicts with the perception of fairness encouraged by the concept of one person, one vote.

In re-evaluating the system of representation, these conflicting views of fairness must be given careful consideration. The deviation from equality of voting power and representation must be justifiable. However, if the deviation is to be reduced, then other considerations must be taken into account. For example, in determining boundaries, the social characteristics of a riding should be accorded greater weight. To maintain northern representation, the Ontario boundary commission extended boundaries to the south (Sancton 1990, 446). Does this dilute the northern and the Aboriginal vote by incorporating more southern and non-Aboriginal people into the district? Perhaps these and similar criteria could be built into the *Representation Act, 1985* more explicitly to meet Charter challenges that might unduly erode the representation of marginalized groups in the Canadian political system. The system must be inclusive to offer adequate protection to minorities, the sine qua non of a liberal democracy.

Representation

The effects of the Charter on representation are less tangible than in the case of one person, one vote.[14] The equality rights section is encouraging Canadians to re-evaluate their institutions. This process encompasses the party and electoral systems as explained above. Recall that women, Aboriginal Canadians, multicultural and multiracial Canadians, and other individuals included in section 15 do not feel adequately represented in the parties or the legislative bodies in Canada. This perception causes them to question the ability and willingness of the traditional parties to respond to their concerns. Given that the groups are often neither cohesive enough nor large enough to organize parties that can contest the traditional parties, the groups are left feeling disillusioned with the party and the electoral system. The fairness and legitimacy of the system is called into question.

A variety of solutions have been proposed to remedy this problem with representation. Proportional representation has been suggested as a cure for sectionalism and regionalism, and to allow for a greater ideological diversity.[15] Proposals to address the exclusiveness of the party system have included dual-member constituencies and quota systems.[16] However, the solution that is attracting the most attention is guaranteed representation as a means of making the House of Commons more representative of particular interests. This has been raised specifically in response to Aboriginal peoples' claims that the system does not adequately respond to the special needs of their communities. It is currently being contemplated at both the federal and provincial levels of government (Platiel 1991; Cox 1991). The following remarks will be addressed to this proposal.

Guaranteed representation for Aboriginal people is an interesting idea, but one that is not without potential problems. Augie Fleras observes that the Maori system of separate representation in New Zealand has been the subject of much criticism from the Maori as well as other New Zealanders (Fleras 1985, 563–70). He cautions that "the applicability of this model for the political aspirations of Canada's Native Indians at the parliamentary level is not encouraging ... given its limitations as an instrument for self-government" (ibid., 576). If guaranteed representation reduced the momentum toward self-government or resulted in a form of representation that was inconsistent with future models of self-government, then it could be a hindrance to the aspirations of Aboriginal people.

There are other potential problems with this system. The guaranteed number of seats will not ensure an effective role in policy development unless these legislators are given a veto over policy. The creation of these seats may remove the onus on parties to be attentive to Aboriginal concerns, given that these representatives will be associated with those issues. Aboriginal representatives may be forced to comply with measures that are antithetical to their interests to build a support basis for other measures in the House. Although not insurmountable, the administrative difficulties are discouraging, beginning with determining how the seats should be allocated among Canada's Aboriginal people. However, many of these problems will vary according to the model chosen.

From another perspective, however, guaranteed representation may be a positive step toward making the system of representation more inclusive and toward increasing perceptions of its legitimacy. As noted in the debate over mirror representation above, there is a symbolic value in including representatives from various groups in society. The legislature acquires a more inclusive appearance, and this is important in inspiring confidence in the institutions of governance. However, for this confidence to hold, material rewards must accompany the symbolic gains. On a practical level, material gains are likely to follow since studies have shown that more inclusive decision-making processes are more attentive to special interests, as discussed above. However, if expectations exceed the realm of realistic material gains, then a more profound disillusionment may occur as has happened in New Zealand. Still, this outcome may be avoided through public education programs.

There is one final benefit to this form of representation. Having Aboriginal representatives in the House may sensitize politicians to Aboriginal concerns and improve their understanding of the goals of Aboriginal communities. It may also help avoid another Oka by having sympathetic spokespersons in the legislature who could act as liaisons between the Aboriginal community and the Canadian government. With a fairer system of representation and more inclusive political institutions, Aboriginal people may be more positively inclined toward the state. In times of crisis, this is especially important.

The solution to the new problems of legitimacy inspired by the Charter consciousness is difficult. Guaranteed representation might provide one answer. However, it should be complemented by encouraging the traditional parties to become more inclusive. The incorporation of Aboriginal people and Charter Canadians into the party structures in greater numbers would force the diverse groups in society to work together. It would open up a dialogue within parties with the possible result that policy initiatives would more directly correspond to public demands, or, at least, inconsistencies between policy and public demands could be more clearly justified. Representation now carried on by interest groups could be subsumed under the parties. The parties should be encouraged to accept guidelines for the full inclusion of these groups. In this way, parties can become both mirrors of society and leaders in integration (not assimilation). The party system would be and appear to be more fair and equitable.

The Public Debate: A Case for Limitations

Election spending has been the cause of considerable review in recent decades. There have been numerous studies of spending limits and the regulation of contributions to parties (Paltiel 1970; 1987; Seidle 1985; Ewing 1988). The problems and prospects for effective regulations are manifold. The influence of the Charter on the regulation of election spending is yet to be determined; however, the Charter has touched directly on one aspect of electoral spending that requires explanation.

Two important perceptions of fairness clashed in a case over election spending. In January 1984, the National Citizens' Coalition launched a case in the Alberta Court of Queen's Bench against sections 70.1 and 72 of the *Election Expenses Act*, which prohibited interest-group spending during elections. The purpose of the legislation was to ensure that the electoral process was fair by maintaining the integrity of spending limits on candidates and parties, and by ensuring that wealthy interests did not dominate the electoral process to the extent of drowning out other voices (Hiebert 1989–90, 74, 78). Despite these admirable goals, the legislation was struck down. Medhurst J. held that the legislation violated the freedom of expression guarantee in the Charter. He decided that the legislation could not be justified under the reasonable limits clause in section 1 of the Charter because the government had not proved that the harm the legislation was intended to avoid would necessarily occur without this restriction in place (*National Citizens' Coalition* 1984). Since freedom of speech is integral to the operation of a liberal democracy, any limits had to be clearly justifiable. The restrictions were not enforced in either the 1984 or the 1988 elections (Canada, Elections Canada 1989, 47).[17]

There is a need for the regulation of interest-group spending during elections if the process is to be fair and equitable. Although it is important to allow open public debate of political issues during elections, it is also important to ensure that one voice or one interest does not dominate others. Spending restrictions ensure that more public interests have fair and equal access to the election debate.[18]

There are three possible responses to interest-group spending in the wake of the Medhurst decision. First, the government could maintain the status quo by leaving the legislation on the books but not enforcing it. This solution is unsatisfactory because it does not guarantee a level playing field during elections. The dominance of the pro–free trade faction in advertising during the 1988 election testifies to the dangers inherent in this approach (Hiebert 1989–90, 80). Unrestricted spending limits on interest groups does not lead to an open and balanced public debate – a basic requirement of a democratic system.

Second, the federal government could prohibit all interest-group advertising. If this action were challenged in the courts, it might fail on the grounds that it was a denial of freedom of expression rather than a limit. The Supreme Court developed this distinction in the *Quebec School Board* case (1984). Otherwise, it could fail under the section 1 test for not impairing the right as little as possible. This option is not realistic.

The third option is for the government to regulate but not prohibit interest-group election spending. One variant of this approach would be to allow issue advertising but not advertising for or against parties or candidates. However, this is a difficult distinction to maintain (Hiebert 1991). Another variant would be to provide a government-regulated environment for election advertising by interest groups. A possible means of regulation would involve the television media, the centrepiece of election advertising (Meisel 1985, 173–74). The government could fund a television program during elections on which interest groups could buy time to air their views to the Canadian population. The fees could be set, and the amount of time allocated to any group or point of view could be regulated. If this were done through the CBC news channel, then a report could be submitted to Parliament through the CBC rather than having elections officials monitor the program. The government could provide a subsidy, along with the fees paid by the interest groups, to the CBC to develop shows for the time slots not used by interest groups on the program.

There are four advantages to this approach. First, a level playing field would be established among interest groups. Once the fees are set, interest groups with the most money would not be able to dominate; also the content of the advertising would be monitored. Second, if the fees were subsidized to allow smaller interest groups to advertise, then the public debate would be more open and balanced. Minority interests would have a better chance of being heard. This would appeal to the new Charter Canadians who often feel that their interests are overlooked by the major parties. The legitimacy of the system would be increased. Third, the CBC, as the national broadcasting agency, would benefit and serve the community. Fourth, elections could be made more accessible to the majority of Canadians. Fill-in shows could include current affairs and issues, electoral education and candidate activities. In sum, this solution could work toward making elections more fair, equitable and open. This accords with the developing trends in Canadian society.

A Ballot for All

The Charter is having an impact on the voting restrictions in the *Canada Elections Act*. The democratic and the equality rights contained in the Charter place the onus upon governments to justify restrictions on the ability of Canadian citizens to participate in the democratic process. Emerging norms of equality and fairness reinforce demands for the system to be more inclusive.

The restrictions on the right to vote or to hold office are fairly limited. Those citizens restricted from voting include: the chief electoral officer, the assistant electoral officer, returning officers unless a tie occurs, federally appointed judges with the exception of citizenship judges, all inmates of penal institutions, all persons restrained of liberty of movement or deprived of the management of property because of mental disease, electors disqualified from voting for corrupt or illegal practices, and persons under the age of eighteen. Challenges have been mounted or contemplated by groups and individuals against the restrictions on judges, prison inmates, persons with mental disabilities, people who are homeless or illiterate, and the young (Greene 1989, 110–17; Beaudoin 1989, 273–81; Canada, Elections Canada 1989, 27–29, 47; Delacourt 1988; Smith 1984, 376–84).

The restrictions on the voting rights of prison inmates and persons with mental disabilities have been under review at least since the early 1970s. However, it was not until the advent of the Charter that the federal government proposed repealing these restrictions in Bill C-79. This bill progressed to second reading in the 33d Parliament but died on the order paper when the 1988 federal election was called (Canada, Elections Canada 1989, 11, 27–28). Although there is variation at the provincial court level, the early cases indicate that the broad language in these sections encompassed individuals whose right to vote could not be reasonably denied. If the vote is to be restricted and the restrictions perceived as fair, then they must be as limited as possible (*Canadian Disability Rights Council* 1988; *Badger* 1988; cf. *Sauvé* 1988; *Grondin* 1988). The Supreme Court will likely be called on to determine this issue if the restrictions are not changed.

The rights of the homeless and the illiterate may also be included by the electoral system without much difficulty. Section 3 applies to the homeless and other citizens equally. The danger with registering the homeless to vote is that election officials are limited in their ability to ensure that homeless voters do not vote more than once. However, under the current system, arrangements could be made for the homeless to register at the address closest to where they sleep (Canada, Elections Canada 1989, 47). In future, computers can be used to monitor voting. A blanket denial of their right to vote is not justifiable. Similarly, the right to vote in our society implies by secret ballot. The denial of the right to vote by secret ballot to persons with literacy problems or to citizens with language barriers could be remedied by placing the party logos on ballots beside the names of the candidates (ibid., 47).

A final area of challenge may come from Canadian youth. Sections 3 and 15 could be used to challenge restrictions on the rights of teenagers to vote. The age limit of eighteen years would be difficult to justify if compared with legislation permitting teenagers to drive and to accept responsibility for their actions at the age of sixteen. However, this limit is not unreasonable if compared with the age limit for the draft into the military, the drinking age in the provinces, and election legislation in other countries. The courts will most likely defer to the legislatures in determining the appropriate voting age.

CONCLUSION

The *Canadian Charter of Rights and Freedoms* is having a significant impact on the operation of the electoral system and citizens' perceptions of both the electoral system and the party system. With the rise in rights consciousness, citizen demands on the state to be more open, more inclusive and more representative of their interests are increasing. However, these demands often conflict.

The different perceptions of fairness and equity in relation to the electoral system were seen most clearly in the cases involving electoral boundaries. Equality of voting power and representation can effectively disenfranchise minority voters, whether rural, northern or otherwise defined. When the vote of any group is severely diluted, then the legitimacy of the voting system is called into question.

The electoral and party systems are not escaping from calls for political institutions to be more open and inclusive. Increasingly, political parties are scrutinized for their degree of representativeness of all Canadians regardless of ancestry and sex. Similarly, restrictions on the right to vote are being challenged. The right to political expression is being defended by various citizen groups. Limits on electoral participation are perceived as being neither fair nor just. To restore the dignity and legitimacy of the system, these limits will have to be carefully examined and defined by legislators.

In the attempt to harmonize the electoral and party systems with the new civic consciousness of Canadians in the Charter era, politicians and bureaucrats should avoid grasping at "quick fixes." Remedies must be carefully developed in accordance with past traditions and future goals. Solutions such as guaranteed representation and reforms developed in other countries should be carefully scrutinized to determine their compatibility with the principles underlying the Canadian political system, political practices and future goals. Only then will they achieve their objectives and increase public confidence in political institutions.

The Charter has posed new challenges for the Canadian system of representation. At times the process seems in disarray as differing rights claims and perceptions of fairness and equity collide. However, embedded in these challenges are the seeds of a new legitimacy for the Canadian political system. The current constitutional situation requires Canadians to rise to this challenge.

ABBREVIATIONS

c.	chapter
C.A.	Court of Appeal
D.L.R. (4th)	Dominion Law Reports, Fourth Series
F.T.R.	Federal Trial Reports
O.R. (2d)	Ontario Reports, Second Series
R.S.C.	Revised Statutes of Canada
S.C.	Statutes of Canada
S.C.R.	Supreme Court Reports
s(s).	section(s)
W.W.R.	Western Weekly Reports

NOTES

This study was completed 25 April 1991.

I wish to thank Janet Hiebert, Patrick Macklem, Paul Thomas, Ian Greene and Eric Bertram for their comments on this paper. Special thanks to Orest Zajcew for his advice and research assistance.

1. One conceivable situation would be if Canada were involved in a protracted war in the Gulf, and the inflationary pressures caused social unrest. Another situation would be if Canada's domestic situation worsened and a stable Parliament was essential to maintaining national order and unity in the face of a social uprising. In either case, Parliament could vote to continue the House of Commons. The Charter does not specify the duration of the continuance. While the period would depend upon the particular circumstances, most likely, the precedence of the House of Commons being continued for an additional year during the First World War would be noted. For an informative discussion of these sections, see Beaudoin (1989, 295–99).

2. See, for example, the review of federal legislation offered in Canada, House of Commons (1985).

3. The importance of the Charter for particular groups is the subject of considerable controversy. For example, compare Beatty (1987), to Petter (1986) and Mandel (1989).

4. The Supreme Court of Canada gave this section a broad reading in *R. v. Sparrow* (1990), 70 D.L.R. (4th) 385 (S.C.C.).

5. The interpretation was based upon the definition of "equality before the law," which is the phrase used in the *Canadian Bill of Rights* to guarantee equality rights. In *Lavell* (1974) the Supreme Court of Canada held that "equality before the law" was a procedural guarantee, not a substantive guarantee. The guarantee did not include the right to equality under the law. As a result, the court concluded that as long as women within a particular group were treated equally, the right to equality before the law would be upheld. In *Bliss* (1979), Stella Bliss was denied unemployment insurance benefits because she had not worked the required period, which was longer for pregnant women than for others. The Supreme Court of Canada held that discrimination based on a pregnancy is not discrimination based on sex because all women do not become pregnant. For a fuller discussion of these cases, see Baines (1988, 171–74; Brodsky and Day (1989, 14–16); Gibson (1990, 28–30, 139–43, 167–73). The *Bliss* decision regarding pregnancy and discrimination was overturned in *Brooks v. Canada Safeway Ltd.* (1989).

6. Morton et al. (1990, tables 5 and 6). Note, however, that if sections 16–22 are combined with section 23, then the number of language cases exceeds the number of equality cases by one. See also Morton and Withey (1987, 75–77).

7. For example, Baines writes that "in the context of Meech Lake, I compared the final *Report* of the first of the male dominated federal committees with the published transcripts of their proceedings, only to learn that the Committee *Report* seriously misrepresented the submissions made by five national women's organisations" (Baines 1990, 19). Although the debate recorded in this paper is drawn from the literature on the Constitution, the criticism of the assumption that men represent the interests of women extends to political and constitutional matters, as Baines observes.

8. See also the comment by Georges Erasmus, National Chief of the Assembly of First Nations to the Special Joint Committee on the Meech Lake Accord as quoted in Alan Cairns (1988, 125). He said that the statement that non-Aboriginal politicians could represent Aboriginal interests is bogus.

9. See also Bashevkin (1989); and Clarke et al. (1991, 11–12). Note the quicker response of the bureaucracy than of the parties to the mobilization of women.

10. See also Russell (1990, 247–51). For a brief account of interest-group use of the courts, see Morton (1987, 39–43).

11. This idea was developed through conversations with Paul Thomas.

12. For a discussion of the history of Canadian departures from the principle of representation by population, see, generally, Roach (1991) and Boyer (1987a, 1987b).

13. For a discussion of the case, see, generally, Roach (1990, 1991).
14. I am not referring to the right to be qualified for membership in the House of Commons or a provincial legislature. This has been raised in a number of cases including *Fraser v. Nova Scotia (Attorney General)* (1986) and *MacLean v. Nova Scotia (Attorney General)* (1987).
15. For a fuller discussion of this idea, see Canada, Task Force on Canadian Unity (1979, 131); and Franks (1987).
16. For a discussion of the systems, see Maillé (1990, 33). Baines also notes other sources which discuss these ideas (1990, 18–19).
17. Legislation proposed in Manitoba that was very similar to the federal legislation never proceeded because of the Medhurst decision. Manitoba is waiting for a resolution of this issue at the federal level before drafting new limits according to the elections office, 4 February 1990.
18. For an informative discussion of interest groups and Canadian federal elections in the context of fairness and equity, see Hiebert (1991). For a useful discussion of interest-group spending and the concept of equality in the United States, see Ashdown (1988). Ashdown contrasts the right to speak with the right to hear as a means of assessing interest-group spending restrictions.

BIBLIOGRAPHY

Allen, Gene. 1991. "Interpreters Make Point for MPP." *Globe and Mail*, 16 March, A4.

Ashdown, Gerald. 1988. "Buying Speech: Campaign Spending, the New Politics, and Election Law Reform." *New England Law Review* 23 (Autumn): 363.

Badger v. Canada (Attorney General) (1988), 55 D.L.R. (4th) 177 (Man. C.A.).

Baines, Beverly. 1988. "Women and the Law." In *Changing Patterns: Women in Canada*, ed. Sandra Burt, Lorraine Code and Lindsay Dorney. Toronto: McClelland and Stewart.

———. 1990. "After Meech Lake: The Ms Representation of Gender in Scholarly Spaces." Paper prepared for "After Meech Lake," a conference sponsored by the College of Law and the Department of Political Studies, University of Saskatchewan, Saskatoon, 1–3 November.

Baker, David. 1987. "The Changing Norms of Equality in the Supreme Court of Canada." *Supreme Court Law Review* 9:497–555.

Bashevkin, Sylvia. 1985. *Toeing the Lines: Women and Party Politics in English Canada*. Toronto: University of Toronto Press.

———. 1989. "Political Parties and the Representation of Women." In *Canadian Parties in Transition: Discourse, Organization, and Representation*, ed. Alain G. Gagnon and Brian Tanguay. Scarborough: Nelson Canada.

Beatty, David M. 1987. *Putting the Charter Back to Work: Designing a Constitutional Labour Code*. Montreal and Kingston: McGill-Queen's University Press.

Beaudoin, Gerald-A. 1989. "Democratic Rights." In *The Canadian Charter of Rights and Freedoms*, ed. Gerald-A. Beaudoin and Ed Ratushny. Toronto: Carswell.

Beckton, Clare. 1989. "Freedom of Expression." In *The Canadian Charter of Rights and Freedoms*, ed. Gerald-A. Beaudoin and Ed Ratushny. Toronto: Carswell.

Bergman, Brian, and Dale Eisler. 1991. "A Hard, Cold Choice." *Maclean's*, 18 March, D2.

Blake, Donald. 1990. Comments at the Learned Societies Panel on "Implications of the Charter for Electoral Redistribution." In *Reform of Electoral Campaigns*. Ottawa: Canadian Study of Parliament Group.

Bliss v. Canada (Attorney General), [1979] 1 S.C.R. 183.

Boyer, Patrick. 1981. *Political Rights: The Legal Framework of Elections in Canada*. Toronto: Butterworths.

———. 1987a. *Election Law in Canada*, vol. I. Toronto: Butterworths.

———. 1987b. *Election Law in Canada*, vol. II. Toronto: Butterworths.

Brodsky, Gwen, and Shelagh Day. 1989. *Canadian Charter Equality Rights For Women: One Step Forward or Two Steps Back?* Ottawa: Canadian Advisory Council on the Status of Women.

Brooks v. Canada Safeway Ltd., [1989] 4 W.W. R. 19 (S.C.C.).

Burton, Randy. 1991. "Ruling Devastates PC Election Plans." *The Star-Phoenix*, 7 March.

Cairns, Alan. 1986. "The Embedded State: State–Society Relations in Canada." In *State and Society: Canada in a Comparative Perspective*, ed. Keith Banting. Vol. 31 of the research studies of the Royal Commission on the Economic Union and Development Prospects for Canada. Toronto: University of Toronto Press.

———. 1988. "Citizens (Outsiders) and Governments (Insiders) in Constitution-Making: The Case of Meech Lake." *Canadian Public Policy* 14 (special supplement): 121–45.

———. 1989a. "The Electoral System and the Party System in Canada, 1921–1965." In *Constitution, Government and Society in Canada*, ed. Douglas

E. Williams. Toronto: McClelland and Stewart.

———. 1989b. "Political Science, Ethnicity and the Canadian Constitution." *Federalism and Political Community: Essays in Honour of Donald Smiley,* ed. David P. Shugarman and Reg Whitaker. Peterborough: Broadview Press.

———. 1989c. "Ritual, Taboo and Bias in Constitutional Controversies in Canada." Paper read as the Timlin Lecture, University of Saskatchewan, Saskatoon, 13 November.

Cameron, James M., and Glen Norcliff. 1985. "The Canadian Constitution and the Political Muskeg of One Person One Vote." *The Operational Geographer,* 8.

Canada. Bill C-79. *An Act to amend the Canada Elections Act,* 2nd Session, 33rd Parliament, 1986–87.

———. *Canada Elections Act,* R.S.C. 1970, c. 14 (1st supp.), ss. 70.1, 72; en. 1973–74, c. 51, s. 12.

———. *Canada Elections Act,* R.S.C. 1985, c. E-2.

———. *Canadian Bill of Rights,* S.C. 1960, c. 44.

———. *Canadian Charter of Rights and Freedoms,* ss. 1, 3–5, 15, 15.1, 16–23, 27, 28, 33, Part I of the *Constitution Act, 1982,* being Schedule B of the *Canada Act 1982* (U.K.), 1982, c. 11.

———. *Constitution Act, 1982,* being Schedule B of the *Canada Act 1982* (U.K.), 1982, c. 11. s. 35(1).

———. *Elections Expenses Act,* S.C. 1973–74, c. 51.

———. *Representation Act, 1985,* S.C. 1986, c. 8 [now R.S.C. 1985, c. 6 (2nd Supp.)].

Canada. Elections Canada. 1989. *Report of the Chief Electoral Officer of Canada as per subsection 195(1) of the Canada Elections Act.* Ottawa: Minister of Supply and Services Canada.

Canada. House of Commons. Sub-committee on Equality Rights. 1985. *Equality for All.* Ottawa: Queen's Printer.

Canada. Task Force on Canadian Unity. 1979. *A Future Together.* Ottawa: Minister of Supply and Services Canada.

Canada (Attorney General) v. Lavell, [1984] S.C.R. 1349.

Canadian Disability Rights Council v. Canada (1988), 21 F.T.R. 268.

Clarke, Harold, Jane Jenson, Lawrence LeDuc and Jon Pammett. 1991. *Absent Mandate: Interpreting Change in Canadian Elections.* 2d ed. Toronto: Gage.

Courtney, John. 1988. "Parliament and Representation: The Unfinished Agenda of Electoral Redistributions." *Canadian Journal of Political Science* 21:675–90.

Cox, Kevin. 1991. "N.B. Seat Proposed for Natives." *Globe and Mail*, 19 March.

Dafoe, John. 1991. "Tories Tremble at the Loss of Supporters in Rural Ridings." *Globe and Mail*, 9 March.

Delacourt, Susan. 1988. "Charter Spurred More to Fight for Their Voting Rights in 1988." *Globe and Mail*, 24 November.

Dickson, The Right Honourable Brian. 1987. "Keynote Address." In *The Cambridge Lectures*, ed. Frank E. McArdle. Montreal: Les Éditions Yvon Blais Inc.

Dixon v. British Columbia (Attorney General) (1989), 59 D.L.R. (4th) 247 (B.C.S.C.).

Dupré, J. Stefan. 1989. "Canadian Constitutionalism and the Sequel to the Meech Lake/Langevin Accord." In *Federalism and Political Community: Essays in Honour of Donald Smiley*, ed. David P. Shugarman and Reg Whitaker. Peterborough: Broadview Press.

Elton, David, and Roger Gibbins. 1980. *Electoral Reform: The Time Is Pressing, The Need Is Now*. Calgary: Canada West Foundation.

———. 1982. "Western Alienation and Political Culture." In *The Canadian Political Process*, ed. Richard Schultz et al. Toronto: Holt Rinehart and Winston.

Ewing, K. D. 1988. "The Legal Regulation of Campaign Financing in Canadian Federal Elections." *Public Law* 577–607.

Fleras, Augie. 1985. "From Social Control towards Political Self-Determination? Maori Seats and the Politics of Separate Maori Representation in New Zealand." *Canadian Journal of Political Science* 18:551–76.

Franks, C.E.S. 1987. *The Parliament of Canada*. Toronto: University of Toronto Press.

Fraser v. Nova Scotia (Attorney General) (1988), 30 D.L.R. (4th) 340 (N.S.T.D.).

Geddes, Ashley. 1990. "Riding for a Fall." *Calgary Herald*, 18 November.

Gibbins, Roger. 1990. *Conflict and Unity*. Scarborough: Nelson Canada.

Gibson, Dale. 1990. *The Law of the Charter: Equality Rights*. Toronto: Carswell.

Greene, Ian. 1989. *The Charter of Rights and Freedoms*. Toronto: James Lorimer.

Grondin v. Ontario (Attorney General) (1988), 65 O.R. (2d) 427 (H.C.).

Heard, Andrew. 1991. *Canadian Constitutional Conventions*. Toronto: Oxford University Press.

Hiebert, Janet. 1989–90. "Fair Elections and Freedom of Expression Under the Charter." *Journal of Canadian Studies* 24 (Winter): 72–86.

———. 1991. "Interest Groups and Canadian Federal Elections." In *Interest Groups and Elections in Canada*, ed. F. Leslie Seidle. Vol. 2 of the research studies of the Royal Commission on Electoral Reform and Party Financing. Ottawa and Toronto: RCERPF/Dundurn.

Hogg, Peter. 1985. *Constitutional Law of Canada*. 2d ed. Toronto: Carswell.

Irvine, William P. 1979. *Does Canada Need a New Electoral System?* Kingston: Queen's University, Institute of Intergovernmental Relations.

Lavell v. Canada (Attorney General), [1974] S.C.R. 1349.

MacLean v. Nova Scotia (Attorney General) (1987), 35 D.L.R. (4th) 306 (N.S.T.D.).

Maillé, Chantal. 1990. *Primed for Power: Women in Canadian Politics*. Ottawa: Canadian Advisory Council on the Status of Women.

Mandel, Michael. 1989. *The Charter of Rights and the Legalization of Politics in Canada*. Toronto: Wall and Thompson.

Meisel, John. 1985. "The Boob-Tube Election: Three Aspects of the 1984 Landslide." In *The Canadian House of Commons: Essays in Honour of Norman Ward*, ed. John Courtney. Calgary: University of Calgary Press.

Mishler, William, and Harold D. Clarke. 1990. "Political Participation in Canada." In *Canadian Politics in the 1990s*. 3d ed., ed. M.S. Whittington and G. Williams. Scarborough: Nelson Canada.

Morton, F.L. 1987. "The Political Impact of the Canadian Charter of Rights and Freedoms." *Canadian Journal of Political Science* 22:31–55.

Morton, F.L., Peter H. Russell and Michael J. Withey. 1990. "The Supreme Court's First 100 Charter of Rights Decisions: A Quantitative Analysis." Paper presented at the annual meeting of the Canadian Political Science Association, 27–29 May, Victoria, BC.

Morton, F.L., and Michael J. Withey. 1987. "Charting the Charter, 1982–1985: A Statistical Analysis." *Canadian Human Rights Yearbook, 1987*. Toronto: Carswell.

National Citizens' Coalition v. Canada (Attorney General) (1984), 11 D.L.R. (4th) 481 (Alta. Q.B.).

Norman, Ken. 1989. "Freedom of Peaceful Assembly and Freedom of Association." In *The Canadian Charter of Rights and Freedoms*, ed. Gerald-A. Beaudoin and Ed Ratushny. Toronto: Carswell.

Olsen, Dennis. 1980. *The State Elite*. Toronto: McClelland and Stewart.

Paltiel, Khayam Z. 1970. *Political Party Financing in Canada*. Toronto: McGraw-Hill Ryerson.

———. 1987. "Canadian Election Expense Legislation 1963–85: A Critical Appraisal or Was the Effort Worth it?" In *Contemporary Canadian Politics*, ed. Robert Jackson et al. Scarborough: Prentice-Hall.

Panitch, Leo. 1990. "Elites, Power and Class in Canada." In *Canadian Politics in the 1990s*. 3d ed., ed. M.S. Whittington and G. Williams. Scarborough: Nelson Canada.

Petter, Andrew. 1986. "The Politics of the Charter." *Supreme Court Law Review* 473–505.

Platiel, Rudy. 1991. "Natives Polled on Senator's Idea." *Globe and Mail*, 18 January.

Poirier, Patricia. 1991. "Spicer Claims Neutral Role in Quebec." *Globe and Mail*, 6 February, A4.

Porter, John. 1972. *The Vertical Mosaic: An Analysis of Social Power in Canada*. Toronto: University of Toronto Press.

Quebec (Attorney General) v. Quebec Association of Protestant School Boards, [1984] 2 S.C.R. 66.

R. v. Sparrow (1990), 70 D.L.R. (4th) 385 (S.C.C.).

Roach, Kent. 1990. "Reapportionment in British Columbia." *UBC Law Review* 24:79–102.

———. 1991. "One Person, One Vote? Canadian Constitutional Standards for Electoral Distribution and Districting." In *Drawing the Map: Equality and Efficacy of the Vote in Canadian Electoral Boundary Reform*, ed. David Small. Vol. 11 of the research studies of the Royal Commission on Electoral Reform and Party Financing. Ottawa and Toronto: RCERPF/Dundurn.

Russell, Peter H. 1983. "The Political Purposes of the Canadian Charter of Rights and Freedoms." *Canadian Bar Review* 61 (March): 30–54.

———. 1990. "The Charter and the Future of Canadian Politics." In *Canadian Politics: An Introduction to the Discipline*, ed. Alain G. Gagnon and James P. Bickerton. Peterborough: Broadview Press.

Sancton, Andrew. 1990. "Eroding Representation-by-Population in the Canadian House of Commons: The *Representation Act, 1985*." *Canadian Journal of Political Science* 23:441–57.

Sauvé v. Canada (Attorney General) (1988), 53 D.L.R. (4th) 595 (Ont. H.C.).

Seidle, F. Leslie. 1985. "The Election Expenses Act: The House of Commons and the Parties." In *The Canadian House of Commons: Essays in Honour of Norman Ward*, ed. John Courtney. Calgary: University of Calgary Press.

Smith, Jennifer. 1990. "Representation and Constitutional Reform in Canada." Paper prepared for "After Meech Lake," a conference sponsored by the College of Law and the Department of Political Studies, University of Saskatchewan, Saskatoon, 1–3 November.

Smith, Lynn. 1984. "Charter Equality Rights: Some General Issues and Specific Applications in British Columbia to Elections, Juries and Illegitimacy." *UBC Law Review* 18:351–406.

Stasiulis, Daiva, and Yasmeen Abu-Laban. 1990. "Ethnic Activism and the Politics of Limited Inclusion in Canada." In *Canadian Politics: An Introduction to the Discipline*, ed. Alain G. Gagnon and James P. Bickerton. Peterborough: Broadview Press.

Thomas, Paul G. 1991. "Parties and Regional Representation." In *Representation, Integration and Political Parties in Canada*, ed. Herman Bakvis. Vol. 14 of the research studies of the Royal Commission on Electoral Reform and Party Financing. Ottawa and Toronto: RCERPF/Dundurn.

United Kingdom. *Constitution Act, 1867*, 30 & 31 Vict., c. 3, ss. 37, 51, 91¶1.

Williams, Robert J. 1981. "Candidate Selection." In *Canada at the Polls, 1979 and 1980*, ed. Howard R. Penniman. Washington, DC: American Enterprise Institute for Public Policy Research.

7

A CODE OF ETHICS FOR POLITICAL PARTIES

Janet Hiebert

AN INTERESTING DEVELOPMENT is taking place in public attitudes toward Canadian political parties. Although survey data indicate that public trust in political parties and those who hold public office is being seriously questioned (Blais and Gidengil 1991), this cynicism has not translated into a lack of interest in the affairs of parties. If anything, public interest in parties is increasing. Public expectations of parties are more extensive and demanding than ever before. Canadians, as they indicated in the hearings of the Royal Commission on Electoral Reform and Party Financing, increasingly feel a stake in how parties nominate candidates and select leaders and in the outcomes of these processes in terms of fair representation – activities which, in the not-so-recent past, have been considered strictly the private interest of parties.

This increased public scrutiny may be puzzling to many within the parties, who question why the activities of private organizations, where individuals with similar views and objectives gather to promote common values, should command such scrutiny by those external to the party. But the extent to which this scrutiny seems puzzling betrays a lack of awareness that Canadians are increasingly asserting an interest in the basic institutions that affect the way we, as a society, order and assess our political priorities. This public interest in political institutions is not confined to parties. The entrenchment of rights in the Charter and the ongoing constitutional debate have contributed to a more critical polity in which individuals and groups are more sensitive to and vocal about the basic assumptions, policies and institutions that affect them.

There are essentially two bases Canadians point to in justifying a legitimate public interest in party activities. Because parties serve as the principal gatekeepers in determining who is selected as candidates and leaders, these activities are understandably scrutinized in accordance with accepted norms and values. Accordingly, there is an expectation that these processes should be conducted in a fair and equitable manner:

> In the Canadian political system, the leadership selection process that goes on in the political parties is a critical part of our whole democratic process. The leader of the political party that gains the most seats in Canada becomes the Prime Minister of this country and it is in his or her sole discretion then to pick a Cabinet ... And so, that process becomes very much a public process ... As a member of a political party who becomes a voting delegate at a convention, I have pre-selected for all Canadians who may become Prime Minister of this country ...
> How he or she is selected becomes critical. If he or she is selected on the basis of dirty tricks, forged signatures on membership cards, the enumeration of tombstones in the local cemetery, then the entire political process becomes weakened or corrupted or tainted because the selection of the leader and the nomination process is the foundation of our democratic institutions. (McCarney 1990, 221–22)

Political parties have a direct influence on how Canadians view their electoral system. Canadians overwhelmingly base their voting decisions on parties (and their positions on national issues) and party leaders rather than constituency issues or candidates (Clarke et al. 1991, 113–16). Thus, if public confidence in the integrity of parties is questioned, this lack of confidence influences perceptions of the legitimacy of the electoral process and system of representation.

The second reason for public concern derives from the extent of state subsidies to parties and candidates. The total public financial contribution to parties and candidates through tax credits and reimbursements of election expenses in the four-year cycle ending in 1988 was $66 658 000, or 31.4 percent of the total expenditures of parties and candidates (Michaud and Laferrière 1991). Many interveners at the Royal Commission's public hearings argued that, given the significant public subsidy of candidates and parties, it is a legitimate public expectation that parties will conduct such activities as nomination and leadership processes in accordance with public norms and expectations.

For these reasons, Canadians feel they have a legitimate stake in how parties perform certain activities, an interest that does not depend on personal or direct involvement with any particular party. This interest has prompted criticism that political parties have not been effective in redressing the behaviour that undermines public confidence in the integrity of parties and the political process. A complaint frequently directed at parties, and which was made during Commission hearings, is that parties are either unwilling or incapable of internally monitoring and enforcing fair procedures for their activities. The concern was that where incidents or allegations of misbehaviour occur, parties have been reluctant to assume responsibility for reviewing and revising the practices which give rise to allegations of misconduct.

The combination of cynicism and enhanced expectations presents a serious challenge to those within political parties who wish to promote a vital and expanding membership. Widespread cynicism may be a serious threat to a party's ability to hold and attract members. With discontent comes also the risk of diminishing electoral appeal for the traditional political parties in favour of new parties or alternative forms of political associations, such as interest groups. Furthermore, the impression that parties do not recognize the seriousness of public concerns encourages suggestions that an increasing range of party activities should be regulated.

CODES OF ETHICS

In responding to this combination of public cynicism and enhanced expectations, parties should look at other organizations that have been faced with similar challenges and have responded by adopting codes of ethics. Codes of ethics are written statements of an organization's basic values and principles of behaviour. Although there is considerable variance in the scope and structure of ethical codes and in the specific values they articulate, codes often contain the following two elements: an explicit statement of the organization's values and principles, grounded in its philosophy, objectives and traditions; and an expectation that all members of the organization will be committed to these values and principles (Berenbeim 1987, 16).

Whereas ethical codes are becoming commonplace for corporations, professional associations and public servants, few political parties have adopted them. The closest example of a party utilizing a code of ethics is the Democratic party in the U.S. which in the early 1970s went through an extensive reform process and codified many of its rules for political conventions and delegate voting (Shafer 1983; Commission on Party Structure 1970, 1973). In Canada the Reform Party has also adopted a code of ethics, but this is more a process for reviewing and screening candidates than a set of rules that binds all members of the organization. More will be said about the Reform Party code later in the study.

Despite the absence of fully articulated codes of ethics for political parties, there is much to commend them. A serious obstacle in reforming political activities is that parties are so decentralized that leaders have difficulties controlling the conduct of their members, particularly at the constituency level. The increasing use of professionals or experts, accompanied by the diminishing role of patronage, means that the leader is effectively deprived of many of the sanctions used in the past to ensure conformity and compliance by the party faithful with the party's rules. The fact that an overwhelming majority of party members are volunteers adds to the difficulties that face leaders in ensuring adherence to the principles of the party.

Given these difficulties it is surprising that more attention has not been paid to similar experiences of other sectors, in particular, large decentralized corporations. Although there are important differences between these organizations, especially the fact that parties consist largely of volunteers whereas corporations have paid employees, some of the problems encountered by the two kinds of organizations are remarkably similar.

CORPORATE USE OF CODES

Many organizations have values that guide the conduct of their members. Whether explicitly articulated or not, these values often reflect the basic assumptions of the organization by addressing the question, "What are the principles that should guide a person's conduct in interactions with other employees or members of the public?" The difficulty facing large, decentralized organizations is how to ensure that these values and rules are understood and followed regularly by everyone throughout the organization.

Unlike political parties, many corporations are no longer willing to rely on chance to ensure that individuals, at all levels of the organization, understand the organization's values and act upon them. Like Canadian political parties, corporations have been subject to increased public scrutiny and heightened public interest in the way they conduct themselves. Much of this increased attention had its origins in the 1970s stemming from a number of investigations and scandals in the United States relating to allegations of illegal or questionable corporate behaviour. Like Canadian political parties today, American corporations in the 1970s were faced with declining public confidence. While polls showed that 55 percent of the American public had "a great deal of confidence" in the leaders of large corporations in 1966, this figure had fallen significantly to 29 percent in 1973 and 15 percent in 1975 (Silk and Vogel 1976, 21).

The decline in public confidence prompted a move toward greater management of the corporate performance at all levels of the organization. Codes of ethics have become an important part of this management process. Corporations have revisited and re-evaluated existing codes and in many circumstances have devised new ones. As many as 93 percent of large American corporations (Center for Business Ethics 1986, 86) and more than half of large Canadian corporations now have codes of ethics (Brooks 1989).

Corporations have viewed codes of ethics as an effective way of helping foster a shared philosophy throughout the organization and to ensure predictable and appropriate behaviour in ambiguous circumstances (White and Montgomery 1980, 80). This objective has been particularly challenging because, like political parties, many corporations have a decentralized structure and are often geographically dispersed. A principal advantage of codes of ethics, according to corporate leaders who have implemented them, is that they enable management to promote the organization's principles and values as the basic standards to be adhered to by everyone in the organization. A New York Conference Board study based on interviews with executives and public statements by chief executive officers reveals that among the reasons identified for adopting codes of ethics is the importance of emphasizing the values of the organization in a manner that allows for greater managerial professionalism and protects against improper conduct by employees (Berenbeim 1987, 13–14). This finding is reinforced by an assessment of corporate excellence that reveals that one of the common traits of the corporations that earn this illustrious assessment is that they possess a set of values that is well known and understood by everyone in the organization and that represents a clear expression of how the organization and everyone associated with it should act (Peters and Waterman 1982, 279).

Many who believe that articulating the values and principles of an organization is important for responsible corporate performance stress the responsibility of leaders to provide the environment in which these values are understood by all and become institutionalized in the corporation's operating procedures. In the words of one corporate leader,

> Ethical organizations make sure that ethical behaviour is built into their operating procedures and that employees are clearly informed about them. This is why in our company we have a written code of ethics. It is important to explain why we have a written code, because people are often sceptical about words on a piece of paper. First, it shows that our company takes ethics very seriously and that management has

focused attention on key principles. Secondly, it instills in all employees a greater awareness of what is right, both in the internal and in the external sense. In other words, it serves as a reminder that our company is an integral part of society. Thirdly, the code makes ethics an ever-present and ongoing activity in the daily life of the corporation, not something to which we merely pay lip-service. Finally, it helps build our team. When people know what is expected of them, they endeavour to meet the standard. (Haynes 1991, 19–20)

In moving toward a greater codifying of values, corporate leaders recognize that codes of ethics will not only help to restore and enhance public confidence in corporations but may also forestall demands for greater regulation:

First, by establishing the benchmarks of what is right and what is wrong, we are more likely to be able to fend off punitive, heavy-handed and possibly damaging legislation that the public will insist on if a degree of self-policing is not seen to be effective. And second, such action more importantly can provide a clear path for restoring confidence in business in our society – by improving the performance, and not merely the image, of our business organizations. Ethical codes are no panacea, of course, even if they are enforced. But they do clarify our thinking and encourage socially useful behavior. The central issue is integrity – and much depends in the coming years, on the forthrightness and courage with which we face up to that issue. (Blumenthal 1975, 2. Copyright © 1975 by The New York Times Company. Reprinted by permission.)

The arguments that corporations need leaders who have both the willingness and institutional capability to promote the values of the organization and to provide a framework for ongoing evaluation are equally applicable to political parties. Parties are faced with similar challenges of ensuring that these values are meaningful and will encourage persons at all levels to pursue the party's mission. Given the decentralized nature of political parties and the high volunteer component, it is currently difficult for leaders to incorporate these values into the members' regular activities.

BENEFITS OF ARTICULATING THE VALUES OF A PARTY

A code of ethics would be an important organizational instrument of party governance that would enable the executive of a party to manage and give coherence to the values, principles and standards of the party. The affirmation of a party's basic precepts and values in a code of ethics would help foster and reinforce agreement with these values among members and would emphasize their importance as the collective standard of the party. The explicit expression of the core values of a political party would enhance the authority and responsibility of party leaders for assessing the activities of members in terms of these shared values and promoting certain behavioural expectations. Furthermore, codification of the party's values would make the imposition of sanctions against those who do not comply with the party's principles, and who by their actions undermine confidence and trust in the party, easier and more justifiable.

By stating specifically how the party's values should inform the basic rules of conduct for all members, a code would help promote a shared culture that would bind members to the common purpose of strengthening the party and affirming its integrity. Thus a code would give a greater emphasis to the principles that encourage individuals to join a particular party and would reinforce their commitment to the party.

With a party's adoption of a code of ethics would come the responsibility of party members to conduct themselves in accordance with the philosophy and values of the party. A code of ethics would encourage behaviour that accorded with the precepts and principles of the party by relying on internal peer pressure to enforce an explicit and generally recognized set of behavioural expectations. The crystallization of the party's basic values and principles in a code of ethics would be particularly valuable to members who must make difficult decisions in the competitive environment of elections. It would enhance the incentives for members to put the party's long-term interests ahead of possible short-term gains by protecting its integrity and reputation.

A greater emphasis on adhering to and promoting the values of a party would facilitate the evaluation of the practices and rules of the party and encourage members to address any disparity between desirable standards and current practices. By providing a framework within which members could assess activities that might undermine confidence in the political party, a code of ethics would provide justification for insisting that the party membership reform procedures and seek ways of correcting existing problems.

For example, a party that may be committed to broadening its representational base to include more women and members of underrepresented groups could encounter unintended barriers to full participation. The recognition, through a code, of the value of promoting greater representation would enable members to criticize existing barriers and those who would maintain them. This commitment, for instance, could be seen as the justification for the party to establish or strengthen search committees or other mechanisms to enhance the representativeness of the party.

The very act of consulting other members and discussing the activities included in a code of ethics would itself foster reflection on members' and parties' practices. It would also provide individual members who have ethical concerns about the practices of others in the party with the justification for criticizing these practices. These steps are crucial for modifying behaviour within parties and for altering perceptions of what considerations should be acted upon when making decisions.

Another important contribution that a code of ethics would make is to endow membership with greater importance than it now has in Canada. Unlike West European party systems, which encourage and promote meaningful membership in party activities, Canadian parties are criticized for placing too great an emphasis on the voting capacity of members in leadership and nomination activities, at the expense of contributing to the more general objectives and functions of the party. A code would encourage parties to evaluate the importance of membership when they are determining what guidelines and principles ought to govern membership, including the role members play in selecting leaders and candidates. Further, the responsibility envisaged in a code of each member to evaluate his or her own practices within the party would itself contribute to the significance of membership by making each member a more vital part of the organization.

In addition to ensuring that the values of the party are more clearly understood and have more salience in the regular activities of members, one of the biggest attractions of a code of ethics should be its potential for forestalling greater regulation of party life. A code of ethics would provide leaders with an effective management resource and members with the guidance and incentive to reform party activities that may otherwise be subject to calls for regulation. In doing so, it would allow parties to retain internal control over their activities.

For example, in the Commission's hearings serious concerns were raised about the way some members of parties conduct themselves during elections. Political advertising attracted considerable criticism from many interveners who expressed the view that parties' advertising is often deceptive, cheapens the electoral system and alienates voters. Unlike the strict guidelines on the content of advertising applied to the private sector, regulations are rarely enforced for political advertising, and parties often fail to restrain themselves or impose their own standards. The sense that "anything goes," whether truthful or not, undermines public respect for the political process and parties. It also enhances the appeal of calls for regulation. The recommendations by interveners in the Commission's hearings included greater controls on election advertising to encourage more substantive content. They also included requirements that candidates and leaders speak on their own behalf, that negative advertising be limited to no more than 25 percent of a party's total advertising budget, and that candidates' and parties' messages be required to adhere to the advertising guidelines regarding truthfulness.

Despite these proposals, criticisms that party members do not conform with normative expectations may not be easily or practically addressed by regulations. Because elections are activities in which parties should be given as much latitude as possible to promote their policies and distinguish them from those of their rivals, it would be difficult and, it can be argued, ill-advised to regulate election tactics. Nevertheless, the public's suspicions that election practices manipulate and exploit certain groups of electors threaten the integrity of the electoral process.

Election advertising is well suited for redress in a code of ethics. For example, though a party may recognize that criticism of political opponents through advertising is a legitimate strategy and that it is expected to challenge its rivals and suggest alternative policies, it may also emphasize that confidence in the party system will be undermined by advertising that distorts the position of others, engages in inflammatory appeals, attacks personal characteristics of political rivals not related to their competence to perform public duties, and is inconsistent with the Canadian Code of Advertising Standards.

CONSIDERATIONS WHEN DEVELOPING A CODE

It is generally recognized that ethical codes are no guarantee that organizations and their employees or members will uphold the principles and values contained in the code. Those who study codes suggest there are at least three factors that have a significant influence on their effectiveness: the extent to which they realistically express the values and principles of the organization; the extent to which all levels of the organization feel bound by the code; and the ability of the organization to enforce the code.

Codes are not technical regulations and should not read as such. On the other hand, moralizing or philosophical statements of principle, without descriptions of the ambiguous situations that are likely to face an individual, are not particularly helpful either. Political parties should consider a balance between statements outlining the party's philosophical and moral foundation and the practical application of these values to the specific activities of the party. In defining these standards, it is important to remember the competitive environment in which parties exist. Though it would be relatively easy to establish a set of optimum behavioural standards, such standards that assume the highest moral conduct possible would run the risk of being little more than empty platitudes. Instead, parties should stress the principles that guide their organization and reflect on how these can be incorporated into the party's various activities. A realistic code would have a better chance of commanding the respect and acceptance of members than one that introduces lofty principles but without any application to the particular situations that give rise to difficult, and often ad hoc, decisions.

A second factor that determines the effectiveness of a code is the extent to which it permeates the entire organization. For a code to become part of the life of the party, the party executive, the executive of the constituency association and all members should feel that it applies equally to them. Given the importance of leaders and the images they project, it is essential that they be seen as validating the principles on which the code is based. It is equally important that members feel sufficiently bound by, and knowledgeable about, the code so they can evaluate their own activities as well as the actions of others in light of the standards of the party. To further this objective, it is important that procedures be implemented at all levels of the party organization (one example would be local or regional review committees) to ensure that the code is accessible to all new and existing members and to promote education in the values and principles in the code. Further, it is important that the code be updated regularly to address changing or new matters of concern.

The third and most important factor in ensuring the effectiveness of codes is enforcement. If codes are to be a useful organizational tool for party leaders, exhortations to engage in appropriate behaviour are insufficient. Parties are faced with a significant challenge in enforcing their codes, particularly in light of the decentralized nature of parties, the large volunteer component, and the fact that levels of party activity may depend on the proximity of a convention or election. Though the nature of the enforcement process will vary with the objectives, structure and culture of the party, there are steps that any party could take to maximize the influence of a code on decision making.

For example, ethics committees at the provincial or national level could establish procedures for appraising complaints from members that the activities of other members, or party officers, have not been in accordance with the code. These committees could also be called upon to provide interpretations of the code and its application to particular circumstances. Parties may wish to implement a division of labour between local associations and the national executive. For example, parties may require that the constituency executives be responsible for making immediate recommendations on whether a nomination convention was conducted fairly whereas the national executive might make the final determination, through an appeal mechanism, and decide on the penalties or sanctions. Penalties for noncompliance by a member with the code could include reprimands, suspension of membership and revoking of membership. In cases where party officers or candidates had violated the code, penalties could include reprimanding the individual, disqualifying candidates for nomination and leadership, prohibiting members from serving in an official party capacity, disqualifying elected delegates, revoking membership or nullifying the result of a selection process.

Whatever enforcement procedures are adopted, it is important to implement procedures to ensure fairness in all enforcement proceedings. When enforcing the code, it is also important to recognize the differences between poor judgement and intentional violation so a member will not be punished unreasonably for a momentary and honest error (Smith 1976, 289).

In addition to creating committees or positions to perform these functions, parties may require ethics committees to submit annual reports to the leadership or general membership of the party. These would provide valuable information on common problems that the party may wish to correct by internal reforms or amendments to the code. In addition, this information would be valuable if the national party wished to hold advisory and educational meetings on the state of compliance with the code.

ADDRESSING THE POLITICAL CONTEXT IN WHICH PARTIES OPERATE

Although the principles and values expressed in the code may vary from party to party, all codes may address a number of common activities. Ethical codes might contain statements about the rights and obligations of membership, establish standards for recruiting candidates and leaders, outline the norms that should govern these processes, establish guidelines for the solicitation of contributions, articulate principles for assessing election advertising campaigns and establish guidelines for mobilizing the vote on election day.

Two of the newer political parties have adopted codes of ethics, but these differ from what is being suggested in this study. These codes define the values of the party but do not go far enough in applying these values to the specific activities where guidance and instruction may be necessary. The values expressed in the Reform Party's code, for example, clearly reflect the principles of the party. Because the Reform Party is committed to grassroots principles, its code expresses a constituency-centred view of politics. In emphasizing the obligation of candidates to represent the views of constituents, the code de-emphasizes party discipline. The Reform Party code also contains a number of general ethical principles, such as retaining personal integrity, respecting the dignity of opponents, being fair in demands on the public purse and keeping an "open mind."

A shortcoming of the Reform Party's code, however, is that the values expressed, such as the importance of the views of constituents and the integrity, dignity and fairness of candidates, are stated so generally that they do not provide the guidance for leaders or members to resolve particular circumstances. For example, recognition of the dignity of others may not offer sufficient guidance to inform a Reform candidate's decision whether or not to engage in particularly harsh forms of negative advertising if he or she truly believes a rival candidate is unworthy of political office. Another serious shortcoming of the Reform code is that it is directed at candidates and does not address other members of the party. Given the general tone of the code and its limited application, it is not a "living" code that would permeate the organization and provide moral suasion or guidance in assessing specific forms of conduct in terms of the values expressed in the code.

The Christian Heritage party has an implicit code of ethics (in the form of a Solemn Pledge) that stresses the religious convictions of the party and its commitment to the Christian faith and family values. Although the philosophy of the party is clear and is understood by all who join and give their pledge, this code does not provide sufficient direction on how recourse to Christian values will resolve the specific conflicts that arise in election campaigns or in nomination and leadership selection processes.

The Reform Party and Christian Heritage party codes reflect the statement of philosophy guiding their organizations. However, they do not adequately address the partisan and competitive circumstances in which parties operate. Furthermore, they do not include any enforcement mechanism. Therefore, they offer little guidance to other parties attempting to improve their performance in activities that have undermined the confidence of party members and of the public.

CONCLUSION

Public confidence requires that the basic election rules be expressed clearly in a fair and transparent regulatory framework. However, normative expectations may not be satisfied simply by conformity with established laws: legal requirements are the minimum standards that have to be obeyed without penalty. Although obeying the law is a requisite for appropriate conduct, it may not, in itself, satisfy public expectations. Consequently, political parties will always be subject to demands that their activities be regulated when these activities appear to depart significantly from public expectations and where parties are believed to be incapable of regulating their own actions or unwilling to do so.

While it is important that legislative reforms accompany changes in ethical expectations, electoral law can and should only go so far in encouraging certain kinds of behaviour. A code of ethics would give party leaders the tools for enforcing the principles of the party, and members a clearer sense of their obligations to those principles. Whether motivated by a new understanding of and responsibility for upholding the values and principles of the party or enlightened self-interest to reform activities before public confidence declines further, the articulation in a code of ethics of the standards of behaviour expected of members, parties and local associations would go a long way toward increasing the confidence of the public and party members in the integrity of political parties. In short, it would give parties an effective way to manage their own conduct and forestall demands for regulation of a greater range of party activities.

APPENDIX: PARTIAL LIST OF INTERVENERS CONCERNED WITH PARTY ACTIVITIES

Adamson, Agar
Adelson, Anne
Barlow, Maude
Blanchard, Tom
Blom, Gerald
Burnham, Elizabeth
Christian, William
Day, M.
de Jong, Simon
Dickinson, Randy
Fillimore, Joanne
Fishman, Anna-Rae
Groody, Eric
Guarnieri, Albina
Kisby, Steve
Landry, Lucien G.
Lee, Derek
Maillé, Chantal
Moddejonge, Bert
Morrison, Jeff
Oliver, Eden
Proctor, Dick
Proulx, Rachel
Quennell, Frank
Regenstreif, Peter
Rhiness, Brian
Saulnier, Alain
Scott, Don
Steeves, Chuck
Thompson, J. Walter
Vickers, Jill
Whelan, Dermot
Woodward, Douglas

ACKNOWLEDGEMENTS

I would like to thank the following individuals who participated in sessions to discuss the effectiveness of a code of ethics for political parties or who contributed ideas on what a code of ethics might look like: Michael Atkinson, Peter Aucoin, Eric Bertram, William Chandler, Elwood Cowley, Ian Greene, Pierre-Marc Johnson, Kenneth Kernaghan, John Langford, Pierre Lortie, David Mac Donald, Maureen Mancuso, Hugh Mellon, Lucie Pépin and David Small.

BIBLIOGRAPHY

Berenbeim, Ronald E. 1987. "Corporate Ethics." Research report. New York: Conference Board.

Blais, André, and Elisabeth Gidengil. 1991. *Representative Democracy: The Views of Canadians*. Vol. 17 of the research studies of the Royal Commission on Electoral Reform and Party Financing. Ottawa and Toronto: RCERPF/Dundurn.

Blumenthal, M. 1975. "New Business Watchdog Needed." *New York Times*, 25 May, sect. 3, p. 2.

Bowie, Norman, and Ronald Duska. 1990. *Business Ethics*. 2d ed. Englewood Cliffs: Prentice-Hall.

Brooks, Leonard. 1989. "Corporate Codes of Ethics." *Journal of Business Ethics* 8:1.

Bucholz, R. 1989. *Fundamental Concepts and Problems in Business Ethics.* Englewood Cliffs: Prentice-Hall.

Center for Business Ethics. 1986. "Are Corporations Institutionalizing Ethics?" *Journal of Business Ethics* 5:85–91.

Clarke, Harold D., Jane Jenson, Lawrence LeDuc and Jon H. Pammett. 1991. *Absent Mandate: Interpreting Change in Canadian Elections.* 2d ed. Toronto: Gage.

Commission on Party Structure and Delegate Selection. 1970. "Mandate for Reform." A report of the Commission on Party Structure and Delegate Selection to the Democratic National Committee. Washington, DC: Democratic National Committee.

———. 1973. "Democrats All." A report of the Commission on Party Structure and Delegate Selection. Washington, DC: Democratic National Committee.

Corporate Ethics Monitor. 1989. Vol. 1.

Cressey, Donald R., and Charles A. Moore. 1983. "Managerial Values and Corporate Codes of Ethics." *California Management Review* 25 (4): 53–77.

De George, Richard T. 1987. "The Status of Business Ethics: Past and Future." *Journal of Business Ethics* 6:201–11.

Drucker, Peter. 1974. *Management: Tasks, Responsibilities and Practices.* New York: Harper and Row.

Epstein, Edwin M. 1989. "Business Ethics, Corporate Good Citizenship and the Corporate Social Policy Process: A View from the United States." *Journal of Business Ethics* 8:45–57.

Haynes, Andrew. 1991. "The Ethical Dimension of Business and Government." *Canadian Public Administration* 34:17–20.

Hill, Ivan, ed. 1976. *The Ethical Basis of Economic Freedom.* Chapel Hill: American Viewpoint.

Kernaghan, Kenneth. 1987. "The Statement of Principles of the Institute of Public Administration of Canada: The Rationale for Its Development and Content." *Canadian Public Administration* 30:331–51.

———. 1991. "Managing Ethics: Complementary Approaches." *Canadian Public Administration* 34:132–45.

Lipset, Seymour Martin, and William Schneider. 1987. "The Confidence Gap during the Reagan Years 1981–1987." *Political Science Quarterly* 102 (1): 1–21.

McCarney, Rosemary. 1990. Comments at Symposium on the Active Participation of Women in Politics. Royal Commission on Electoral Reform and Party Financing. Montreal, 1 November.

Michaud, Pascale, and Pierre Laferrière. 1991. "Economic Analysis of the Funding of Political Parties in Canada." In *Issues in Party and Election Finance in Canada*, ed. F. Leslie Seidle. Vol. 5 of the research studies of the Royal Commission on Electoral Reform and Party Financing. Ottawa and Toronto: RCERPF/Dundurn.

Nitkin, David. 1989. "Corporate Codes of Ethics: Learning, Leading, Lying and Loyalty." *The Corporate Ethics Monitor* 1 (4): 57–60.

Peters, Thomas, and Robert Waterman, Jr. 1982. *In Search of Excellence: Lessons from America's Best-Run Companies*. New York: Harper and Row.

Purcell, Theodore. 1976. "Electing an 'Angel's Advocate' to the Board." *Management Review* (May): 4–11.

Securities and Exchange Commission. 1976. *Report of the Securities and Exchange Commission on Questionable and Illegal Corporate Payments and Practices*. Special Supplement. Submitted to the Senate Banking, Housing and Urban Affairs Committee. Washington, DC: Bureau of National Affairs.

Shafer, Byron. 1983. *Quiet Revolution: The Struggle for the Democratic Party and the Shaping of Post-Reform Politics*. New York: Russell Sage Foundation.

Silk, Leonard, and David Vogel. 1976. *Ethics and Profits: The Crisis of Confidence in American Business*. New York: Simon and Schuster.

Simon, William. 1976. "A Challenge to Free Enterprise." In *The Ethical Basis of Economic Freedom*, ed. Ivan Hill. Chapel Hill: American Viewpoint.

Smith, Rea. 1976. "Commentary on Code of Ethics of Public Relations Society of America." In *The Ethical Basis of Economic Freedom*, ed. Ivan Hill. Chapel Hill: American Viewpoint.

White, Bernard, and B. Ruth Montgomery. 1980. "Corporate Codes of Conduct." *California Management Review* 23 (Winter): 80–87.

CONTRIBUTORS TO VOLUME 12

Kathy L. Brock	University of Manitoba
Pierre Fortin	Université du Québec à Rimouski
Ian Greene	York University
Janet Hiebert	Commission Research Coordinator
Jane Jenson	Carleton University
Vincent Lemieux	Université Laval
Richard G. Price	University of Windsor
Walter I. Romanow	University of Windsor
Walter C. Soderlund	University of Windsor

ACKNOWLEDGEMENTS

The Royal Commission on Electoral Reform and Party Financing and the publishers wish to acknowledge with gratitude the permission of the following to reprint and translate material:

Broadview Press Ltd.; Institute of Public Administration of Canada, *Canadian Public Administration;* Nelson Canada; The New York Times Company; Thomson Professional Publishing Canada – Carswell/Richard De Boo Publishers.

Care has been taken to trace the ownership of copyright material used in the text, including the tables and figures. The authors and publishers welcome any information enabling them to rectify any reference or credit in subsequent editions.

Consistent with the Commission's objective of promoting full participation in the electoral system by all segments of Canadian society, gender neutrality has been used wherever possible in the editing of the research studies.

THE COLLECTED RESEARCH STUDIES*

VOLUME 1
Money in Politics: Financing Federal Parties and Candidates in Canada

W.T. STANBURY	Money in Politics: Financing Federal Parties and Candidates in Canada

VOLUME 2
Interest Groups and Elections in Canada
F. Leslie Seidle, Editor

JANET HIEBERT	Interest Groups and Canadian Federal Elections
A. BRIAN TANGUAY AND BARRY J. KAY	Political Activity of Local Interest Groups

VOLUME 3
Provincial Party and Election Finance in Canada
F. Leslie Seidle, Editor

LOUIS MASSICOTTE	Party Financing in Quebec: An Analysis of the Financial Reports of Parties, 1977–89
DAVID JOHNSON	The Ontario Party and Campaign Finance System: Initiative and Challenge
TERRY MORLEY	Paying for the Politics of British Columbia
HUGH. MELLON	The Evolution of Political Financing Regulation in New Brunswick
DOREEN P. BARRIE	Party Financing in Alberta: Low-Impact Legislation

VOLUME 4
Comparative Issues in Party and Election Finance
F. Leslie Seidle, Editor

HERBERT E. ALEXANDER	The Regulation of Election Finance in the United States and Proposals for Reform

---

* The titles of studies may not be final in all cases.

ROBERT E. MUTCH	The Evolution of Campaign Finance Regulation in the United States and Canada
JANE JENSON	Innovation and Equity: The Impact of Public Funding
MICHAEL PINTO-DUSCHINSKY	The Party Foundations and Political Finance in Germany

VOLUME 5
Issues in Party and Election Finance in Canada
F. Leslie Seidle, Editor

LISA YOUNG	Toward Transparency: An Evaluation of Disclosure Arrangements in Canadian Political Finance
MICHAEL KRASHINSKY AND WILLIAM J. MILNE	Some Evidence on the Effects of Incumbency in the 1988 Canadian Federal Election
R. KENNETH CARTY	Official Agents in Canadian Elections: The Case of the 1988 General Election
D. KEITH HEINTZMAN	Electoral Competition, Campaign Expenditure and Incumbency Advantage
THOMAS S. AXWORTHY	Capital-Intensive Politics: Money, Media and Mores in the United States and Canada
PETER P. CONSTANTINOU	Public Funding of Political Parties, Candidates and Elections in Canada
ERIC BERTRAM	Independent Candidates in Federal General Elections
DONALD PADGET	Large Contributions to Candidates in the 1988 Federal Election and the Issue of Undue Influence
PASCALE MICHAUD AND PIERRE LAFERRIÈRE	Economic Analysis of the Funding of Political Parties in Canada

VOLUME 6
Women in Canadian Politics: Toward Equity in Representation
Kathy Megyery, Editor

JANINE BRODIE, WITH THE ASSISTANCE OF CELIA CHANDLER	Women and the Electoral Process in Canada

SYLVIA BASHEVKIN — Women's Participation in Political Parties

LISA YOUNG — Legislative Turnover and the Election of Women to the Canadian House of Commons

LYNDA ERICKSON — Women and Candidacies for the House of Commons

GERTRUDE J. ROBINSON AND ARMANDE SAINT-JEAN, WITH THE ASSISTANCE OF CHRISTINE RIOUX — Women Politicians and Their Media Coverage: A Generational Analysis

VOLUME 7
Ethno-cultural Groups and Visible Minorities in Canadian Politics: The Question of Access
Kathy Megyery, Editor

DAIVA K. STASIULIS AND YASMEEN ABU-LABAN — The House the Parties Built: (Re)constructing Ethnic Representation in Canadian Politics

ALAIN PELLETIER — Politics and Ethnicity: Representation of Ethnic and Visible-Minority Groups in the House of Commons

CAROLLE SIMARD, WITH THE ASSISTANCE OF SYLVIE BÉLANGER, SERGE TURMEL, NATHALIE LAVOIE AND ANNE-LISE POLO — Visible Minorities and the Canadian Political System

VOLUME 8
Youth in Canadian Politics: Participation and Involvement
Kathy Megyery, Editor

RAYMOND HUDON, BERNARD FOURNIER AND LOUIS MÉTIVIER, WITH THE ASSISTANCE OF BENOÎT-PAUL HÉBERT — To What Extent Are Today's Young People Interested in Politics? Inquiries among 16- to 24-Year-Olds

PATRICE GARANT — Revisiting the Voting Age Issue under the *Canadian Charter of Rights and Freedoms*

JON H. PAMMETT AND JOHN MYLES — Lowering the Voting Age to 16

VOLUME 9
Aboriginal Peoples and Electoral Reform in Canada
Robert A. Milen, Editor

ROBERT A. MILEN	Aboriginal Constitutional and Electoral Reform
AUGIE FLERAS	Aboriginal Electoral Districts for Canada: Lessons from New Zealand
VALERIE ALIA	Aboriginal Peoples and Campaign Coverage in the North
ROGER GIBBINS	Electoral Reform and Canada's Aboriginal Population: An Assessment of Aboriginal Electoral Districts

VOLUME 10
Democratic Rights and Electoral Reform in Canada
Michael Cassidy, Editor

JENNIFER SMITH	The Franchise and Theories of Representative Government
PIERRE LANDREVILLE AND LUCIE LEMONDE	Voting Rights for Inmates
YVES DENONCOURT	Reflections concerning Criteria for the Vote for Persons with Mental Disorders
PATRICE GARANT	Political Rights of Public Servants in the Political Process
KENNETH KERNAGHAN	The Political Rights of Canada's Federal Public Servants
PETER MCCORMICK	Provision for the Recall of Elected Officials: Parameters and Prospects
DAVID MAC DONALD	Referendums and Federal General Elections
JOHN C. COURTNEY AND DAVID E. SMITH	Registering Voters: Canada in a Comparative Context
CÉCILE BOUCHER	Administration and Enforcement of the Elections Act in Canada

VOLUME 11
Drawing the Map: Equality and Efficacy of the Vote in Canadian Electoral Boundary Reform
David Small, Editor

KENT ROACH	One Person, One Vote? Canadian Constitutional Standards for Electoral Distribution and Districting
HOWARD A. SCARROW	Apportionment, Districting and Representation in the United States
ALAN STEWART	Community of Interest in Redistricting
MUNROE EAGLES	Enhancing Relative Vote Equality in Canada: The Role of Electors in Boundary Adjustment
DOUG MACDONALD	Ecological Communities and Constituency Districting
ALAN FRIZZELL	In the Public Service: Representation in Modern Canada
DAVID SMALL	Enhancing Aboriginal Representation within the Existing System of Redistricting

VOLUME 12
Political Ethics: A Canadian Perspective
Janet Hiebert, Editor

PIERRE FORTIN	Ethical Issues in the Debate on Reform of the *Canada Elections Act*: An Ethicological Analysis
VINCENT LEMIEUX	Public Sector Ethics
IAN GREENE	Allegations of Undue Influence in Canadian Politics
WALTER I. ROMANOW, WALTER C. SODERLUND AND RICHARD G. PRICE	Negative Political Advertising: An Analysis of Research Findings in Light of Canadian Practice
JANE JENSON	Citizenship and Equity: Variations across Time and in Space
KATHY L. BROCK	Fairness, Equity and Rights
JANET HIEBERT	A Code of Ethics for Political Parties

VOLUME 13
Canadian Political Parties: Leaders, Candidates and Organization
Herman Bakvis, Editor

KEITH ARCHER	Leadership Selection in the New Democratic Party
GEORGE PERLIN	Attitudes of Liberal Convention Delegates toward Proposals for Reform of the Process of Leadership Selection
R. KENNETH CARTY AND LYNDA ERICKSON	Candidate Nomination in Canada's National Political Parties
WILLIAM M. CHANDLER AND ALAN SIAROFF	Parties and Party Government in Advanced Democracies
RÉJEAN PELLETIER, WITH THE COLLABORATION OF FRANÇOIS BUNDOCK AND MICHEL SARRA-BOURNET	The Structures and Operations of Canadian Political Parties
KEITH ARCHER	The New Democrats, Organized Labour and the Prospects of Electoral Reform

VOLUME 14
Representation, Integration and Political Parties in Canada
Herman Bakvis, Editor

DAVID J. ELKINS	Parties as National Institutions: A Comparative Study
MAUREEN COVELL	Parties as Institutions of National Governance
RAND DYCK	Links between Federal and Provincial Parties and Party Systems
PAUL G. THOMAS	Parties and Regional Representation
DONALD E. BLAKE	Party Competition and Electoral Volatility: Canada in Comparative Perspective
JOHN FEREJOHN AND BRIAN GAINES	The Personal Vote in Canada
S.L. SUTHERLAND	The Consequences of Electoral Volatility: Inexperienced Ministers 1949–90

NEIL NEVITTE   New Politics, the Charter and Political
                              Participation

RÉJEAN LANDRY   Incentives Created by the
                              Institutions of Representative
                              Democracy: Their Effect on Voters,
                              Political Parties and Public Policy

VOLUME 15
Voter Turnout in Canada
  Herman Bakvis, Editor

MUNROE EAGLES   Voting and Non-voting in Canadian
                              Federal Elections: An Ecological
                              Analysis

JON H. PAMMETT   Voting Turnout in Canada

JEROME H. BLACK   Reforming the Context of the Voting
                              Process in Canada: Lessons from
                              Other Democracies

VOLUME 16
Polls and the Media in Canadian Elections: Taking the Pulse

GUY LACHAPELLE   Polls and the Media in Canadian
                              Elections: Taking the Pulse

VOLUME 17
Representative Democracy: The Views of Canadians

ANDRÉ BLAIS AND   Representative Democracy:
ELISABETH GIDENGIL   The Views of Canadians

VOLUME 18
Media and Voters in Canadian Election Campaigns
  Frederick J. Fletcher, Editor

JEAN CRÊTE   Television, Advertising and
                              Canadian Elections

ROBERT MACDERMID   Media Usage and Political Behaviour

CATHY WIDDIS BARR   The Importance and Potential of
                              Leaders Debates

ROBERT BERNIER AND   The Organization of Televised
DENIS MONIÈRE   Leaders Debates in the United States,
                              Europe, Australia and Canada

LYNDSAY GREEN — An Exploration of Alternative Methods for Improving Voter Information

VOLUME 19
Media, Elections and Democracy
Frederick J. Fletcher, Editor

JACQUES GERSTLÉ — Election Communication in France

HOLLI A. SEMETKO — Broadcasting and Election Communication in Britain

KLAUS SCHOENBACH — Mass Media and Election Campaigns in Germany

KAREN SIUNE — Campaign Communication in Scandinavia

JOHN WARHURST — Campaign Communication in Australian Elections

DORIS A. GRABER — The Mass Media and Election Campaigns in the United States of America

FREDERICK J. FLETCHER AND ROBERT EVERETT — Mass Media and Elections in Canada

VOLUME 20
Reaching the Voter: Constituency Campaigning in Canada
David V.J. Bell and Frederick J. Fletcher, Editors

DAVID V.J. BELL AND FREDERICK J. FLETCHER — Electoral Communication at the Constituency Level: A Framework for Analysis

ANTHONY M. SAYERS — Local Issue Space at National Elections: Kootenay West–Revelstoke and Vancouver Centre

ANDREW BEH AND ROGER GIBBINS — The Campaign–Media Interface in Local Constituencies: Two Alberta Case Studies from the 1988 Federal Election Campaign

DAVID V.J. BELL AND CATHERINE M. BOLAN — The Mass Media and Federal Election Campaigning at the Local Level: A Case Study of Two Ontario Constituencies

LUC BERNIER — Media Coverage of Local Campaigns: The 1988 Election in Outremont and Frontenac

THE COLLECTED RESEARCH STUDIES

LEONARD PREYRA	Riding the Waves: Parties, the Media and the 1988 Federal Election in Nova Scotia
DAVID V.J. BELL, FREDERICK J. FLETCHER AND CATHERINE M. BOLAN	Electoral Communication at the Constituency Level: Summary and Conclusion

VOLUME 21
Election Broadcasting in Canada
Frederick J. Fletcher, Editor

DAVID RALPH SPENCER, WITH THE ASSISTANCE OF CATHERINE M. BOLAN	Election Broadcasting in Canada: A Brief History
PIERRE TRUDEL AND FRANCE ABRAN	The Legal and Constitutional Framework for the Regulation of Election Campaign Broadcasting
DAVID HOGARTH AND WILLIAM O. GILSDORF	The Impact of All-News Services on Elections and Election Coverage
PETER DESBARATS	Cable Television and Federal Election Campaigns in Canada
STEPHEN KLINE, ROVIN DEODAT, ARLENE SHWETZ AND WILLIAM LEISS	Political Broadcast Advertising in Canada
LORNA ROTH	CBC Northern Services and the Federal Electoral Process: Problems and Strategies for Improvement

VOLUME 22
Reporting the Campaign: Election Coverage in Canada
Frederick J. Fletcher, Editor

WILLIAM O. GILSDORF AND ROBERT BERNIER	Journalistic Practice in Covering Federal Election Campaigns in Canada
JEAN CHARRON	Relations between Political Parties and the Media in Quebec Election Campaigns
CHRISTOPHER DORNAN	Free to Be Responsible: The Accountability of the Print Media
ROBERT A. HACKETT	Smaller Voices: Minor Parties, Campaign Communication and the News Media

EILEEN SAUNDERS   Mass Media and the Reproduction
                       of Marginalization

VOLUME 23
Canadian Political Parties in the Constituencies:
A Local Perspective

R. KENNETH CARTY   Canadian Political Parties in the
                        Constituencies: A Local Perspective

COMMISSION ORGANIZATION

CHAIRMAN
Pierre Lortie

COMMISSIONERS
Pierre Fortier
Robert Gabor
William Knight
Lucie Pépin

SENIOR OFFICERS

Executive Director
Guy Goulard

Director of Research
Peter Aucoin

Special Adviser to the Chairman
Jean-Marc Hamel

Research
F. Leslie Seidle,
 Senior Research Coordinator

Coordinators
Herman Bakvis
Michael Cassidy
Frederick J. Fletcher
Janet Hiebert
Kathy Megyery
Robert A. Milen
David Small

Assistant Coordinators
David Mac Donald
Cheryl D. Mitchell

Legislation
Jules Brière, Senior Adviser
Gérard Bertrand
Patrick Orr

Communications and Publishing
Richard Rochefort, Director
Hélène Papineau, Assistant
 Director
Paul Morisset, Editor
Kathryn Randle, Editor

Finance and Administration
Maurice R. Lacasse, Director

Contracts and Personnel
Thérèse Lacasse, Chief

EDITORIAL, DESIGN AND PRODUCTION SERVICES

ROYAL COMMISSION ON ELECTORAL REFORM AND PARTY FINANCING

Editors   Denis Bastien, Susan Becker Davidson, Ginette Bertrand, Louis Bilodeau, Claude Brabant, Louis Chabot, Danielle Chaput, Norman Dahl, Carlos del Burgo, Julie Desgagners, Chantal Granger, Volker Junginger, Denis Landry, André LaRose, Paul Morisset, Christine O'Meara, Mario Pelletier, Marie-Noël Pichelin, Kathryn Randle, Georges Royer, Eve Valiquette, Dominique Vincent.

LE CENTRE DE DOCUMENTATION JURIDIQUE DU QUÉBEC INC.

Hubert Reid, *President*

Claire Grégoire, *Comptroller*

Lucie Poirier, *Production Manager*
Gisèle Gingras, *Special Project Assistant*

Translators   Pierre-Yves de la Garde, Richard Lapointe, Marie-Josée Turcotte.

Technical Editors   Stéphane Côté Coulombe, *Coordinator*; Josée Chabot, Danielle Morin.

Copy Editors   Martine Germain, Lise Larochelle, Elisabeth Reid, Carole St-Louis, Isabelle Tousignant, Charles Tremblay, Sébastien Viau.

Word Processing   André Vallée.

Formatting   Typoform, Claude Audet; Linda Goudreau, *Formatting Coordinator*.

WILSON & LAFLEUR LTÉE

Claude Wilson, *President*

DUNDURN PRESS

J. Kirk Howard, *President*
Ian Low, *Comptroller*
Jeanne MacDonald, *Project Coordinator*

Avivah Wargon, *Managing and Production Editor*
Beth Ediger, *Managing Editor*
John St. James, *Managing Editor*
Karen Heese, *Special Project Assistant*

Ruth Chernia, *Tables Editor*
Victoria Grant, *Legal Editor*
Michèle Breton, *Special Editorial Assistant*

Editorial Staff   Elliott Chapin, Peggy Foy, Lily Hobel, Marilyn Hryciuk, Madeline Koch, Elizabeth Mitchell, John Shoesmith, Nadine Stoikoff, Shawn Syms, Anne Vespry.

Copy Editors   Carol Anderson, Elizabeth d'Anjou, Jane Becker, Diane Brassolotto, Elizabeth Driver, Curtis Fahey, Tony Fairfield, Freya Godard, Frances Hanna, Kathleen Harris, Andria Hourwich, Greg Ioannou, Carlotta Lemieux, Elsha Leventis, David McCorquodale, Virginia Smith, Gail Thorson, Louise Wood.

Formatting   Green Graphics; Joanne Green, *Formatting Coordinator;*
Formatters   Linda Carroll, Mary Ann Cattral, Gail Nina, Eva Payne, Jacqueline Hope Raynor, Andy Tong, Carla Vonn Worden, Laura Wilkins.

Printed and bound in Canada by
Best Gagné Book Manufacturers